CH

WORKING TOGETHER
TO REDUCE HARMFUL DRINKING

Marcus Grant & Mark Leverton

Editors

Routledge
Taylor & Francis Group
New York   London

Routledge
Taylor & Francis Group
270 Madison Avenue
New York, NY 10016

Routledge
Taylor & Francis Group
27 Church Road
Hove, East Sussex BN3 2FA

© 2010 by International Center for Alcohol Policies
Routledge is an imprint of Taylor & Francis Group, an Informa business

Printed in the United States of America on acid-free paper
10 9 8 7 6 5 4 3 2 1

International Standard Book Number: 978-0-415-80087-7 (Hardback)

Library of Congress Cataloging-in-Publication Data

Working together to reduce harmful drinking / edited by Marcus Grant and
  Mark Leverton.
       p. cm.
  Includes bibliographical references and index.
  ISBN 978-0-415-80087-7 (hbk. : alk. paper)
     1. Drinking of alcoholic beverages--Social aspects. 2. Alcoholic
  beverage industry--Social aspects. 3. Social responsibility of business. 4.
  Alcoholism--Prevention. I. Grant, Marcus. II. Leverton, Mark. III. Title.

  HV5035.W67 2009
  362.292'7--dc22   2009016166

Visit the Taylor & Francis Web site at
http://www.taylorandfrancis.com

and the Routledge Web site at
http://www.routledgementalhealth.com

Contents

About the Editors

Marcus Grant is President of the International Center for Alcohol Policies (ICAP). He has worked in the alcohol field for over 30 years, first as Director of a U.K.-based nongovernmental organization, the Alcohol Education Center, which provided national coordination of postqualification training on alcohol problems for health and social service staff, and then for the World Health Organization (WHO), where he was responsible for global activities on the prevention of alcohol and drug abuse. He resigned from WHO in 1994 to set up ICAP.

Mark Leverton is Director of Alcohol Policy and Industry Issues at Diageo, the world's leading beer, wine, and spirits company. He has been a member of the ICAP Board of Directors since 1997 and was Board Chair from 2004 to 2006. He has held a number of senior management positions in Diageo in London, Brussels, and Asia. He has also held a number of industry positions, including Chair of the Scotch Whisky Association International Affairs Committee and Chair of the Alcohol and Society Standing Committee of the Confédération Européenne des Producteurs de Spiritueux (CEPS); he also was a long-standing member of the Scotch Whisky Association Council. Mr. Leverton has represented Diageo in formal industry consultations with WHO on how to reduce harmful drinking.

Contributors

Brett Bivans, International Center for Alcohol Policies (ICAP), USA
Brett Bivans is ICAP's Vice President. He is a specialist in public-private partnerships, project management, and corporate social responsibility. Prior to joining ICAP in 2004, Mr. Bivans was the first manager of the Global Road Safety Partnership (GRSP) and a member of the World Bank's Finance and Private Sector Development team, working on corporate social responsibility and partnership initiatives.

Adrian Botha, Industry Association for Responsible Alcohol Use (ARA), South Africa
Adrian Botha, formerly of SABMiller and an ICAP Board member, is Executive Director of the Industry Association for Responsible Alcohol Use (ARA), a social aspects organization in South Africa.

Marjana Martinic, ICAP, USA
Dr. Marjana Martinic is Senior Vice President at ICAP, where her work focuses on the nexus between the scientific evidence base and international alcohol policy development. Prior to joining ICAP in 1996, she worked in developmental neuroscience research. Dr. Martinic has published extensively in the fields of neuroscience and alcohol policy. Her most recent book, coedited with Dr. Fiona Measham, is

Swimming with Crocodiles: The Culture of Extreme Drinking, which takes a cross-cultural look at young people's drinking. She currently serves on the Science Group that advises the European Commission's Alcohol and Health Forum.

John Orley, Clifford Beers Foundation, United Kingdom

Dr. John Orley is a psychiatrist and anthropologist who worked for 15 years in the Division of Mental Health of the World Health Organization (WHO) in Geneva, latterly as the Programme Manager. Since retiring from WHO, he has worked as a consultant for ICAP on a number of projects. From 2000 to 2009, Dr. Orley was Chair of the Clifford Beers Foundation, a society devoted to the promotion of mental health and the prevention of mental disorders; he continues as a Board Member.

Godfrey Robson, ICAP Consultant, United Kingdom

Godfrey Robson is Chair of Scotland's largest independent company of management consultants, a Director of LloydsTSB Bank Scotland, and a Trustee of a major Scottish charity providing health advice and services to young people. He was Head of Economic and Industrial Affairs for Scotland and subsequently Director of Health Policy in the Scottish government. The first Scottish Executive Plan for Action on Alcohol Problems was drawn up under his direction.

Ronald Simpson, ICAP Consultant, USA

Dr. Ronald Simpson has 25 years of experience in the food and beverage industries. Prior to retirement, he was Vice President of Corporate Scientific Affairs at Joseph E. Seagram and Sons (and an ICAP Board Member), responsible for developing and implementing strategies to gain a better understanding of the role of alcohol consumption in health and social issues. He received his doctorate in nutrition at the University of California at Davis (USA).

Roger Sinclair, University of the Witwatersrand, South Africa

Dr. Roger Sinclair is Professor of Marketing at the University of the Witwatersrand, Johannesburg, South Africa. Since September 2005, he has been independent external Chair of the SABMiller code of responsible marketing compliance committee.

Graeme Willersdorf, ICAP Consultant, Australia

Graeme Willersdorf has over 25 years of experience in the alcohol industry. He spent two decades at Foster's Group, where his final position prior to retirement was Senior Vice President, Corporate Affairs, and where he oversaw the development of the company's programs on responsible alcohol consumption. Mr. Willersdorf was also Chairman of the Australian Associated Brewers when they funded the University of Melbourne to develop a national alcohol education program for secondary school students. He was member of the ICAP Board of Directors and served as ICAP Chairman for three years. Since his retirement, Mr. Willersdorf has been an advisor to industry and government.

Disclaimer

The opinions expressed in this book are those of the individual authors and do not necessarily reflect the views of the International Center for Alcohol Policies (ICAP) or its sponsor companies.[1]

---

[1] ICAP is dedicated to promoting understanding of the role of alcohol in society and to helping reduce the abuse of alcohol worldwide through dialogue and partnerships involving the beverage alcohol industry, governments, the public health community, and others with an interest in alcohol policy. ICAP is a not-for-profit organization supported by major international beverage alcohol companies: Anheuser-Busch InBev, Asahi Breweries, Bacardi, Beam Global Spirits & Wine, Brown-Forman Corporation, Diageo, Heineken, Molson Coors Brewing Company, Pernod Ricard, and SABMiller.

Acknowledgments

We wish to acknowledge the contributions made to the preparation of this book by a number of individuals. Trevor Estelle, Brad Krevor, Andy Pearce, Gaye Pedlow, and Nick Soper all provided text on specific issues, which has been incorporated into the relevant chapters. Above all, however, we wish to thank Daniya Tamendarova, who has worked patiently with all the authors to help them find the most accurate and elegant way to convey what they wished to express. The book has benefited greatly from her tireless attention to detail.

1

INTRODUCTION

MARCUS GRANT AND MARK LEVERTON

What Is This Book Setting Out to Achieve?

This book lays out for the international community a coherent view of what it is that beverage alcohol producers can do to help reduce harmful drinking. It does not pretend to present complete solutions that will work for all people in all places. Indeed, one of its main messages is that very few strategies are universally applicable. Rather, what is required is a range of options so that different countries and communities can select which combination of measures is likely to work best for them given their drinking culture and health priorities. Alcohol producers are under no illusion that they are the most important players in developing and implementing balanced alcohol policies. Governments, health professionals, and civil society must occupy center stage. But, equally, alcohol producers are convinced that they do have a role to play. This book aims to demonstrate just how positive that role can be.

Of course, the beverage alcohol industry is diverse and complex (International Center for Alcohol Policies [ICAP], 2006), including many companies, trade associations, and others with no direct hand in the preparation of this book. Although the views presented here are those of individual authors, they broadly reflect the perspectives of those major international drink producers that sponsor ICAP.[1] The experience of other companies and other parts of the

---

[1] Anheuser-Busch InBev, Asahi Breweries, Bacardi, Beam Global Spirits & Wine, Brown-Forman Corporation, Diageo, Heineken, Molson Coors Brewing Company, Pernod Ricard, and SABMiller.

industry—particularly retailers—may differ from what is included here. Nevertheless, even if this is not *the* view of the industry, it does represent a significant international consensus among leading producers. In this connection, the terms *industry* and *producers* are not used interchangeably in the text.

The immediate impetus for this book arose from a renewed interest by the international community in balancing the positive and negative effects of alcohol. The World Health Assembly (WHA), which has over the years adopted a number of resolutions, particularly on the development of national alcohol policies, turned its attention in 2008 to strategies to reduce the harmful use of alcohol. The resolution adopted by the 61st WHA calls for the development by 2010 of a draft global strategy, based on all available evidence and existing best practices, to reduce the harmful use of alcohol. In responding to this challenge, the World Health Organization (WHO) Secretariat has been requested "to collaborate and consult with Member States, as well as to consult with intergovernmental organizations, health professionals, nongovernmental organizations and economic operators on ways they could contribute to reducing harmful use of alcohol" (WHO, 2008, p. 8).

Clearly, the terms of the resolution give pride of place to Member States as the primary constituents of WHO. However, the importance of the other stakeholders is acknowledged by being explicitly listed in the text of the resolution. As a consequence, in the latter part of 2008, WHO initiated a web-based open consultation for all interested parties and then convened two roundtable meetings, one for economic operators and the other for health professionals and representatives of nongovernmental organizations. In the early part of 2009, WHO organized a series of six regional consultations with Member States and went on to produce the draft global strategy, taking into account the results of its broad consultative process, for submission to the WHO Executive Board and, through them, to the WHA.

One effect of this process, which has been conducted in a clear and transparent manner, is to stimulate a wide-ranging international debate about alcohol policy and how it can best be implemented. The goal of this book is to contribute to that debate in a positive and considered way. The governing bodies of WHO will make decisions based on their assessment of whether the draft global strategy, as presented to them, adequately reflects the available evidence and charts a prudent and reasonable course through the competing claims and counterclaims made by the proponents of different points of view. A litmus test of these claims must be the extent to which they seem to offer practical solutions to persistent problems. WHO has been asking stakeholders what they can actually *do* to help reduce harmful use of alcohol. It is often a great deal easier to explain what others should do than to make specific commitments involving one's own resources and energies, particularly if these commitments may result in some inconvenience or discomfort. What goes into the global strategy may turn out to be quite predictable. The challenge, as the world moves from planning to implementation, will be to ensure that what comes out of it really does provide a context for multi-stakeholder efforts to reduce harmful drinking.

What Is Harmful Drinking?

Alcohol consumption has the potential to be either harmful or beneficial, depending on the drinkers' individual characteristics and circumstances, consumption patterns, and drinking context. The term *harmful use* was introduced in 1992 in WHO's *International Classification of Diseases* (10th revision, *ICD-10*) to supplant "nondependent use" as a diagnostic term. In relation to alcohol, it refers to any drinking pattern that causes damage to health. The damage may be physical or mental. Harmful use commonly, but not invariably, has adverse social consequences. As applied in *ICD-10*, however, adverse social consequences are not in themselves sufficient to justify a diagnosis of harmful use. The closest equivalent in the other main diagnostic system, the American Psychiatric Association's (2000) *Diagnostic and Statistical Manual of Mental Disorders* (fourth edition, text revision, *DSM-IV-TR*), is *substance abuse*, which usually does include social consequences.

Not included in either *ICD-10* or *DSM-IV-TR* but often referred to in public health discussions is the term *hazardous use*, which—in relation to alcohol—refers to a pattern of drinking that increases the *risk* of harmful consequences. This is sometimes limited to physical and mental health consequences but is often used to include social consequences. It can, therefore, include potential harm to the drinkers or others who might be adversely affected by their behavior.

For the purposes of this book, it will be important to cast the net wide to encompass all aspects of drinking behavior that can be reasonably taken to cause harm to individuals, their families and associates, and the society. It will also sometimes be relevant, particularly from the point of view of prevention programs and public policy, to consider drinking behavior that carries a significantly elevated risk of causing harm, even when it is not possible to document specific negative consequences in every instance. In other words, we need to go beyond narrowly defined diagnostic criteria to embrace a concept of harmful drinking that includes both harmful and hazardous use.

A similarly broad approach is necessary when attempting to define *responsible drinking*. There is no single source on which we can rely for a generally accepted definition since use of the term commonly reflects the characteristics of the cultures in which it is used. Broadly, it can be considered as a synonym for the term *moderate drinking* and usually denotes a drinking pattern that does not exceed a culturally accepted daily volume, carrying little or no risk of harm. For example, the Industry Association for Responsible Alcohol Use (ARA) in South Africa defines responsible drinking as "the enjoyable consumption of alcohol beverages within the limits set by your health, circumstances, and obligations to family, friends, and society."[2] Of course, this is a rather fluid definition since what counts as responsible drinking at a meeting of Presbyterian churchmen in Scotland will likely be quite different from what counts as responsible drinking at a fiesta in Brazil. Nevertheless, for the purposes of this book, responsible drinking can probably be taken to encompass those patterns of alcohol consumption that do not, or are highly unlikely to, lead to any of the negative consequences described here as associated with harmful drinking.

It is beyond the scope of this book to describe specific health and social benefits that derive from responsible drinking. These have been extensively reviewed elsewhere, both in relation to protective effects

---

[2] Personal communication with Adrian Botha, Industry Association for Responsible Alcohol Use (ARA), January 14, 2009.

for specific diseases, such as coronary heart disease and some metabolic disorders, and in relation to social and cognitive functioning (e.g., Ellison, 2007).[3] The relationship between alcohol and subjective pleasure has also been analyzed, with particular attention given to issues such as sociability, relaxation, and quality of life (e.g., Baum-Baicker, 1985; Peele & Brodsky, 2000; Peele & Grant, 1999; Stranges et al., 2006; Valencia-Martin, Galán, & Rodríguez-Artalejo, 2009). Taking that literature into account, the basic premise of this book is that there is a clear and useful distinction between harmful and responsible drinking.

This distinction is important because it speaks to opportunities to develop policy approaches that are relevant to both individuals and societies. From a public health point of view, alcohol policy is one part of a broad approach to health and social policy that is intended to promote equity and improved quality of life at the same time as it eliminates preventable disease and injury. The WHO definition of health, enshrined in the constitution of the organization, states that it is "a state of complete physical, mental and social well-being and not merely the absence of disease or infirmity" and goes on to note that "the enjoyment of the highest attainable standard of health is one of the fundamental rights of every human being without distinction of race, religion, political belief, economic or social condition" (WHO, 1946, p. 1).

More recently, the aspirational language of the WHO Constitution has been taken up and given additional traction through the work of the Commission on Social Determinants of Health (2008). This approach, which stems from earlier work on health inequalities (for a review, see WHO, 2005), identifies socioeconomic factors as powerful determinants of health and advances the notion that the social

---

[3] See also the *ICAP Health Briefings* at http://www.icap.org/PolicyTools/ICAPHealthBriefings. The *ICAP Health Briefings* offer overviews of the relationship between drinking patterns and specific health outcomes, compile the key literature, and provide a bibliography that refers to original research on each topic. The topics addressed include: drinking patterns and health outcomes, drinking and cancer, drinking and cardiovascular health, drinking and cognitive function, drinking and metabolic disorders, fetal alcohol exposure, drinking and liver disease, and drinking and HIV/AIDS risk.

and economic structure of society shapes the health of populations. It is important to recognize that this approach sees the potential for both positive and negative effects. On the one hand, a vigorous and successful alcohol production industry can contribute significantly to the economic health of a society and thus to the health status of its population. On the other hand, since some patterns of drinking clearly carry increased risk of harm, reasonable regulation and other interventions are required to protect populations, especially vulnerable groups, including the young.

What Is the Case for Industry Involvement?

Interventions aimed at reducing the potential harm associated with drinking have traditionally been divided into two basic categories. One is the population-level approach to prevention, consisting of across-the-board measures that rely mainly on controlling the volume of drinking in society as a whole. The other approach involves interventions that are applied in a targeted way, focusing on particular groups, behaviors, drinking patterns, or settings where the potential for harm is elevated. Increasingly, these two approaches have come to be seen as complementary, with population-level measures providing a context within which targeted interventions can be developed (Stimson, Grant, Choquet, & Garrison, 2007).

This book includes a discussion of population-level measures, such as the control of price and access to alcohol (e.g., through setting and enforcing a minimum purchase age). It is worth making clear at the outset that alcohol producers do not favor an exclusive reliance on such measures. Even if they can be demonstrated to have a positive impact on alcohol-related harm, they are usually difficult to introduce and often have detrimental unintended effects (Stimson et al., 2007, pp. 173–191). In addition, their implementation requires elaborate political negotiation, and they are frequently unpopular, at least in part because they are perceived to be discriminatory. However, producers certainly acknowledge the need for a reasonable regulatory framework with opportunities for interventions that address particular groups, settings, and behaviors. How the balance between population-level measures and targeted interventions is created will vary from one country to another, reflecting prevailing attitudes, social and economic circumstances, and culture.

Major alcohol producers understand that reducing harmful drinking is in the enlightened self-interest of their enterprises and their shareholders as well as other stakeholders. While it has been argued that some of their profits derive from excessive or irresponsible drinking, the fact is that such behaviors create a negative image of drinking—and even of producing companies and their brands—that is bad for business. Moreover, left unaddressed, excessive or irresponsible drinking results in calls for high, even punitive, taxes and restrictions. Add to this the fact that *people* manage and operate alcohol-producing companies, and they also wish to prevent harmful drinking and its ill effects, just as we believe most citizens do. Alcohol producers, therefore, support a range of efforts to encourage responsible drinking. These begin with effective self-regulatory mechanisms so that product marketing promotes only responsible drinking. They also support appropriate governmental regulation in areas such as licensing, purchase age restrictions, and drink-driving laws, as well as reasonable taxation. Further, industry can and should partner with governments, public health, and other civil society organizations that provide effective alcohol misuse prevention and harm reduction programs. In this context, public health and economic interests need not be at odds—they are quite complementary.

There is considerable variation among countries in the salience of alcohol as an issue of public concern. In some, there is little attention paid to it at the political level, whereas in others it is a high priority on the political and public agendas. Not only are there different views among the various stakeholders in each country—governments, industry, the scientific and health communities, and nongovernmental organizations—but also there are many shades of opinion within each sector. The challenge in developing alcohol policy is to balance these different interests by both meeting their many demands and harnessing the contributions they can make.

We have noted that WHO perceives Member States to be its main partners in developing the draft global strategy. But, the governments of Member States are not single entities. Different departments of government have distinct and sometimes competing perspectives on alcohol. Finance departments are likely to be conscious of their significant reliance on alcohol taxes and may be reluctant to raise them as a means of regulating consumption if there is a risk that total revenue will fall. Agriculture and industry departments may have a general inclination against regulation and may promote the alcohol production and hospitality industries as important contributors to the economy. Tourism and culture departments may wish to support the role of alcohol consumption as a contributory factor to quality of life and leisure. Justice departments are likely to focus on public order and, thus, on the regulation of retail drinking establishments. All of these are legitimate perspectives, reflecting a concern for the public good.

Of course, public health is an important component of the public good, and health departments, more than any other sector of government, are likely to give priority to preventing harmful drinking as well as to treating alcohol-related diseases and injuries. The cost of health services, whether privately or publicly funded, tends to increase at rates well beyond those of general inflation or many other government programs. This tends to lead to resistance from other government departments that may see their own budgets threatened. The response of health departments is often, at least at the rhetorical level, to focus on disease prevention, which is compatible with the goals of a global alcohol strategy, but the reality is that politicians tend to take a short-term view of their options and favor policies that are most likely to prove popular in the short term. Whether this is a fair assessment is open to dispute, but no alcohol policy can be sustained unless it balances the perspectives of different government departments and other important stakeholders from outside government.

Beyond government, the health and scientific communities exercise significant influence over the terms in which alcohol policy is debated. Again, this is not a homogeneous group. It includes medical practitioners and medical scientists, other health professionals, psychologists, epidemiologists and public health specialists, social scientists (including anthropologists), pharmacologists, biochemists, geneticists, and others from a laboratory science background. The science that lies behind alcohol policy is certainly not free from personal, disciplinary, and ideological considerations. Indeed, the intensity of views on the causes and nature of alcohol problems and appropriate responses to them is greater than is typically seen in other comparable areas of scientific endeavor. As a consequence, in seeking to accumulate the best available evidence, as the WHA resolution mandates, there is some tension between those who interpret "best" to mean "most complete" and those who interpret it to mean "most supportive of a particular perspective."

This tension is even more prevalent within the nongovernmental community. In seeking to gather the views of nongovernmental organizations, WHO is faced with at least three distinct categories. First, there are bodies, often community-based, that focus on prevention, treatment, or both. They generally provide counseling and support services to people with alcohol problems and their families and seek to increase public awareness about alcohol-related health and social problems. Such organizations may or may not be sympathetic to industry interests. Second, there are advocacy organizations with the goal to promote particular views on alcohol policy. They are usually, although not invariably, focused on an approach that favors population-level measures designed to restrict the availability of alcohol and are often highly critical of industry positions. Third, there are social aspects organizations (SAOs), supported by the beverage alcohol industry. SAOs play an active role in prevention of harmful drinking, focusing, for example, on drink-drive countermeasures and underage drinking. There is, frankly, often much contentiousness in the relations among these three categories of nongovernmental organizations, although all have legitimate and relevant contributions to make to policy discussions and subsequent policy implementation.

This book presents the views of another important stakeholder: beverage alcohol producers. As noted at the opening of this chapter, it is worth recognizing that producers are only one part of the supply chain that stretches from farmers who grow the crops forming the basis of the beverages to producers, wholesalers, retailers, and the hospitality sectors—all the way to the consumer. But, producers tend to be particularly active in alcohol policy, if only because branded products are well known and highly visible. As will become apparent from subsequent chapters, producers are very conscious of the roles of all members of the supply chain but, nevertheless, recognize their special position as the catalyst and focus for much private sector involvement. Subsequent chapters discuss the core business models in the beverage alcohol industry, looking at the nature of the products and how they are developed, marketed, and distributed to consumers. Considerations of important public health concerns relating to alcohol need to take account of the local business models, and this is as true for emerging markets as it is for mature economies.

Particular drinking patterns have a special place in many cultures (e.g., Heath, 2000). These patterns are not static and will change as new influences emerge. The lesson that needs to be kept in mind is that producers, retailers, and consumers have a shared obligation to treat alcohol with respect. In this book, we look at efforts to achieve consistency across sectors, regions, and cultures, but always with the recognition that each country—and sometimes even each community—has its own traditions and drinking styles. In seeking common solutions, it is essential to maintain and respect the richness of diversity.

Although it is not a particular focus of this book, it is worth acknowledging that, for major alcohol producers, commitment to sound and balanced alcohol policy is also part of commitment to good practice in corporate social responsibility generally. Most of the companies that sponsor ICAP are, for example, members of the UN Global Compact, with its wide-ranging commitments in such areas as the environment, human rights, labor practices, and anticorruption initiatives.[4] Equally, most of the companies have proud records of corporate philanthropy, including ambitious programs of aid in developing countries.

Despite this, there are some, notably a number of vocal health advocates and public health activists, who take the view that there is a fundamental conflict of interest between industry's profit motive and its involvement in public policy (e.g., Anderson, 2008; Casswell, 2009). This view mirrors a concern about the integrity of scientific research funded by the private sector, for which the concern is that researchers who are financially dependent on a particular funding source are less likely to reveal findings that might prove unpopular with that funding source. A number of measures have been put in place over recent years to protect the integrity of scientific research, most of which have to do with full disclosure of financial ties and relationships with the private sector at the time of publication of results. Within the alcohol field, there

---

[4] See http://www.unglobalcompact.org/

are already two such instruments: "The Farmington Consensus" (1997) and the *Dublin Principles* (ICAP & National College of Ireland, 1997). The former was produced by a group of addiction journal editors, and the latter is a consensus document prepared by ICAP and the National College of Ireland, reflecting input from a wide range of interested parties. Despite their different provenance, these two documents are strikingly similar on the key points of transparency and full disclosure.

The view that industry has no place at the table when alcohol policy is discussed is, of course, unlikely to be answered to the satisfaction of all parties by a simple declaration of interest. After all, potential conflicts of interest can relate to many issues beyond the economic interests of producers. Ideological and religious convictions, for example, which are likely to be deeply and sincerely held by advocacy organizations, can exert a powerful influence on what is and is not considered an appropriate component of alcohol policy. Equally, government-sponsored research may also be following a political agenda. This is a fundamental question about whether *all* those with a legitimate interest in alcohol policy should be involved in its development and implementation or whether only those who assert, rightly or wrongly, their "independence" should participate. The question can be addressed at the ethical level, and here the competing voices of those who support industry's involvement and those who are opposed to it are likely to be raised in loud, long, and heated debate. It is, however, also possible to address the question from a more pragmatic perspective. The answer may be, "Industry should be involved if industry has something to contribute." That is a simple inclusion criterion that can be applied equally to all stakeholders seeking a place at the table. Using this approach, this book is, in a sense, the best response to those who would seek to exclude industry from the policy discussion. Given the range and diversity of contributions that industry members are prepared to make, how can they possibly *not* be part of the solution?

How Can This Book Contribute to More Effective Implementation of Alcohol Policy?

Mention was made of the web-based open consultation process, initiated by the WHO Secretariat as part of its effort to gather views from a wide range of stakeholders about what they could do to help reduce harmful alcohol consumption. Recognizing that we had a unique opportunity to bring together the views of major international alcohol producers and relate them to defined public health goals, ICAP commissioned individuals with extensive knowledge and expertise in relevant fields to work with representatives of our sponsoring companies to produce evidence-based papers in the areas of production, distribution, availability, price, and marketing. In each case, the individual selected had broad experience over many years of the topical area he was asked to address. In three cases (production, distribution, and availability), that experience was within the alcohol production industry, encompassing all major industry sectors, although none of the individuals selected is currently employed by an alcohol production company. For the discussion of price, we selected an individual whose main experience has been within government (although, again, he is not currently a government employee); for marketing, we selected an academic with extensive experience in the area of branding. The individuals came from Australia, South Africa, the United Kingdom, and the United States. We also produced an additional paper looking at partnerships and targeted interventions, which was prepared by ICAP staff members. All six papers were submitted to WHO by their authors on behalf of the ICAP sponsors (WHO, 2009).[5] However, because of the constraints on the length of submissions, reasonably imposed by WHO to make the consultation process manageable, we recognized that the evidence and argumentation included in these six papers had to be severely constrained.

The ICAP Board, therefore, agreed to produce this book, expanding these papers so that they could become full-length chapters and including additional contextual material to support them. The structure of the book relies to a considerable extent on the original six papers. All authors graciously agreed to take their original contributions and work them into full chapters. These form the core of the book, which moves through the supply chain from producing beer, wine, and spirits to the choice consumers make to purchase them. In a sense, each of

---

[5] For referenced versions of the six papers submitted to the WHO consultation, see www.icap.org/Publications/ICAPPapersforWHOConsultation/

these core chapters tells a similar story: Reasonable regulation provides the context for good alcohol policy; excessive regulation often leads to unanticipated negative consequences; leading producers have a proud record of making positive contributions to implementing effective alcohol policies, but there are opportunities to do much more.

A firm conviction of all those who have been involved at the various stages of developing this book is that a great deal more can be achieved by individual stakeholders working together than any one can achieve in isolation. There are many examples of the public and private sectors working together productively, and the book therefore includes some of these examples, drawn from a wide range of cultural contexts and different parts of the world. Because this book is about the role of producers, we have chosen to focus particularly on examples in which producers have played a significant role. Although the main focus is on what can be achieved working together with other stakeholders, there are also examples for which companies have chosen to take a particular initiative alone. We have included these where they can reasonably be taken to represent best practice examples, particularly when independent evaluation has been undertaken. Clearly, it would be good to see more such independent evaluations—if only to counter the claim made by some advocacy groups that industry initiatives of this sort are simply marketing exercises in another guise. Good intentions on the part of industry are insufficient; the challenge is to find ways of working together with public health practitioners and researchers to strengthen the evaluation component of industry programs, whether conducted alone or in partnership. Our hope is that the publication of this book will stimulate even greater enthusiasm for the private and public sectors to work together to reduce harmful drinking and to measure the effectiveness of their efforts. ICAP is currently developing a new generation of policy tools that are intended to promote and provide support for such initiatives.[6]

Finally, it is in the concluding chapter that we hope to come closest to answering the question of how this book—and, therefore, how

---

[6] See *ICAP Blue Book: Practical Guides for Alcohol Policy and Prevention Approaches, ICAP Policy Guides, ICAP Health Briefings, ICAP Issues Briefings,* and *Toolkits* at www.icap.org (under "ICAP Policy Tools").

alcohol producers—can contribute to implementing effective alcohol policy. It is worth acknowledging that many countries limit the extent to which industry members are permitted to work together. Competition laws, antitrust laws, and other legal safeguards sometimes act to restrict opportunities for collective industry action, even if it could be in pursuit of the public good. Nevertheless, the concluding chapter presents both an integrated vision of a future in which producers have a key and continuing role and a menu of options for specific actions that they are willing and able to take, where permitted and appropriate, in countries around the world. Some are extensions of action that they are already taking; others are new proposals, offered in the spirit of breaking down traditional divisions between the private and public sectors. All are based on the experience, competence, and resources of the industry. As such, the last chapter demonstrates the willingness of alcohol producers to play a positive role in both helping to develop effective strategies to reduce harmful drinking and—even more importantly—working on their implementation.

References

American Psychiatric Association (APA). (2000). *Diagnostic and statistical manual of mental disorders* (4th ed., text revision). Washington, DC: Author.

Anderson, P. (2008). Consulting with the industry. *Drug and Alcohol Review, 27*, 463–465.

Baum-Baicker, C. (1985). The psychological benefits of moderate alcohol consumption: A review of the literature. *Drug and Alcohol Dependence, 15*, 305–322.

Casswell, S. (2009). Alcohol industry and alcohol policy—the challenge ahead. *Addiction, 104*, 3–5.

Commission on Social Determinants of Health (CSDH). (2008). *Closing the gap in a generation: Health equity through action on the social determinants of health. Final report of the Commission on Social Determinants of Health.* Geneva, Switzerland: World Health Organization.

Ellison, R. C. (Ed.). (2007, May). Health risks and benefits of moderate alcohol consumption: Proceedings of an international symposium. *Annals of Epidemiology, 17*(Suppl.), S1–S116. Retrieved on February 9, 2009, from http://www.annalsofepidemiology.org/issues

The Farmington Consensus. (1997). *Addiction, 92*, 1617–1618.

Heath, D. B. (2000). *Drinking occasions: Comparative perspectives on alcohol and culture.* Philadelphia: Brunner/Mazel.

International Center for Alcohol Policies (ICAP). (2006). *The structure of the beverage alcohol industry* (ICAP Report 17). Washington, DC: Author.

International Center for Alcohol Policies (ICAP) & National College of Ireland. (1997). *The Dublin principles: Principles of cooperation among the beverage alcohol industry, governments, scientific researchers, and the public health community.* Dublin, Ireland: National College of Ireland.

Peele, S., & Brodsky, A. (2000). Exploring psychological benefits associated with moderate alcohol use: A necessary corrective to assessments of drinking outcomes? *Drug and Alcohol Dependence, 60,* 221–247.

Peele, S., & Grant, M. (Eds.). (1999). *Alcohol and pleasure: A health perspective.* Philadelphia: Brunner/Mazel.

Stimson, G. V., Grant, M., Choquet, M., & Garrison, P. (Eds.). (2007). *Drinking in context: Patterns, interventions, and partnerships.* New York: Routledge.

Stranges, S., Notaro, J., Freudenheim, J. L., Calogero, R. M., Muti, P., Farinaro, E., et al. (2006). Alcohol drinking pattern and subjective health in a population-based study. *Addiction, 101,* 1265–1276.

Valencia-Martin, J. L., Galán, I., & Rodríguez-Artalejo, F. (2009). Alcohol and self-rated health in a Mediterranean country: The role of average volume, drinking pattern, and alcohol dependence. *Alcoholism: Clinical and Experimental Research, 33,* 240–246.

World Health Organization (WHO). (1946). *Constitution of the World Health Organization.* Geneva, Switzerland: Author.

World Health Organization (WHO). (1992). *The ICD-10 classification of mental and behavioural disorders: Clinical descriptions and diagnostic guidelines* (10th revision). Geneva, Switzerland: Author.

World Health Organization (WHO). (2005). *Action on the social determinants of health: Learning from previous experiences. A background paper prepared for the Commission on Social Determinants of Health.* Geneva, Switzerland: Author.

World Health Organization (WHO). (2008). WHA 61.4. Strategies to reduce the harmful use of alcohol. In *Sixty-first World Health Assembly: Geneva, 19–24 May 2008. Resolutions and decisions* (pp. 7–8). Retrieved February 9, 2009, from http://www.who.int/gb/ebwha/pdf_files/WHA61-REC1/A61_REC1-en.pdf

World Health Organization (WHO). (2009). *WHO public hearing on harmful use of alcohol. Volume IV: Received contributions from individuals.* Retrieved March 8, 2009, from http://www.who.int/substance_abuse/activities/6individuals.pdf

2

PRODUCING BEER, WINE, AND SPIRITS

RONALD SIMPSON

Introduction

This chapter is included to help provide an overview of the key issues and processes involved in the production of beer, wine, and spirits and because some of these activities have significant public health implications. It describes those implications that involve product quality and safety, new product development and packaging, the production of drinks with different alcohol strengths, and the economic and social contributions producers make to local economies and sustainable development.

The History and Process of Alcohol Production

The production of beverage alcohol has a long and colorful history. The first step in producing an alcohol beverage is fermentation, the conversion of sugars to carbon dioxide and ethanol (alcohol) by yeast (Tini, 1994). Because yeast and sugars are so widely distributed in nature, the early discoveries of alcohol were mostly by chance. Agricultural products such as grains, vegetables (potatoes), and fruits (grapes) are common sources of sugar or carbohydrates for producing beer, wine, and spirits.

Beer is an ancient beverage. Archeological excavations have brought to light Assyrian and Babylonian bas-reliefs that depict early brewing techniques and date back 6,000 BCE. From ancient Egypt, across the

Middle East, beer spread to central-northern Europe and became the social drink typical of the barbarian populations living there. Beer was also known to ancient Romans, who even attributed therapeutic properties to it (Sbuelz, 1991).

The manufacturing process for beer starts with grains, such as barley, corn, or sorghum. The carbohydrates (starches in the grain) must be converted to sugars to facilitate fermentation. This process is called *malting*. Once the sugars are released from the grains, yeast is added. It ferments the sugars to carbon dioxide and alcohol. The amount of alcohol in the beverage is dependent on the amount of sugar in the fermentation mix (*mash*) and the length of time fermentation is allowed to proceed. The result of this simple process is beer in its raw form. At this stage, home-brewers may simply separate the beer from the mash and bottle it for local sale.

Wine has probably existed as long as humankind itself; the methods for its production have changed and evolved over the centuries (Zonin, 1994). For example, while Romans adopted Greek winemaking techniques, they added some interesting innovations and new varieties of wines in the process.

Wine is generally made from grapes. Grapes contain sugars that are easily fermented. The basic winemaking procedure is simple: Grapes are crushed to release the juice, and yeast is added into the mix; the fermentation proceeds until all of the sugar in the grapes is converted to alcohol. The type of grape and the length of time the skins stay in contact with the fermented juice determine the color of the wine. Many procedures and processes affect the taste of the finished product. Some wines are stored and aged for taste and quality purposes; others are bottled very soon after processing.

Distilling flourished among the early Arabs, Greeks, and Romans and was primarily used for the production of medicine, essential oils, and perfumes. The use of distilling to make beverage alcohol dates to the mid-1300s in Italy (Ford, 1983).

Spirits are produced by a process similar to beer—up through fermentation. The sources of fermentable carbohydrates may be different for spirits than for beer, depending on which beverage is being made. For example, grains are used to make whisk(e)y,[1] a range of raw materials is used to make vodka, and sugar cane is used to make rum. Once the fermentation is complete, the beer is separated from the mash and made ready for distillation. The distilling process separates the alcohol from water by heating the liquid to a temperature hot enough to vaporize the alcohol while the water remains liquid. The vaporized alcohol is cooled, recondensed, and collected in another container. The final alcohol content depends on the quality of the distillation process and intended use of the product. Some distillates, such as those intended for whisk(e)y, are put in barrels at high alcohol content and aged, to be further processed and bottled later. Distillates intended for nonaged products, such as vodka, may be processed directly into a finished product.

The basic steps in the production of beer, wine, and spirits are relatively simple. The ingredients are readily available, and the rudimentary equipment to make these products can be found in most places. So, it is not surprising that so much noncommercial production of these beverages takes place, particularly in poorer areas where people cannot afford to purchase commercial alcohol. Informal producers generally do not have the technology to check the quality and safety of their drinks, which may lead to contamination (see the quality control and safety discussion on pp. 26–28). Meanwhile, commercial brewers, winemakers, and distillers are regulated by strict hygiene and health codes (Carnacini & Riponi, 1998; Cremonini, 1991; Sbuelz, 1991); in addition to the procedures described, their products undergo a series of tests to ensure quality and consumer safety before beverages can be bottled and distributed.

---

[1] The spelling of this spirit varies according to the origin of the product. For example, drinks made in Ireland or the United States are spelled "whiskey," while it is Scotch, Canadian, and Japanese "whisky." This book uses whisk(e)y when speaking about the drink in general and applies the regional spelling when referring to a particular type.

The Structure of the Beverage Alcohol Producers

Global beverage alcohol production is rather heterogeneous and includes both recorded and unrecorded beer, wine, and spirits.

Unrecorded Beverage Alcohol

The volume of unrecorded alcohol production is large, found in virtually every country around the world. In some areas, particularly in low- and middle-income economies, it may account for more than half of total alcohol consumed, but this varies widely from community to community (World Health Organization [WHO], 2004). It appears that local low-volume products make up an overwhelming share of unrecorded consumption. However, the informal market also includes counterfeit beverages; illicit drinks made by clandestine, usually small-scale, outfits; and alcohol that is unregistered to evade taxation (see Chapter 3). Some of these beverages can pose serious health risks as they tend to have unknown alcohol content and may contain hazardous ingredients. Untaxed and often made from cheap materials, such drinks remain popular, however, because they are offered at lower prices than legitimate products.

Recorded Beverage Alcohol

The majority of beverage alcohol in the formal sector is produced by a plethora of domestic manufacturers catering to local traditions and tastes. These products—sometimes called "commodity drinks"—are not traded internationally, but their levels of production are generally recorded by governments for tax purposes. Commodity drinks reflect the local alcohol culture and, in some countries, comprise a significant share of recorded consumption (International Center for Alcohol Policies [ICAP], 2006).

Multinational producers of beer, wine, and spirits account for a surprisingly small portion of total alcohol produced. The top 10 global beer companies make up approximately 23% of the recorded beer market, and the top 10 global spirits producers form approximately 20% of the recorded spirits market. Wine production is more fragmented.

The top 10 winemakers produce approximately 10% of the global wine volume (ICAP, 2006).

To improve its ability to monitor drinking internationally, WHO has a stated objective of collecting the best available data on beverage alcohol production and trade flows. The alcohol producers that sponsor ICAP agreed to ask trade data collection companies to provide top-level data as specified by WHO. ICAP, on behalf of the industry, is making this information available on its website (www.icap.org). The data have been gathered by consulting companies Canadean and the International Wine and Spirit Record (IWSR) and are to be made public annually in the period between 2008 and 2013. The rest of the chapter explores other areas of multi-sector interaction at the alcohol production stage and suggests opportunities for the future.

Opportunities for Working Together

Formal alcohol production is usually a locally based operation with many technical resources. Most production facilities have experts in engineering, chemistry, quality control, and safety. In addition, these local technical experts have access to resources at corporate laboratories. This expertise is available and can be consulted when local officials are confronted with alcohol-related technical issues and problems beyond their capabilities. Companies have demonstrated their willingness to advise and help when asked by governments.

However, long-term industry contributions cannot be sustained in a vacuum. For example, the producers are willing to assist governments in developing quality and safety procedures and training police and quality assurance inspectors, but this process cannot be sustained without a strong and effective enforcement mechanism. Governments have to institute a clear regulatory system that would hold producers, big and small, accountable for the quality of their products and impose adequate penalties for noncompliance. One step forward may be to create an international technical resource pool and make it available to local officials to help them address specific technical problems related to alcohol production. Additional ideas for multi-stakeholder cooperation are identified next, as we consider the economic and social impact of alcohol production, quality controls and safety, and new product development. The production of lower alcohol products is then discussed to illustrate the producers' willingness to meet consumer demand and health considerations.

Economic and Social Impact of Alcohol Production

In both developed and developing countries, commercial alcohol producers provide stable employment to many people and are a significant source of public revenue to governments (Grant & O'Connor, 2005; ICAP, 2006). For example, an economic impact study conducted for Heineken in Sierra Leone demonstrated that, for every job created at the Sierra Leone Brewery (SLB), approximately 40 jobs were generated in indirect employment (Triple Value Strategy Consulting, 2006). In the European Union (EU), the spirits sector directly employs about 50,000 people and indirectly 250,000. The 2,800 European brewers directly employ 164,000 people and indirectly 26 million. It is estimated that, for each job in the brewing sector, one job is generated in retail, two in the supplies sector, and 12 in the hospitality sector. The industries normally linked to alcohol production are advertising, packaging, capital equipment, and agriculture (ICAP, 2006).

Since most alcohol beverages require some type of fermentation, agricultural products are an important component of production. This offers opportunities to source raw materials locally, thus benefiting rural communities, especially women, who are predominantly engaged in farming in many countries. The experience of the SLB (Triple Value Strategy Consulting, 2006) demonstrates the positive impact a company can have on economic development by engaging local farmers. Barley is traditionally used in the production of beer, but it does not grow in the tropics. Therefore, SLB developed a program to substitute locally grown sorghum for imported barley. Approximately 3,000 farmers participate in this program; the production of locally grown grain generates significant local revenue (Triple Value Strategy Consulting, 2006). In addition, local production of legal beverages is likely to reduce the prevalence of noncommercial alcohol, thus increasing government revenue and minimizing the public health risks of contaminated drinks. The box presents another example of how a producer can contribute to local development.

NILE BREWERIES' EAGLE LAGER PROJECT, UGANDA

Nile Breweries' Eagle Lager Project is rooted in a partnership between SABMiller and the Ugandan government. It demonstrates the producer's commitment to encouraging responsible alcohol consumption and illustrates how the private sector can act as a catalyst for economic development.

The project was designed to respond to specific characteristics of the Ugandan alcohol market. The local population cannot afford commercially produced beverages. Many communities therefore produce their own, noncommercial alcohol, which tends to be high in alcohol content and, because it evades quality controls, can be toxic. In addition, these informal beverages are untaxed, diverting funds from state revenue.

In this context, Nile Breweries introduced Eagle Lager, an affordable and quality beer, made from a locally produced primary raw material, sorghum. The project's objectives were to stimulate agricultural research and development into the use of sorghum for brewing and create a market for local farmers. In four years since its launch, this beer is Nile Breweries' top-selling brand. The use of sorghum in production has created a permanent market for 5,800 Ugandan farmers.

An evaluation by local officials in the Soroti District (one of the poorest in Uganda) confirmed that the Eagle Lager Project has directly contributed to the government's Poverty Eradication Action Plan, which is aligned with the poverty alleviation objectives of the United Nations Millennium Development Goals (SABMiller, 2005).

Another essential ingredient for beverage alcohol production is water. Most producers establish their own water source, particularly in developing countries. As part of this process, they work with communities to develop and maintain safe and reliable drinking water systems that can be used by the local population. Such programs go beyond encouraging economic growth to address the broader goals of environmental stewardship and sustainable development.

An early definition of *sustainability* comes from the United Nations World Commission on Environment and Development (1987): "Sustainable development ... implies meeting the needs of the present without compromising the ability of future generations to meet their own needs" (para. 2). Driven by growing public anxieties about climate change and the impact of globalization, governments and citizens increasingly demand social and environmental benefits of sustainable business practices. As a result, each year companies in all industries place more and more information about their business operations in the public domain. Corporate reports on economic, social, and environmental responsibilities have several uses. They address society's interest in the potential positive and negative impacts of an industry; enable companies to learn from each other about successful management practices and benchmark performance and best practice; and ensure accountability and dialogue with a wide range of partners and stakeholders. Today, reporting on sustainable practices is as important to companies as financial reporting, and many leading alcohol producers support global reporting standards that promote transparency. The box offers two examples of industry activities in this area.

SUSTAINABLE DEVELOPMENT INITIATIVES

- Diageo, Molson Coors, and SABMiller have endorsed the United Nations CEO Water Mandate to address water sustainability in the companies' operations and supply chain. It is an initiative developed in partnership among the United Nations Global Compact (n.d.), the government of Sweden, and a group of committed companies and specialized organizations dealing with the problems of water scarcity and sanitation.
- As part of its corporate social responsibility efforts, the Asahi Breweries Group (2008) has been adopting a

multistage program to reduce the environmental impact of its operations. The company is employing a range of energy-saving programs to cut the use of electricity and boiler combustion. These sources of power are being replaced with cogeneration systems and solar and wind power. The company also promotes the collection and recycling of carbon dioxide. As a result of these initiatives, Asahi achieved an annual reduction of about 19,000 tons in carbon dioxide emissions in 2008 compared to 2007. The company is also improving its capability to recycle waste and byproducts, working toward recycling 100% of waste at all 33 group manufacturing sites by 2010; in 2007, this goal was achieved at 28 factories. Finally, by holding public events, such as Environmental Culture Seminars and Education Seminars, Asahi promotes environmental awareness in the communities where it operates.

Such activities contribute positively to social development by improving daily living conditions, thus alleviating poverty and improving the local physical environment. This helps to tackle inequalities in health recognized by WHO (2005, 2009) and identified by the Commission on Social Determinants of Health (2008). These outcomes of commercial alcohol production may be especially important in difficult economic times.

Going forward, areas for multi-stakeholder cooperation in this area may include working with local authorities to develop and maintain safe and reliable sources of drinking water, necessary not only for factory operation but also crucial for the health of the local community. In addition, where appropriate, the leading producers will continue training local farmers to grow crops for ingredients in commercial beverage production, contributing to poverty alleviation, government revenue, and economic development.

Quality Control and Safety

Quality control and safety are a significant part of any production process. A company's license to operate typically covers both of these aspects; it is granted and may be supervised by government in accordance with existing regulations. There are no universally accepted quality and safety controls for alcohol beverages, but many governments establish national or regional standards and product definitions. The rationales for creating these regulations vary but generally include the following: protecting traditional beverages that have acquired a reputation; shielding consumers and producers from deceptive and unfair trade; ensuring that products are safe to consume—that is, that they do not contain inappropriate or harmful levels of, for example, methanol or heavy metals; and providing a yardstick against which the authorities may check for product safety and authenticity.

Two broad approaches to setting product standards exist: defining the necessary raw materials and production processes for a given beverage and specifying its chemical composition. Generally, producers prefer the former as there are serious limitations in defining some beverages by their chemical composition. The EU definitions for spirits are an excellent example of the preferred approach as they establish maximum acceptable levels of methanol and heavy metals, such as lead (European Parliament & European Council, 2008). Major alcohol producers support product standards and definitions and work with governments around the world to promote and encourage their adoption where they do not already exist or where they are inadequate. Producers also work with authorities to ensure that such standards are observed internationally to protect consumers and trade.

Within companies, brand manuals require hundreds of quality and safety checks. Cremonini (1991) described the modern technical approach to beverage alcohol production. In addition to internal checks, all brand manuals must abide by the established national and regional regulations for manufacturing, hygiene, and health. Quality control is applied to all phases of the production cycle, from the purchase of raw materials to their transformation into semiworked and then finished products. Analysis is carried out in well-equipped laboratories by specialized personnel (Cremonini, 1991). The concept of quality not only focuses on the product itself but also on everything that goes into making it and then delivering it to consumers (Carnacini & Riponi, 1998; Sbuelz, 1991). While such safety and quality checks are standard among big producers, they may be limited among small legitimate manufacturers and altogether absent in the unregulated informal market. Absence of set safety checks for illicit products—from counterfeit drinks to homebrews—makes such beverages vulnerable to possible contamination or adulteration.

In the informal sector, the vast majority of contaminated products are spirits, although there are occasional reports of contaminated wine and beer. The primary source of contamination in spirits is methanol (wood alcohol). It is important to note that small amounts of methanol are produced naturally during distillation; this is closely monitored during official quality checks. Research showed that small quantities of methanol are not harmful for health (Lachenmeier, Rehm, & Gmel, 2007). The real health risk comes when methanol is added to an alcohol beverage to increase its strength. Methanol has historically been used to produce denatured alcohol for industrial uses as a solvent and as an ingredient in many household products. The denatured or methylated alcohol is not subject to the same taxation as commercial alcohol and is therefore much cheaper. Because of its ready availability and low price, methanol has become an inexpensive way to increase the potency of noncommercial beverages. Other common sources of contamination in illicit drinks are ethylene glycol (antifreeze), higher alcohols (fusel alcohols), acetic acid, and lead.

The primary source of contamination in beer is moldy grains used during fermentation. For example, a chemical analysis of traditional Xhosa maize beer in South Africa discovered a high concentration of fumonisin mycotoxins, harmful chemicals produced by fungi that are common in maize (Shephard et al., 2005). Although not thought to be acutely toxic, mycotoxins have been found to cause chronic liver damage.

Fungi in ingredients and chemicals added during production or bottling can cause contamination in wine. Thus, the Ministry of Health of Vietnam reported widespread poisoning in Ho Chi Minh City from methanol in wine ("Vietnam Inspects," 2008). Overall, methanol and ethylene glycol are considered the most common sources of acute poisoning among consumers of noncommercial alcohol.

Community leaders have decried the consumption of beverage alcohol products containing dangerous substances, including methanol, bacterial and fungal contaminants, and substances added deliberately to increase alcohol strength. Numerous police, health, and media reports have described incidences of poisoning from noncommercial alcohol beverages (e.g., Nuzhnyi, 2004; see also Chapter 3). From a production point of view, most health-related issues arise from poor-quality alcohol produced in an unsafe environment.

All major producers of beer, wine, and spirits are willing to share their expertise of developing strict quality and safety controls with governments. They are willing to collaborate with local authorities in providing training to help legitimate small producers make safe products and, where home production is widespread, in informing the public about potential risks for contamination and the health consequences of consuming toxic beverages.

New Product Development

The development and introduction of new products require a significant commitment of financial, technical, and creative resources. The process of new product development, at one point or another, involves almost every function in a corporation. Yet, the chances of a new product succeeding are very small.

The process usually begins with a new product idea or concept designed to fill a gap in the market or respond to an emerging consumer trend. These ideas can come from almost anywhere in the company; usually, however, a team from marketing and research departments develops a collection of concepts that can be tested. These concepts may include a new flavor of an existing product, a new package size or shape, a new packaging material (e.g., plastic instead of glass), or an idea for a new product that requires new technology to make (e.g., lower alcohol drinks, discussed in a separate section).

The next step is testing. This involves showing the concepts or new product ideas to a sample of potential consumers in the form of storyboards or product mock-ups. The sample participants are asked whether they like the concept and would buy the new product if it were available. Testing concepts with consumers helps the researchers refine the new ideas and select those that will continue into the product development stage.

The approved concept is generally assigned to a research-and-development team to address the technical issues. The extent of the technical assessment depends on the complexity of the product. Some new products require simple changes in flavor or package style that can be accomplished relatively easily; others must rely on new technology or processes—potentially a long and expensive option.

After the technical issues have been resolved, the research team produces samples that can be taken through another round of consumer testing. Market researchers then provide these samples to a group of potential consumers to see and taste. This usually determines the fate of a new product. If the consumer test is positive—meaning that the consumers like the product and express an interest in buying it—the product will go to the next phase. If the test is negative, the concept may be refined and retested, or the project may be stopped.

Once the new product has been approved by consumer tests, most companies conduct a "full test market," which involves producing a quantity of the new product large enough to be placed in real stores in selected markets. The product is placed on the same shelves as its existing counterparts and is offered for sale. This is the final test to determine if the consumers are interested in buying the new beverage, drinking it, and, it is hoped, purchasing it again. If the test is successful, the new product will be manufactured in large enough quantities to be sent to national or international markets.

Producers recognize that, in developing new products, they need to take into account public health considerations, such as ensuring that new products do not primarily appeal to those under the legal drinking age or that undue emphasis is not placed on the alcohol content of higher-strength drinks. In practice, producers usually apply the provisions of their internal marketing codes and use internal review processes to check code compliance systematically at various stages of product development.

The formality of the review varies among producers, with some having relatively informal processes and others requiring formal sign-off from a range of departments (e.g., corporate social responsibility and legal) beyond the groups normally responsible for developing the product. Where it is implemented, formal sign-off is required at every stage of development; the product cannot proceed to the next stage unless it has received all relevant approvals and is deemed in compliance with marketing codes.

This approach is also often applied to product packaging, which has the potential to encourage irresponsible drinking. Producers accept that such irresponsible containers as syringes and sprays are unsuitable for beverage alcohol and avoid their use. Containers with large quantities of alcohol that cannot be resealed also raise public health issues. A number of industry codes govern the naming and packaging of products and have been effective in preventing or removing irresponsible products from the market. The Portman Group's *Code of Practice on the Naming, Packaging and Promotion of Alcoholic Drinks* (2008) in the United Kingdom (U.K.) is an excellent example of one such code.

PORTMAN GROUP'S CODE, PRODUCT DEVELOPMENT, AND PACKAGING

First introduced in 1996, the Portman Group's *Code of Practice* applies to all prepackaged alcohol beverages and addresses their naming, packaging, point-of-sale advertising, brand websites, merchandise, and other promotional activities (see also Chapter 4). Currently in its fourth edition, the code relies on an independent Complaints Panel to influence, regulate, and control actions of producers, retailers, and others within the industry. The code is publicly available online (www.portman-group.org. uk), and anyone can make a complaint. There are over 140 code signatories from all parts of the industry, but the ruling of the Complaints Panel applies regardless of the signatory status.

Of relevance to the discussion on new product development is the provision by the Portman Group of a free and confidential Advisory Service, offered to companies and importers to ensure code compliance before product launch. Code requirements specific to beverage naming and packaging—all important considerations during new product development—are as follows:

3.1 The alcoholic nature of the drink should be communicated on its packaging with absolute clarity.

3.2 A drink, its packaging, and any promotional material or activity should not in any direct or indirect way:

(a) have the alcoholic strength, relatively high alcohol content, or the intoxicating effect, as a dominant theme;

(b) suggest any association with bravado, or with violent, aggressive, dangerous or anti-social behaviour . . . ;

(c) suggest any association with, acceptance of, or allusion to, illicit drugs;

(d) suggest any association with sexual success;

(e) suggest that consumption of the drink can lead to social success or popularity;

(f) encourage illegal, irresponsible or immoderate consumption, such as drink-driving, binge-drinking or drunkenness;

(g) urge the consumer to drink rapidly or to "down" a product in one;

(h) have a particular appeal to under-18s [the minimum drinking age in the U.K.] . . . ;

(i) incorporate images of people who are, or look as if they are, under 25 years age . . . ;

(j) suggest that the product can enhance mental or physical capabilities. (Portman Group, 2008, p. 7)

A company found incompliant with the code is asked to take necessary action—for example, redesign the packaging in accordance with the code or withdraw the product from the market—as directed by the Complaints Panel. The companies must respond to this ruling within a set time, normally no more than 3 months. In case of continued breach, the Code Secretariat may contact retailers, Internet service providers, trade associations, relevant licensing authorities, the media, and others to enforce the panel's decision. Details of complaints, rulings, and follow-up are published and distributed to government, industry, the media, and the general public.

An example of the code in action is the ruling on Wee Beastie and Big Beastie, carbonated vodka drinks flavored with raspberry and blackcurrant. The Wine and Spirit Trade Association complained in 2006 that these drinks break the code "in terms of packaging and the content and style of the website. They use childish images of dancing and laughing spiders and we feel it is designed to have specific appeal to under-18s" (Portman Group, 2006, p. 5). After review and communication with the producers, the panel concluded that "the combination of the garish pink and yellow colours, the cartoon-style grinning spider and the [large] 'Adults Only' warning meant that, overall, both products and the brand website were likely to have a particular appeal to under-18s," in breach of code paragraph 3.2(h) (Portman Group, 2006, p. 5). In response to the ruling, the producers took down the brand website and were liaising with the Advisory Service for guidance on amending the products' packaging. Big Beastie was removed from the market in 2009.

This is a simplified summary of some of the key steps involved in identification, development, and introduction of a new product. It should be reemphasized that the vast majority of such beverages fail despite the time and expense involved in their creation. Throughout the process, the leading alcohol producers rely on a series of checks to ensure compliance with internal marketing codes. Going forward, they will strengthen their efforts to address public health issues explicitly during existing corporate reviews of new product and package development.

Lower Alcohol Products

Producers of beverage alcohol have been willing to invest in new technology to meet consumer demand for low- and mid-strength drinks (ICAP, 2007). However, there will only be demand for such products if they meet quality and taste expectations equal to or better than other products on the market.

Considerable progress has been made in building technology to reduce the alcohol content of beer and wine. Various aspects of this process were described by Giovanelli (1993) and Buiatti and Zironi (1997). Although the authors found that it is economically possible to reduce alcohol content of beer and wine, Giovanelli warned that one of the main problems of the various methods employed is the loss of aromatic constituents. The recovery of aroma is of crucial importance to retaining a well-balanced taste and flavor in the treated beverages. This research underlined the fact that developing high-quality lower alcohol products is more than simply removing alcohol.

While specific product definitions vary by market or country, "regular-strength" alcohol content is generally as follows: 4.6 to 6.0% of alcohol by volume (ABV) for lager beers, 12.0 to 15.0% ABV for wines, 37.5 to 40.0% for spirits, and 15.0% and above for liqueurs (ICAP, 2007). Drinks with lower alcohol content are produced in each of the major beverage alcohol categories. However, legal product standards (defining, among other things, minimum alcohol content of different spirits and beer types and forbidding intervention into the wine fermentation process) may limit a broad trend of lowering content for these beverage categories.

Non-alcohol brews and reduced-alcohol beers have been available in some markets for decades and have gained acceptance. These products range from zero alcohol to approximately 4.5% ABV. From 1995 to 2005, there was a significant shift in the United States (U.S.) in consumption from regular lager-type beer (4.6 to 6.0% ABV) to "light beer" (4.2 to 4.5% ABV). The volume of beer at 6.0% ABV or higher now makes up less than 10% of the total alcohol sold in the U.S. (ICAP, 2007).

Spirits-based drinks with lower alcohol content have been developed in an attempt to provide a broader choice for spirits drinkers. For example, a producer of a leading vodka brand with 40% ABV launched a brand extension with 21% ABV. Although this new beverage belongs to the same brand, it can no longer be called "vodka" for regulatory reasons but is called a "spirit drink."

Another category of lower alcohol products is "ready-to-drink" (RTD) beverages, which are often extensions of well-known brands developed to respond to consumer trends for taste, variety of flavors, and convenience of packaging. These premixed, spirits-based or malt-based drinks, sold in single-serve packaging, generally reflect common cocktails or mixed drinks consumed in licensed premises. Alcohol content of RTDs is similar to such mixed spirits—for example, around 5.5% ABV—although this varies from country to country. Unfortunately, in some countries, RTDs have become embroiled in the public health controversy surrounding so-called alcopops due to the perception that they appeal to minors or are a cause of binge drinking by young adults.

Some effort has been made by wine producers to make lower alcohol and non-alcohol wines. The lower alcohol wines must meet regulatory definitions or be called by a fanciful name, thus limiting their appeal. The EU has set a definition for wine in its legislation (Giovanelli, 1993). In France, a zero-alcohol wine has been on the market since 1989. The producer had defined the drink "non-alcohol wine," while the public authorities wanted to label it "grape juice." The disagreement was resolved in favor of the producer, confirming that the product represents a healthy innovation for French viticulture. Non-alcohol sweet and sparkling wines can be found in European stores, whereas non-alcohol red wines are sold outside Europe.

Lower alcohol products have a definite place in the market and a public health role to play in moderating consumption, but this latter point should not be overstated and is, in practice, rather limited. In a small experimental study, Segal and Stockwell (2009) found that male students were unable to readily distinguish low- and regular-strength beers. The authors concluded that these students could enjoy socializing equally with either type of product. On the other hand, producers' experience with some lower alcohol products has made them cautious, following consumers' resentment at finding their drink "watered down" and feeling "ripped off." It is also incorrect to assume that higher-strength drinks automatically result in higher or excessive alcohol consumption. For example, full-strength spirits are mostly consumed with mixers—including soft drinks, tonic, or water—making a typical serving significantly less potent; equally, a common drinking pattern for some spirits is to sip a small amount slowly over a long period.

Consumers choose products of different strengths depending on their mood and the occasion; alcohol content thus tends to be a secondary consideration to taste. Many consumers make their own decisions about the strength of their drink, regardless of the initial alcohol content of a particular product. In the United Kingdom, for example, some consumers "regulate" their drinks by adding a shot of spirit (especially to an RTD or a beer) to increase alcohol content or to adjust the flavor. Meanwhile, nightclub-goers in Spain commonly dilute their drinks by adding more mixer to make them less potent or just make them last longer. The existence of lower alcohol products points to an interest on the part of the industry to provide an expanded range of goods that reflect consumer lifestyle choices, health consciousness, and price sensitivity—as well as taste.

Conclusion

Producing beer, wine, and spirits is an almost ubiquitous activity that has a deep social, economic, and cultural impact on society. Examination of the structure of the industry reveals a great variety of sources for the production of beverage alcohol. Some producers are large corporations with operations in many countries; others—the majority—are domestic producers serving the local market. Moreover, a significant portion of all alcohol produced, particularly in developing countries, is noncommercial, unregulated, untaxed, and unrecorded. The large multinational producers have strict quality control and safety programs to ensure that the highest-quality products are available to all consumers. In countries where these major corporations operate, they contribute to economic growth, improved public health, education, and sustainable development. As this chapter attempted to demonstrate, these companies accept that a number of public health issues may be involved in making their products and are willing to work with others to benefit the consumers.

References

Asahi Breweries Group. (2008). *Corporate social responsibility report.* Tokyo: Author.
Buiatti, S., & Zironi, R. (1997). Technological innovation and improved beer quality. *Alcologia, 9,* 55–59.

Carnacini, A., & Riponi, C. (1998). Biotechnologies in winemaking: Ensuring good quality, natural products. *Alcologia, 10*, 62–65.

Commission on Social Determinants of Health (CSDH). (2008). *Closing the gap in a generation: Health equity through action on the social determinants of health. Final report of the Commission on Social Determinants of Health.* Geneva, Switzerland: World Health Organization.

Cremonini, G. (1991). The manufacture and quality control of liquors. *Alcologia, 3*, 71–73.

European Parliament & European Council. (2008, February 13). Regulation (EC) No. 110/2008 of the European Parliament and the Council of 15 January 2008 on the definition, description, presentation, labelling and the protection of geographical indications of spirit drinks and repealing Council Regulation (EEC) No. 1576/89. *Official Journal of the European Union, 51*(L 39), 16–54.

Ford, G. (1983). *Ford's illustrated guide to wines, brews and spirits.* Dubuque, IA: Brown.

Giovanelli, G. (1993). Reducing the alcohol content of fermented beverages: Improvements in technology. *Alcologia, 5*, 61–67.

Grant, M., & O'Connor, J. (Eds.). (2005). *Corporate social responsibility and alcohol: The need and potential for partnership.* New York: Routledge.

International Center for Alcohol Policies (ICAP). (2006). *The structure of the beverage alcohol industry* (ICAP Report 17). Washington, DC: Author.

International Center for Alcohol Policies (ICAP). (2007). *Lower alcohol beverages* (ICAP Report 19). Washington, DC: Author.

Lachenmeier, D., Rehm, J., & Gmel, G. (2007). Surrogate alcohol: What do we know and where do we go? *Alcoholism: Clinical and Experimental Research, 31*, 1613–1624.

Nuzhnyi, V. (2004). Chemical composition, toxic, and organoleptic properties of noncommercial alcohol samples. In A. Haworth & R. Simpson (Eds.), *Moonshine markets: Issues in unrecorded alcohol beverage production and consumption* (pp. 177–199). New York: Brunner-Routledge.

Portman Group. (2006). *The annual code report 2006. The Portman Group's code of practice on the naming, packaging and promotion of alcoholic drinks.* Retrieved February 28, 2009, from http://portman-group.org.uk/assets/documents/ACR%202006.pdf

Portman Group. (2008). *The code of practice on the naming, packaging and promotion of alcoholic drinks* (4th ed.). Retrieved February 28, 2009, from http://portman-group.org.uk/?pid=18&level=2

SABMiller. (2005). *Submission prepared for Oracle International Award: Eagle-Lager project, Uganda.* Retrieved February 28, 2009, from http://www.SABMiller.com

Segal, D., & Stockwell, T. (2009). Low alcohol alternatives: A promising strategy for reducing alcohol related harm. *International Journal of Drug Policy, 20*, 183–187.

Shephard, W. G., van der Westhuizen, L., Gatyeni, P. M., Somdyala, N. I. M., Burger, H.-M., & Marasas, W. F. O. (2005). Fumonisin mycotoxins in traditional Xhosa maize beer in South Africa. *Journal of Agricultural and Food Chemistry, 53,* 9634–9637.

Sbuelz, R. (1991). The manufacture of beer: Aspects of modern technology. *Alcologia, 3,* 63–69.

Tini, V. (1994). The role of yeast in the production of fermented beverages. *Alcologia, 6,* 43–44.

Triple Value Strategy Consulting. (2006). *Economic impact of Heineken in Sierra Leone.* Amsterdam: Author.

United Nations Global Compact. (n.d.). *The CEO water mandate.* Retrieved February 28, 2009, from http://www.unglobalcompact.org/docs/news_ events/8.1/Ceo_water_mandate.pdf

United Nations World Commission on Environment and Development. (1987). *Report of the World Commission on Environment and Development.* Retrieved February 28, 2009, from http://www.un.org/documents/ga/ res/42/ares42-187.htm

Vietnam inspects alcohol markets amid increasing of wine poisoning cases. (2008, October 22). *Viet Nam News.* Retrieved October 22, 2008, from http://vietnamnews.vnagency.com.vn

World Health Organization (WHO). (2004). *Global status report on alcohol.* Geneva, Switzerland: Author.

World Health Organization (WHO). (2005, March). *Action on the social determinants of health: Learning from previous experiences. A background paper prepared for the Commission on Social Determinants of Health.* Geneva, Switzerland: Author.

World Health Organization (WHO). (2009, January 23). *Reducing health inequities through action on the social determinants of health* (EB124/SR/8). Retrieved February 28, 2009, from http://www.who.int/gb/ebwha/pdf_ files/EB124/B124_R6-en.pdf

Zonin, G. (1994). Wine and its development. *Alcologia, 6,* 39–42.

3

UNDERSTANDING ALCOHOL AVAILABILITY

Noncommercial Beverages

ADRIAN BOTHA

Introduction

Reasonable regulations concerning alcohol availability—or where, when, and by whom alcohol can be sold, obtained, and consumed— are a necessary component of any balanced alcohol policy. A balanced policy avoids excessive regulation and relies on promoting the wellbeing of society without infringing on individual freedom and choice of the moderate-drinking majority. How this balance is created will vary internationally, reflecting socioeconomic circumstances and culture (Stimson, Grant, Choquet, & Garrison, 2007).

In mature economies, laws and regulatory frameworks are generally in place, but enforcement may be uneven; in many developing countries, both the legal framework and enforcement may be lacking (World Health Organization [WHO], 2004b). In this context, proper enforcement of laws should be backed by education of the general public about drinking patterns and outcomes, other prevention and intervention initiatives, and the involvement of the broader community. Importantly, excessive regulations on the availability of alcohol run the risk of generating unintended and often negative consequences, such as driving consumers toward the informal—and completely unregulated—market (Adelekan, Razvodovsky, Liyanage, & Ndetei, 2008).

In most countries, a license is required to produce and sell alcohol beverages. Yet, for example, many alcohol outlets—such as *shebeens*, small local bars widespread in African countries like South Africa—remain beyond the reach of licensing authorities. In many countries, particularly in the developing world, much of the alcohol consumption (and production) follows established traditions, and the complexities of cultural and social contexts tend to resist attempts at government oversight (Haworth & Simpson, 2004).

Whereas the rest of this book focuses on legal alcohol production and sale, this chapter considers the availability of *noncommercial alcohol*—drinks whose manufacture, sale, and consumption are not reflected in official alcohol statistics, such as sales, revenue, or trade figures. Although the production of many noncommercial beverages meets high standards of quality (Haworth & Simpson, 2004), some of what is included under this heading is of poor quality and may be contaminated and toxic. This latter category may pose a public health problem in many countries, particularly in the developing world and in countries undergoing rapid social and economic transition (e.g., Grant, 1998; Ryan, 1995). As one observer noted, "The popularity of noncommercial beverages . . . is driven by the significant price differential between commercial and noncommercial alcohol: The latter is cheaper because such beverages avoid taxation and are normally manufactured with low-cost ingredients, unchecked by official quality controls" (Liyanage, 2008, p. 24). In the many countries where such beverages are prevalent, any consideration of alcohol policy and interventions to address harmful drinking must consider the dynamics of the informal market.

What Is Noncommercial Alcohol?

Drinks from the informal sector have been variously referred to as "moonshine," "local alcohol," "bootleg," "unrecorded," or "home-brewed." There is often confusion about the terminology. Our term *noncommercial alcohol* refers to three beverage categories: traditional homemade drinks; mass-produced illicit beverages, including counterfeit and unregistered products; and nonbeverage—or surrogate—alcohols. A brief description of the three categories is in order.

- *Traditional Drinks:* Produced for home consumption or limited local trade, these drinks include such traditional favorites as *arrack* (India), *cachaça* (Brazil), *kachasu* (Zambia), *palinka*

(Hungary), *pulque* (Mexico), *sahti* (Finland), and *samogon* (Russia), to name a few. Production, distribution, and consumption of such beverages form an integral part of many cultures (Heath, 2000; Mateos, Paramo, Carrera, & Rodriguez Lopez, 2002). Some countries (e.g., Hungary) therefore legally permit production and sale of specified volumes of home-produced alcohol. In some areas, these beverages are an important part of the local economy. For example, in rural Africa,

> a majority of women engage in the production and sale of these beverages as their main commercial activity and as a means of supporting their families. In some [African] countries, home-made beer may be the most widely consumed alcohol and is quite significant in economic terms. (Adelekan, 2008, p. 3)

Whether produced legally or illegally, traditional beverages tend to be of high quality and enjoy widespread popularity (see, e.g., Adelekan et al., 2008; Nuzhnyi, 2004). In fact, many such beverages undergo informal quality controls that help those producing them stay in business (Haworth & Simpson, 2004). However, despite the informal producers' best efforts, the production process itself may pose considerable risk (see Chapter 2), even when one excludes the deliberate adulteration of beverages (to increase their strengths or, as some informal producers believe, speed up fermentation) and the use of dangerous and low-quality ingredients to make cheap drinks. For example, there have been reports of local beers brewed in old oil drums, thereby introducing toxic contaminants. Similarly, the fermentation process of pulque, a Mexican beverage made from the fermented juice of the agave or maguey plant, often relies on the use of animal excrement, resulting in high levels of bacterial contamination in the drink and significant health risks (Rosovsky, 2004).

- *Mass-produced Illicit Alcohol:* Counterfeit beverages packaged as legitimate commercial products, and illicit drinks mass produced by clandestine outfits, coexist with legal production in many countries, particularly in the context of inadequate legal protection for intellectual property, poor law enforcement (where laws exist), corruption by authorities, and unmet consumer demand because of very high prices or strict availability restrictions on the formal alcohol sector.

Counterfeiting of beverage alcohol can take two forms: substitution/refill (typically, when a genuine premium brand is substituted for a cheaper, inferior-quality generic brand in bars by refilling of empty bottles) and organized criminal counterfeit (where small operations or large-scale organized enterprises manufacture fake packaging and liquid or recycle packaging with their own liquid to distribute locally or internationally). Sometimes, counterfeiters use fake labels and closures. In addition to the serious public health concern that these drinks may pose from contamination and low-quality ingredients, their link to organized crime presents a threat to public order.

Also included in this category are unregistered beverages produced at licensed alcohol factories. For example, state inspections in Russia revealed a number of cases when factories worked in two shifts: Daytime production was registered, while nighttime production remained unregistered—and untaxed, diverting revenue from state coffers (Nemtsov, 2001).

- *Surrogate Alcohol:* A relatively widespread phenomenon in some areas, consumption of liquids derived from medicinal compounds, automobile products, cosmetics, and other non-beverage substances is particularly prevalent among problem drinkers in the lowest socioeconomic brackets (McKee et al., 2005). In addition, as noted, drinks made illicitly are at times adulterated with surrogate alcohol, for example, to increase alcohol concentration. The high alcohol content and toxicity of such liquids have been linked to negative health outcomes among drinkers.

We are thus looking at a subsection of what WHO terms *unrecorded alcohol*.[1] This chapter does not address the instances when high-quality

---

[1] WHO's term *unrecorded alcohol* covers the following: home production (licit and illicit), travelers' imports and cross-border shopping, smuggling, surrogate alcohol, tourist consumption, and beverages with alcohol content below the legal definition of alcohol (WHO, 2004a, p. 15).

global brands are bought in one market and sold in another without the involvement of the global brand owner, sometimes illegally. Tourist consumption (drinking during visits to other countries), travelers' imports, and cross-border purchases, all considered part of WHO's "unrecorded consumption," are also outside the scope of this discussion.

Because it is not taxed, regulated, or recorded, little scientific evidence is currently available about noncommercial alcohol and its production, consumption, and related outcomes. When estimates have been made, a number of methodological problems weaken conclusions and—because of differences in measurement, infrastructure, and accessible data sources in different countries—impair international comparison (e.g., Razvodovsky, 2008; Webb & Block, 2008). The box reviews some of the methods that have been applied to gauge the informal alcohol market in Europe, with emphasis on central and eastern Europe (CEE), where the prevalence of noncommercial alcohol remains high.

METHODS TO ASSESS NONCOMMERCIAL ALCOHOL CONSUMPTION IN EUROPE

Assessing the magnitude of noncommercial alcohol consumption is a challenge. Assessment methods can be either direct or indirect. Direct methods include population surveys, which may draw on national screenings. Such surveys are often employed to measure real levels of alcohol consumption in western Europe (Simpura, Karlsson, & Leppänen, 2002). Researchers in CEE must overcome serious obstacles in using self-reported responses given cultural tendencies to hide alcohol-related problems (Nemtsov, 2003).

Several indirect methods to measure the informal sector have been developed and implemented in CEE. In 1980, the State Statistics Service began examining noncommercial alcohol consumption in the former Soviet Union (Nemtsov, 2000). The estimates were based on an analysis of sugar sales, sugar being the main raw material for samogon, the traditional homemade spirit. Other agricultural raw materials, such as grain and fruits, as well as grapes used for home wine production, were not considered. These assessments ceased in 1988 because of sugar shortages on the Soviet market.

Nemtsov (2000) assessed the real level of alcohol consumption in Russia by examining forensic reports on accidental and violent deaths and using blood alcohol coefficients (BACs), estimated from the ratio of BAC-positive and BAC-negative cases. Results indicated that, in the period between 1981 and 2001, the level of unregistered alcohol consumption fluctuated from 4.2 liters per capita in 1984 to 8.9 liters in 1993, which comprised 40 and 178% of official sales figures, respectively.

In areas where noncommercial alcohol is produced from grapes, the informal market can be estimated by calculating the difference between the total area of vineyards and the area of vineyards cultivated for commercial purposes. Thus, in Bulgaria the total area of vineyards is estimated to range from 96,000 to 110,000 hectares. According to available records, 71,500 hectares are cultivated for commercial purposes, while the rest are likely used for noncommercial alcohol production (FAO Investment Centre & European Bank for Reconstruction and Development Cooperation Programme, 2005).

A study in Belarus—which used the autoregressive integrated moving average (ARIMA) time series analysis and focused on the dynamics of such indicators as the level of violent deaths involving alcohol intoxication, incidence of acute alcohol poisoning, and prevalence of alcohol psychosis—reported that the rates of noncommercial alcohol consumption fluctuated significantly in the period between 1980 and 2005 (Razvodovsky, 2003). After leveling off in the mid-1980s, such consumption rose sharply in the second half of the 1980s and early 1990s, after which it began to diminish gradually. In 2003, this figure was 4 liters per capita (4.3 liters per capita of the adult population) or 43% of official alcohol sales in Belarus.

In western Europe, Norström (1998) proposed the now-classic indirect method of assessment based on the data for per capita recorded alcohol consumption and alcohol-related mortality. The method is based on the difference between the actual mortality figures and those that may be predicted from the official consumption data. This difference (the so-called white noise) reflects the influence of factors beyond recorded drinking. This method has helped assess the magnitude of the informal sector in western Europe (Leifman, 2002).

Limitations of the approaches that base the estimates of the informal sector on alcohol-related mortality and official records of per capita drinking should be noted. Mortality is affected not only by how much alcohol is consumed—particularly across a population—but also by the kind of beverages consumed, the drinking patterns, and other factors, such as the number of treatment and counseling facilities available to problem drinkers (e.g., WHO, 2004b). These variables can change significantly, influencing the quality of estimates and hampering cross-country comparison.

Source: Razvodovsky (2008, p. 18)

The figures of unrecorded consumption derived by WHO (2004a) rely in large part on expert estimates and specialized surveys in some countries (Rehm & Gmel, 2001; Rehm et al., 2003). As far as conclusions can be drawn, Table 3.1 presents the estimates for a selection of countries. Although WHO data focus on the broader category of unrecorded alcohol, regional experts suggest that noncommercial beverages, as defined here, account for much of unrecorded drinking in many low- and middle-income countries (Adelekan et al., 2008).

Public Health, Social Issues, and Policy

Strategies to address the informal market have important social implications, not least because noncommercial beverages are produced or consumed primarily by low-income segments of the population. Governments in developing countries sometimes ignore noncommercial alcohol production, knowing that it may be an important source of income for their people.

Table 3.1 Estimates of Unrecorded Alcohol Consumption and Total Recorded Alcohol Consumption in Low- and Middle-income Countries, WHO Data (after 1995)

COUNTRY	RECORDED ALCOHOL CONSUMPTION (LITERS)	UNRECORDED ALCOHOL CONSUMPTION (LITERS)	TOTAL ALCOHOL CONSUMPTION (LITERS)	RELATIVE WEIGHT OF UNRECORDED CONSUMPTION (%)
Belarus	8.1	4.9	13.0	37.7
Botswana	5.4	3.0	8.4	35.7
Brazil	5.3	3.0	8.3	36.1
Bulgaria	7.1	3.0	10.1	29.7
Burkina Faso	4.4	3.3	7.7	42.9
China	4.5	1.0	5.5	18.2
Croatia	12.7	4.5	17.2	26.2
El Salvador	3.5	2.0	5.5	36.4
Estonia	9.9	5.0	14.9	33.6
Hungary	11.9	4.0	15.9	25.2
India	0.8	1.7	2.5	68.0
Kenya	1.7	5.0	6.7	74.6
Lithuania	12.3	4.9	17.2	28.5
Mauritius	3.2	11.0	14.2	77.5
Mexico	4.6	3.0	7.6	39.5
Nigeria	10.0	3.5	13.5	25.9
Philippines	3.8	3.0	6.8	44.1
Poland	8.7	3.0	11.7	25.6
Republic of Korea	7.7	7.0	14.7	47.6
Republic of Moldova	13.9	12.0	25.9	46.3
Romania	7.6	4.0	11.6	34.5
Russian Federation	10.6	4.9	15.5	31.6
Rwanda	6.8	4.3	11.1	38.7
Slovenia	6.6	1.3	7.9	16.5
South Africa	7.8	2.2	10.0	22.0
Sri Lanka	0.2	0.5	0.7	71.4
Thailand	8.5	2.0	10.5	19.0
Uganda	19.5	10.7	30.2	35.4
Ukraine	4.0	8.0	12.0	66.7
Zimbabwe	5.1	9.0	14.1	63.8

Note: Consumption is in liters of pure alcohol per capita for population aged over 15 years.
Source: From WHO (2004a); see also Rehm and Gmel (2001). Reproduced with permission of S. Karger AG, Basel.

At the same time, noncommercial alcohol may represent a public health hazard as both traditional and mass-produced illicit drinks are of inconsistent quality. Some such drinks are contaminated, adulterated, and toxic (Holstege, Ferguson, Wolf, Baer, & Poklis, 2004; McKee et al., 2005; Mosha, Wangabo, & Mhinzi, 1996). Surrogate alcohols, meanwhile, are very high in ethanol content and contain harmful chemicals. Reports from around the world have featured stories about mass poisonings, blindness, and even deaths from bad batches of local drinks, tainted with methanol, lead, arsenic, and other toxins (Haworth & Simpson, 2004, pp. 6–7; Holstege et al., 2004; Hudson, Crecelius, & Gerhardt, 1980; Silverberg, Chu, & Nelson, 2001; Tonkabony, 1975; Willis, 2003). Exploratory investigations of homemade spirits in CEE found higher concentrations of methanol and long-chain alcohols than in products from commercial sources (Lang, Vali, Szucs, & McKee, 2006; Szucs, Sárváry, McKee, & Adany, 2005).

HEADLINES FROM AROUND THE WORLD

Brazil: Death by Methanol Poisoning

A cluster of 13 fatal cases of methanol poisoning after drinking the sugar cane spirit known as *cachaça* or *pinga* was reported in November 1997 in Serrinha, Bahía, Brazil. All the cases had a history of heavy cachaça consumption followed by progressive symptoms of nausea, vomiting, thirst, palpitations and blindness. Analysis of samples of the suspect *cachaça* by the Ministry of Agriculture revealed levels of methanol of 17%, 68-fold the accepted level. Two hypotheses have been put forward to account for the high levels of methanol in the *cachaça*. The first is that the *cachaça* became contaminated with methanol after being stored in large plastic containers which had previously been used for storage by the local chemical industry. The second, more likely, hypothesis is that the *cachaça* was produced in a clandestine distillery, where it was deliberately mixed with industrial alcohol to produce a cheap, low quality product. (adapted from Laranjeira & Dunn, 1998, p. 1103)

Estonia: Bootleg Vodka Makes Up Third of Market

A report from the Estonian Institute of Economic Research estimates that bootleg vodka amounts to 30% of all alcohol sold. The report estimates that over half of the illegal sales are made from private residences, a fifth from street vendors, 13% from small retail outlets, and 11% from open-air markets. In 2001, 68 people died in a town of Parnu after drinking methanol alcohol.... (adapted from O'Connell, 2003, paras. 2–3, 6)

Cameroon: Illicit Brews Flood Cameroonian Market

In Yaounde, Cameroon, the underprivileged population are increasingly turning to potentially lethal, illicit alcoholic brews, because they cannot afford conventional ones.... [I]n November 1997, about 20 people died in the capital from drinking *odontol*, a locally produced gin which is popular amongst the poor. Following the tragedy, the government attempted to prohibit the distilling and consumption of the liquor, however the operations simply moved underground to become even more crude and even more popular. Many people rely on selling odontol and other illicit brews in order to survive and support their families. In the past, this distribution was punishable with a prison sentence but now the public authorities are edging towards complacence. ("Illicit Brews," 2002, paras. 3, 4, 5)

India: Poison Moonshine Kills 110 of India's Poor

The poison hooch has claimed at least 110 lives in recent days. A vast majority of the dead came from slums here [Bangalore], but several dozen deaths were also reported in nearby rural areas and across the state border in Tamil Nadu.... The hooch deaths, as they are called, are occurring a year after the government prohibited the sale of arrack, or country liquor, arguing that it was ruinous to the poor, but left other kinds of alcohol untouched. Since then, plastic sachets of illegal brew have turned up occasionally in Bangalore's poorest neighborhoods.... [T]he state police chief said the liquor was spiked with camphor and tobacco and was suspected to have contained toxic methyl alcohol. The state's top liquor enforcement official ... said that it contained 40% alcohol, but that its exact contents would not be known until lab tests results were released. (Sengupta, 2008, paras. 3, 7, 11)

Nicaragua and El Salvador: Nicaragua Tainted Brew Kills 22

Nicaraguan police have been raiding bars and stores in search of adulterated alcohol that is so far believed to have killed 22 people. Extra doctors have been sent to the city of Leon, where more than 100 people are in hospital. The tainted liquor is thought to have been mixed with methanol, which can cause blindness and organ failure. A similar outbreak of methanol poisoning in El Salvador six years ago left at least 120 people dead. ... Illegally brewed alcohol is much cheaper than commercially produced beer or rum. ("Nicaragua Tainted Brew," 2006, paras. 1–4, 12)

Russian Federation: More Than a Thousand Moscow Residents Died of Counterfeit Alcohol in 2008

[Six thousand forty-one] people were intoxicated by counterfeit alcoholic beverages in Moscow in 2008, the capital's Board of Health's press release read. 1,069 of the intoxicated died, Interfax informed. According to the data from police, 2 million bottles of counterfeit alcohol were confiscated in Moscow in 2008. Nine underground distilleries were shut down. "The Board of Consumer Market and Services reported suspending 343 and cancelling 556 licenses for manufacturing and sales of alcoholic beverages," press release noted. ("More than a Thousand," 2009, paras. 1–2)

Vietnam: Vietnam Inspects Alcohol Markets Amid Increasing Wine Poisoning Cases

The Ministry of Health has set up inspection teams to check hygiene and food safety in wine production and trading establishments in Ho Chi Minh City, following an alarming number of cases of alcohol poisoning. In almost every case high methanol levels in the wine caused the poisoning, and 27 people have been hospitalised up to October 21st, with 9 fatalities. According to statistics released by the Food Safety and Hygiene Department, wine poisoning accounts for almost 42% of food poisoning cases every year. ("Vietnam Inspects," 2008, para. 1)

Regular consumption of noncommercial alcohol can also result in long-term chronic problems. For example, high levels of liver cirrhosis have been reported among those who drink noncommercial beverages—largely from the drinks' bacterial contamination—even when these individuals are not heavy or frequent drinkers (Lovelace & Nyathi, 1977). In the United States, "moonshine" has been reported to have elevated lead levels that, over time, can have adverse health consequences for consumers (Holstege et al., 2004). Studies of emergency room patients in Atlanta, Georgia (Morgan, Todd, & Moore, 2001), and rural counties in southeastern United States (Pegues, Hughes, & Woernle, 1993) reached similar conclusions. Widespread consumption of illicitly produced alcohol in the 1980s and 1990s (Stickley et al., 2007; Szucs et al., 2005), coupled with surrogate alcohol consumption (Lang et al., 2006; McKee et al., 2005), have been linked to high mortality rates in the republics of the former Soviet Union.

In addition, as noted, illicit alcohol production and trade can be associated with organized crime and thus represent a significant public order and safety issue (Junninen & Aromaa, 2000). For example, counterfeiting of beverage alcohol has been a major source of income to the Irish Republican Army (IRA), Chinese triads throughout Asia, and the Russian mafia in many countries. The cumulative effect of counterfeiting, beyond its threat to consumer health, includes consumer deception, loss of confidence in and reduction in sales of genuine products, and loss of government revenue.

When setting and implementing alcohol policies, governments must be aware of the impact they may have on the production and consumption of noncommercial drinks. Policies aimed at curtailing the availability of commercially produced alcohol—whether through physical availability controls or price increase—can boost the production of noncommercial beverages (McKee, 1999) and may shift trade toward the gray and black markets (Hauge & Amundsen, 1994; Single, 2004). Where large price disparities exist between neighboring countries, smuggling and cross-border trade of both legally produced and noncommercial alcohol have been routinely reported. The experience of many alcohol campaigns, including those in the early-1980s in Poland and the mid-1980s in the Soviet Union, showed that restrictive policies inevitably lead to an increase in unregistered alcohol production and consumption (Moskalewicz & Simpura, 2000; Nemtsov, 2001; Reitan, 2000; Treml, 1997). In western Europe, the level of unrecorded drinking is high in countries with strict alcohol policies and high alcohol taxation (Leifman, 2002).

Neither industry nor public health authorities have sufficient data to accurately assess the full scale of the informal market and its outcomes. However, enough is known to suggest that the existence of noncommercial alcohol should be factored into any national alcohol policy. This is an area in which industry, governments, and public health share common objectives, and the potential for multi-sector involvement is significant. As a first step, it is necessary to develop a common methodology to describe and gauge production and consumption of noncommercial alcohol and their outcomes, which then can be used as a standard tool in different countries. Industry members are particularly well placed to help with data gathering. Companies operating internationally may have access to data from many markets—or to channels for collecting such data—that would be useful for conducting cross-cultural comparisons. These data can be made available to governments and public health experts. The International Center for Alcohol Policies (ICAP) website, for example, already offers access to global commercial production data (ICAP, 2009). Current initiatives and other possibilities for promising multi-sector action are explored next.

Current Responses to the Informal Sector

Some patterns of beverage alcohol consumption have the potential for health, social, and economic complications. However, individuals who choose *noncommercial* alcohol may face additional risks, partly because of impurities and indeterminate alcohol levels of such products and partly because these drinkers tend to be more vulnerable than the mainstream on account of other extraneous factors, such as socioeconomic background and access to services. Moreover, the alcohol content and traditional serving sizes of many noncommercial beverages may be impossible to measure (e.g., when drinks are served in communal vessels), thus ruling out prevention efforts based on self-monitoring of drinking.

It is important for the state to gain effective oversight over informal alcohol production and distribution, not least because these beverages are not affected by regulation and are therefore accessible to minors. Licensing and inspection of production—whether home production, small factory operation, or full-scale industrial enterprise—is an important means of eliminating adulterants. In markets where price drives consumer choice for noncommercial alcohol, some governments have provided incentives for legal producers to sell quality low-cost commercial drinks to protect public health and safety (see next box). If this is seen as a useful approach, care should be taken to ensure that an introduction of such measures does not distort the market.

SENATOR KEG IN KENYA

The Kenyan government and health authorities have been looking for ways to address the public health problems associated with illicit alcohol consumption. Regulatory options were limited. By definition, when dealing with an informal sector, measures such as raising taxes or banning advertising have no impact. Instead, the government decided to focus on the main reason why consumers chose to drink illicit alcohol: price and affordability relative to income. Legal alcohol brands normally sell for USD 1 to USD 3 a bottle, out of reach for the majority of Kenyan consumers, 46% of whom live under the poverty line on less than USD 1 a day. Home-produced drinks *busaa* (a traditional brew from finger millet malt) and *chang'aa* (a cornmeal-based gin), sold for a fraction of what commercial drinks cost, fill the gap. For example, *chang'aa* usually costs as little as USD 0.13 per glass. These beverages are frequently adulterated with harmful substances. Use of battery acid, fertilizers, and methanol has been reported.

In this context, the government granted the East African Breweries Limited (EABL) a special tax rate, which enabled the company to offer low-income consumers an affordable, quality alternative to illicit alcohol. Senator Keg, barley-based beer, was launched in November 2004, priced at USD 0.27 per glass. The product immediately began to gain popularity with consumers, who welcomed their newfound inclusion into the branded alcohol market. In June 2006, the government made keg beer duty exempt to enable it to further penetrate the illicit market. The price of Senator Keg has subsequently fallen to USD 0.20 per 300-milliliter glass. While no formal evaluation has yet been undertaken into the public health consequences of this initiative, anecdotal evidence and media reports indicate a marked reduction in the incidence of alcohol poisoning in areas where the brand is popular and widely available.

Senator Keg is distributed through over 2,900 outlets serving *busaa*. *Busaa* is normally consumed from old tins and plastic containers. EABL provides the outlets with glasses and cleaning kits for storage. A cleaning technician regularly checks the equipment. In addition, EABL provides training for venue owners in quality management, hygiene standards, and stock control; for many of these proprietors, it is the first formal training they have ever received.

It should be noted that, in many countries, regulatory options and resources are limited, while the prevalence of noncommercial alcohol is such that it is unrealistic to expect law enforcement to close down an entire sector. Because of the economic and cultural significance of traditional drinks in many instances and in many countries, governments should not rely only on police enforcement but also explore policies that give informal producers incentives to join the legal sector or ensure safety of their products. Particularly in instances when the production of noncommercial beverages is surrounded by other dangerous behaviors—such as high-risk sexual practices involving alcohol producers and sellers and their customers—creating alternative income-generating activities may bring different community actors together, empower marginalized segments of society, and minimize problems (for an example of one such initiative, see Adelekan, 2008).

Reaching venues that sell noncommercial alcohol is often crucial for minimizing harm as many such establishments have been characterized by irresponsible serving practices and high likelihood of heavy drinking and sexual and interpersonal violence (Adelekan et al., 2008). If legal producers of beverage alcohol have little influence over the practices of licensed retailers (see Chapter 6), they have even less over those who sell noncommercial and often-illicit beverages. However, efforts have been made by major legal producers to encourage unlicensed retailers to adhere to codes of conduct and ensure the quality and integrity of products they sell. An example of such an initiative comes from South Africa, where the Industry Association for Responsible Alcohol Use (ARA) has developed a code for retail traders (see Figure 3.1). This code is aimed at those who sell and serve beverage alcohol within a legitimate framework and in licensed premises. However, in a country where the consumption of noncommercial beverages in shebeens is widespread and exceeds that in legal venues, this code represents a pragmatic effort to adapt to everyday reality and to encourage those operating outside the legal framework to adhere to certain standards of operation.

In contrast to addressing traditional drinks, reducing large-scale illegal production and counterfeiting inevitably relies on legal, penal, and enforcement actions. Producers have encouraged legislators to

CODE OF PRACTICE FOR THE SUPPLY, SALE AND CONSUMPTION OF ALCOHOL BEVERAGES

The producers, distributors and all other traders in alcohol beverages undertake to abide by the following practices:

1. **PRACTICES RELATING TO MINORS (PERSONS UNDER 18 YEARS OF AGE)**

    1.1 Minors will not be supplied with alcohol beverages.
    1.2 If uncertain, traders will request evidence of age.

2. **PRACTICES PROMOTING A RESPONSIBLE ATTITUDE TO THE CONSUMPTION OF ALCOHOL BEVERAGES**

    2.1 The rapid and / or excessive consumption of alcohol beverages will be discouraged and promotions with this objective will not be allowed.
    2.2 Where practical, information about taxi and public transport services will be displayed.
    2.3 Food and non-alcoholic drinks should be available.

3. **PRACTICES RELATING TO INTOXICATION AND DISORDERLY BEHAVIOUR**

    3.1 A trader will guard against the supply of alcohol beverages to intoxicated persons.
    3.2 Disorderly, offensive or criminal behaviour on the part of customers will not be tolerated.
    3.3 A trader will ensure that activities on the premises will not result in undue offence, annoyance, disturbance, noise or inconvenience to people who reside, work or worship in the vicinity of the premises.

4. **PRACTICES PROMOTING RESPONSIBLE ATTITUDE TO ADVERTISING AND PROMOTION**

    Traders will subscribe to the Advertising, Packaging and Promotions Code of the Industry Association for Responsible Alcohol Use or the Code of the Advertising Standards Authority.

5. **PRACTICES RELATING TO THE PURCHASE OF ILLICIT AND STOLEN ALCOHOL BEVERAGE PRODUCTS**

    Traders will not purchase or supply illicit or stolen alcohol beverages.

Figure 3.1   ARA Code of Conduct. Reproduced with permission from the Industry Association for Responsible Alcohol Use (ARA).

enhance legal protection for intellectual property and backed anti-counterfeiting efforts with technological innovation in packaging. Partnerships with local authorities are a common and effective approach; these typically include industry support of education and training programs for police, customs officers, and trading standards officials. In many countries, the beverage alcohol industry (like many other industries) is united in its approach against counterfeiters and recognizes that protecting consumers from such illegal products is not a competitive issue.

For many years, producers have developed a variety of devices that inhibit refilling of bottles. They invested in technology to help rapid authentication of brands and protect packaging by using packaging signifiers, infrared identifiers, and holographic inks. For example, in 2004 the industry's first miniaturized spectroscopic portable testing device was launched to help crack down on counterfeit Scotch whisky. The kit uses ultraviolet technology to test the authenticity of Scotch whisky brands and allows rapid analysis of liquid instead of lengthy and costly laboratory tests—a process that previously took up to 2 weeks can now be done in less than 1 minute. The rapid results allow trading standards officers and other enforcement officials, to whom this device has been distributed for free, to take immediate action against poor-quality and at times dangerous imitations.

There are a number of examples of government efforts to control the sale and distribution of counterfeit beverage alcohol. Under a 2007 law in China, alcohol wholesalers are required to attach identification cards to each product when supplying a retailer. The purpose of this regulation is to prevent counterfeit alcohol from entering the market. In Russia, the state alcohol producer, Rosspirtprom, plans to make discount "national vodka" in an effort to stamp out counterfeit and unregistered alcohol. The goal is to produce quality vodka at a price the population can afford.

Economic crisis in many countries may encourage consumers to seek less expensive drinks and become tempted by "discounted" famous brands, which could well be counterfeit. Areas for multi-stakeholder cooperation in this area include continuing to develop simple, inexpensive, and rapid tests to identify contaminants in beverages and supporting local authorities in random tests and identification of sources of contaminated or counterfeit products before they reach the consumers.

Going Forward

Regulating the production and consumption of noncommercial alcohol presents a challenge and a balancing act. On the one hand, there is the need to reduce problems by increasing regulation of these products. On the other, policy-makers must ensure the wellbeing and safety of the population and minimize the potential for harm (Single, 2004). A number of interventions can help reduce the potential negative impact of noncommercial alcohol if undertaken by governments, nongovernmental organizations, and industry members working together.

For example, experts from various sectors can help develop and pilot an international methodology to gauge noncommercial alcohol production, consumption, and outcomes so that the interaction between policies and drinking can be better observed and evaluated, and cross-country comparisons can be made. Governments, meanwhile, should enforce laws against the production and sale of illegal alcohol, where such legislation exists (e.g., through random testing of beverages suspected to be illicit), and institute punitive measures where appropriate. Producers and others can support such initiatives by raising public awareness of these measures and providing consumer education and information about noncommercial alcohol, potential risks, and drinking patterns.

In some cultural contexts, competitions and awards for quality can serve as incentives to legal home-producers to raise and maintain the standards of their beverages. This approach is being used in Hungary to target noncommercial brandy-makers who are allowed to sell allotted amounts of their products on the market. Legal economic operators and local authorities can also offer training and funding to help noncommercial producers establish alternative income-generating businesses. Governments may also provide incentives for legal producers (e.g., through tax breaks) to provide affordable alternatives to illicit alcohol.

Clear government standards for commercial alcohol production, distribution, and retail practices are prerequisites for a reasonable legal framework around alcohol. Where such standards are absent, major producers can help with their development, based on their experience and practices in other markets. In countries with widespread consumption of surrogate alcohol, reasonable government oversight of commonly used substances may help reduce harm—for instance, in reviewing package sizes and shapes, labels, and general availability (Gil et al., 2009; Lang et al., 2006; McKee et al., 2005). In areas where toxicity of noncommercial alcohol is a problem, kits for testing toxins in noncommercial beverages already exist, but their use can be expanded and sensitivity strengthened. Chemical markers that indicate product integrity can be added for identification of commercially produced beverages. Finally, economic operators can support interventions to address the linkage between unlicensed venues and transactional sex, violence, and other social risks.

Overall, to be successful, governments must recognize and appreciate all the interplaying factors (social, cultural, economic, and political) that enable the informal alcohol sector. While the enactment and enforcement of legislation are crucial, they are unlikely to trigger the desired results when implemented on their own. Addressing issues around noncommercial alcohol is in the best interest of governments, law enforcement, and the alcohol industry. As a result, there is ample room for cooperation and initiatives based on partnership and directed at a common goal.

References

Adelekan, M. (2008). Noncommercial alcohol in sub-Saharan Africa. In M. Adelekan, Yu. Razvodovsky, U. Liyanage, & D. Ndetei, *Noncommercial alcohol in three regions* (ICAP Review 3, pp. 3–16). Washington, DC: International Center for Alcohol Policies.

Adelekan, M., Razvodovsky, Yu., Liyanage, U., & Ndetei, D. (2008). *Noncommercial alcohol in three regions* (ICAP Review 3). Washington, DC: International Center for Alcohol Policies.

FAO Investment Centre & European Bank for Reconstruction and Development Cooperation Programme. (2005). *Bulgaria: Bank lending to small and medium sized enterprises in rural areas. An analysis of supply and demand.* Retrieved March 8, 2009, from ftp://ftp.fao.org/docrep/fao/008/af101e/af101e01.pdf

Gil, A., Polikina, O., Koroleva, N., McKee, M., Tomkins, S., & Leon, D. (2009). Availability and characteristics of non-beverage alcohols sold in 17 Russian cities in 2007. *Alcoholism: Clinical and Experimental Research*, 33, 79–85.

Grant, M. (Ed.). (1998). *Alcohol and emerging markets: Patterns, problems, and responses.* Philadelphia: Brunner/Mazel.

Hauge, R., & Amundsen, A. (1994). *Effects of increased availability of alcohol. A study of the effects of opening wine/liquor monopoly outlets in the county of Sogn og Fjordane* (SIFA Report Series No. 2/94). Oslo, Norway: National Institute for Alcohol and Drug Research.

Haworth, A., & Simpson, R. (Eds.). (2004). *Moonshine markets: Issues in unrecorded alcohol beverage production and consumption.* New York: Brunner-Routledge.

Heath, D. B. (2000). *Drinking occasions: Comparative perspectives on alcohol and culture.* Philadelphia: Brunner/Mazel.

Holstege, C. P., Ferguson, J. D., Wolf, C. E., Baer, A. B., & Poklis, A. (2004). Analysis of moonshine for contaminants. *Journal of Toxicology: Clinical Toxicology, 42,* 597–601.

Hudson, J. B., Crecelius, E. A., & Gerhardt, R. E. (1980). Moonshine-related arsenic poisoning. *Archives of Internal Medicine, 140,* 211–213.

Illicit brews flood Cameroonian market. (2002, 6 September). *Panafrican News Agency Daily Newswire.* Retrieved July 7, 2009, from http://www.pana-press.com/

International Center for Alcohol Policies (ICAP). (2009). *Data on production and consumption.* Retrieved July 7, 2009, from http://www.icap.org/AboutICAP/PolicyApproach/DrinkingPatterns/DataonConsumptionandProduction/

Junninen, M., & Aromaa, K. (2000). Professional crime across the Finnish–Estonian border. *Crime Law and Social Change, 34,* 319–347.

Lang, K., Vali, M., Szucs, A., & McKee, M. (2006). The consumption of surrogate and illegal alcohol products in Estonia. *Alcohol and Alcoholism, 41,* 446–450.

Laranjeira, R., & Dunn, J. (1998). Death by methanol poisoning in Brazil. *Addiction, 93,* 1103–1104.

Leifman, H. (2002). Trends in population drinking. In T. Norström (Ed.), *Alcohol in postwar Europe: Consumption, drinking patterns, consequences and policy responses in 15 European countries* (pp. 49–82). Stockholm: Almqvist & Wiksell.

Leon, D. A., Chenet, L., Shkolnikov, V. M., Zakharov, S., Shapiro, J., Rakhmanova, G., et al. (1997). Huge variation in Russian mortality rates 1984–94: Artefact, alcohol, or what? *Lancet, 350,* 383–388.

Liyanage, U. (2008). Noncommercial alcohol in southern Asia: The case of *kasippu* in Sri Lanka. In M. Adelekan, Yu. Razvodovsky, U. Liyanage, & D. Ndetei, *Noncommercial alcohol in three regions* (ICAP Review 3, pp. 24–34). Washington, DC: International Center for Alcohol Policies.

Lovelace, C. E., & Nyathi, C. B. (1977). Estimation of the fungal toxins, zearalenone and aflatoxin, contaminating opaque maize beer in Zambia. *Journal of the Science of Food and Agriculture, 28,* 288–292.

Mateos, R., Paramo, M., Carrera, I., & Rodriguez Lopez, A. (2002). Alcohol consumption in a southern European region (Galicia, Spain). *Substance Use and Misuse, 37,* 1957–1976.

McKee, M. (1999). Alcohol in Russia. *Alcohol and Alcoholism, 34,* 824–829.

McKee, M., Szucs, S., Sárváry, A., Adany, R., Kiryanov, N., Saburova, L., et al. (2005). The composition of surrogate alcohols consumed in Russia. *Alcoholism: Clinical and Experimental Research, 29*, 1884–1889.

More than a thousand Moscow residents died of counterfeit alcohol in 2008. (2009, March 26). *MosNews.com* [Online]. Retrieved July 7, 2009, from http://www.mosnews.com/society/2009/03/26/561/

Morgan, B. W., Todd, K. H., & Moore, B. (2001). Elevated blood lead levels in urban moonshine drinkers. *Annals of Emergency Medicine, 37*, 51–54.

Mosha, D., Wangabo, J., & Mhinzi, G. (1996). African traditional brews: How safe are they? *Food Chemistry, 57*, 205–209.

Moskalewicz, J., & Simpura, J. (2000). The supply of alcoholic beverages in transitional conditions: The case of central and eastern Europe. *Addiction, 95*(Suppl. 4), 505–522.

Nemtsov, A. (2000). Estimates of total alcohol consumption in Russia, 1980–1994. *Drug and Alcohol Dependence, 58*, 133–142.

Nemtsov, A. (2001). *Alcohol related mortality in Russia, 1980–1990s*. Moscow: Nalex.

Nemtsov, A. (2003). Alcohol consumption level in Russia: A viewpoint on monitoring health conditions in the Russian federation (RLMS). *Addiction, 99*, 369–370.

Nicaragua tainted brew kills 22. (2006, September 10). *BBC News* [Online]. Retrieved July 7, 2009, from http://news.bbc.co.uk/2/hi/americas/5331760.stm

Norström, T. (1998). Estimating changes in unrecorded alcohol consumption in Norway using indicators of harm. *Addiction, 93*, 1531–1538.

Nuzhnyi, V. (2004). Chemical composition, toxic and organoleptic properties of noncommercial alcohol samples. In A. Haworth & R. Simpson (Eds.), *Moonshine markets: Issues in unrecorded alcohol beverage production and consumption* (pp. 177–199). New York: Brunner-Routledge.

O'Connell, M. (2003, 11 July). Bootleg vodka makes up third of market. *The Baltic Times* [Online]. Retrieved July 7, 2009, from http://www.baltictimes.com/news/articles/8376/

Pegues, D. A., Hughes, B. J., & Woernle, C. H. (1993). Elevated blood lead levels associated with illegally distilled alcohol. *Archives of Internal Medicine, 153*, 1501–1504.

Razvodovsky, Yu. E. (2003). *Indicators of alcohol-related problems in Belarus*. Grodno, Belarus: Medical University Press.

Razvodovsky, Yu. E. (2008). Noncommercial alcohol in central and eastern Europe. In M. Adelekan, Yu. E., Razvodovsky, U. Liyanage, & D. M. Ndetei, *Noncommercial alcohol in three regions* (ICAP Review 3, pp. 17–23). Washington, DC: International Center for Alcohol Policies.

Rehm, J., & Gmel, G. (2001). Alcohol per capita consumption, patterns of drinking and abstention worldwide after 1995. Appendix 2. *European Addiction Research, 7*, 155–157.

Rehm, J., Rehn, N., Room, R., Monteiro, M., Gmel, G., Jernigan, D., et al. (2003). The global distribution of average volume of alcohol consumption and patterns of drinking. *European Addiction Research, 9*, 147–156.

Reitan, T. C. (2000). Does alcohol matter? Public health in Russia and the Baltic countries before, during, and after the transition. *Contemporary Drug Problems, 27*, 511–560.

Rosovsky, H. (2004). The reporting of alcohol use through personal diaries in two Mexican communities. In A. Haworth & R. Simpson (Eds.), *Moonshine markets: Issues in underecorded alcohol beverage production and consumption* (pp. 103–124). New York: Brunner-Routledge.

Ryan, M. (1995). Alcoholism and rising mortality in the Russian Federation. *British Medical Journal, 310*, 646–648.

Sengupta, S. (2008, May 21). Poison moonshine kills 110 of India's poor. *The New York Times* [Online]. Retrieved July 7, 2009, from http://www.nytimes.com/2008/05/21/world/asia/21india.html?_r=1&scp=1&sq=Poison+moonshine+kills+110+of&st=nyt

Silverberg, M., Chu, J., & Nelson, L. (2001). Elevated blood lead levels in urban moonshine drinkers. *Annals of Emergency Medicine, 38*, 460–461.

Simpura, J., Karlsson, T., & Leppänen, K. (2002). European trends in drinking patterns and their socioeconomic background. In T. Norström (Ed.), *Alcohol in postwar Europe: Consumption, drinking patterns, consequences and policy responses in 15 European countries* (pp. 83–144). Stockholm: Almqvist & Wiksell International.

Single, E. (2004). Key economic issues regarding unrecorded alcohol. In A. Haworth & R. Simpson (Eds.), *Moonshine markets: Issues in unrecorded alcohol beverage production and consumption* (pp. 167–175). New York: Brunner-Routledge.

Stickley, A., Leinsalu, M., Andreev, E., Razvodovsky, Y., Vagero, D., & McKee, M. (2007). Alcohol poisoning in Russia and the countries in the European part of the former Soviet Union, 1970–2002. *European Journal of Public Health, 17*, 444–449.

Stimson, G., Grant, M., Choquet, M., & Garrison, P. (Eds.). (2007). *Drinking in context: Patterns, interventions, and partnerships.* New York: Routledge.

Szucs, S., Sárváry, A., McKee, M., & Adany, R. (2005). Could the high level of cirrhosis in central and eastern Europe be due partly to the quality of alcohol consumed? An exploratory investigation. *Addiction, 100*, 536–542.

Tonkabony, S. E. H. (1975). Post-mortem blood concentration of methanol in 17 cases of fatal poisoning from contraband vodka. *Forensic Science, 6*, 1–3.

Treml, V. G. (1997). Soviet and Russian statistics on alcohol consumption and abuse. In J. L. Bobadilla, C. A. Costello, & F. Mitchell (Eds.), *Premature death in the new independent states* (pp. 220–238). Washington, DC: National Academy Press.

Vietnam inspects alcohol markets amid increasing of wine poisoning cases. (2008, October 22). *Viet Nam News.* Retrieved October 22, 2008, from http://vietnamnews.vnagency.com.vn

Webb, P., & Block, S. (2008). *Illicit alcohol in Mexico: A pilot study of what we know and what we need to know.* Unpublished paper prepared for Steven Block Economic Consulting.

Willis, J. (2003). New generation drinking: The uncertain boundaries of criminal enterprise in modern Kenya. *African Affairs, 102,* 241–260.

World Health Organization (WHO). (2004a). *Global status report on alcohol.* Geneva, Switzerland: Author.

World Health Organization (WHO). (2004b). *Global status report: Alcohol policy.* Geneva, Switzerland: Author.

4

MARKETING BEVERAGE ALCOHOL

ROGER SINCLAIR

What Is the Issue?

Evidence regarding the relationship between marketing and drinking patterns has led researchers to quite different conclusions. For example, two articles sum up the opposing opinions: According to Henriksen, Feighery, Schleicher, and Fortmann (2008), "Alcohol advertising and promotions are associated with the uptake of drinking" (p. 28); meanwhile, Ringold (2008) found that alcohol advertising "does not exert a material influence on total consumption or abuse" and that "[i]ndustry-sponsored responsibility efforts . . . appear to affect desired changes . . . , model desired drinking behaviors, and may be more effective with heavier drinkers" (p. 127). These two conclusions illustrate a real lack of consensus. The proponents of greater government control of the drinks industry and its marketing efforts draw on a body of research that supports their position, while those who favor liberalization are able to counter this with a parallel flow of work indicating the opposite.

This is not merely a debate among academics; the discussion has important practical implications for alcohol policy. Thus, for example, a World Health Organization (WHO) Expert Committee on Problems Related to Alcohol Consumption warned in 2007 that unless alcohol marketing activities "come under a legal framework . . . , governments may find . . . loss of policy control of the marketing of a product that seriously affects public health" (p. 30). Meanwhile, as discussed in this chapter, major producers are making significant efforts to strengthen the efficacy and reach of self-regulatory schemes designed to promote high standards in beverage alcohol marketing.

The alcohol industry certainly does not dispute that serious problems can arise from the misuse of its products. That is well documented elsewhere in a substantial body of literature and in this book. The questions to be examined here are whether the industry's marketing activities contribute to the problem and whether severe controls on marketing would achieve the objective of reducing harm. This chapter explores the evidence for different views and examines the proposition that the steps taken by the industry to limit the promotion of its brands to underage youth and remove messages that encourage adults to drink irresponsibly are effective. Further, statutory control of the industry's marketing activities is compared to other approaches, such as self- and co-regulation.

What Do We Know?

What Is Marketing?

Modern marketing developed from the age-old human process of exchange. During the Industrial Revolution and aided by the invention of movable type, it evolved from a person-to-person event in a public marketplace to large producers promoting their goods to consumers en masse in robust competition with rivals. The development of the current world economic system has been built on this tripartite relationship. Mass sales of products have led to job creation, increased government revenue from taxation, infrastructure construction, and a rapid and unprecedented growth in intellectual capital. Since World War II, marketing has become more sophisticated, but it essentially remains a process by which a supplier of goods or services makes these available to people who wish to own or use them. Marketers employ message arguments to convince consumers in the product category to buy their brands in favor of the alternative choices.

The ability to persuade people to buy what they do not want is no more developed now than it was at the start of the 20th century when British businessman Lord Leverhulme—the founder of Unilever, one of the biggest multinational companies today—reportedly said that half of his advertising allocation was wasted, but he did not know which half.[1] Marketing can claim success in opening up new market segments, such as the ballpoint pen, the microwave oven, and the Apple iPod—these are new categories in which manufacturers responded to consumer needs. Where marketing has failed its sponsors is in building aggregate consumption. This strategy is rarely attempted because it is very expensive and has a low probability of success.[2] If it is successful, the market expansion benefits all brands in the product category, including those of competitors, who stand to gain according to their proportional market shares. A search on the topic in the database of the World Advertising Research Center (2008) revealed 96 campaign case studies, mostly involving conversion of non-users to users of, for example, apples, milk, and types of meat. There were three examples of alcohol products: single malt whisky, sherry, and lower alcohol beer. None of the three campaigns could claim to have converted non-drinkers to drinking but tried to attract consumers of one category and quality of alcohol beverage to another.

There is a saturation of demand in many markets. Marketers therefore live by the maxim, "Fish where the fish are." This is particularly the case for beverage alcohol. Marketers utilize their financial resources to promote their brands; their focus, however, is the possible. For example, it is much simpler to persuade existing whisk(e)y drinkers to switch from one brand to another than to persuade a gin or a wine drinker to choose whisk(e)y instead. A considerable body of literature demonstrates that the tools of marketing, especially advertising, are ineffective in building overall category consumption (e.g., Dickerson & Dorsett, 2004; Houghton & Roche, 2001, p. 231; Lipsitz, Brake, Vincent, & Winters, 2003; National Institute on Alcohol Abuse and

---

[1] Harris and Seldon (1959) attributed the following quotation to Lord Leverhulme: "Probably half of every advertising appropriation is wasted, but nobody knows which half" (preface). In the United States, this idea, stated slightly differently, is attributed to department store pioneer John Wanamaker. He is reputed to have said, "I know half the money I spend on advertising is wasted. The problem is I don't know which half."

[2] According to Reichheld (1996) and as cited in Kotler and Keller (2006, p. 156), it costs at least five times more to acquire a new customer as it does to retain existing customers of a brand. No estimate is made of how this ratio would increase to convert product category non-users to category users.

Alcoholism, 2000; Nelson & Young, 2001; Ringold, 2008). When there is evidence, it is of small effects only (e.g., Grube, 2003).

The Purpose of Marketing

The focus of modern marketing is the relationship between the consumer and the brand. Increasingly, brands are being seen as assets, and in keeping with finance theory, an asset derives its value from future economic benefits or cash flows (Brealey & Myers, 1996, p. 11; Financial Accounting Standards Board, 2001). The solitary source of cash flows for a brand is the consumer (e.g., Keller, 2008, pp. 427–428). Boards invest funds in marketing to ensure that the company keeps its existing customers in the face of aggressive competition, and that it builds the customer base by convincing individuals who might not be committed to their present brand to shift loyalties. Kotler and Keller (2006) defined marketing's purpose as follows: "the art and science of choosing target markets and getting, keeping, and growing customers through creating, delivering, and communicating superior customer value" (p. 6). Brealey and Myers (1996) explained that "firms with a strong competitive advantage tend to be those with very strong brand images or know-how" (pp. 775–776).

Beverage alcohol companies rely heavily on marketing to protect and build their brands. Because there is a finite market for alcohol, each company must fight to retain its share. Normative sector dynamics are well known and established: As old consumers exit, they are replaced by young drinkers, who are generally initiated into alcohol consumption by their families and peers in mid- to late adolescence. The WHO (2004a) *Global Status Report on Alcohol* illustrated flat trends in consumption since the mid-1980s. This suggests that industry marketing efforts have not significantly influenced the established and consistent trend in drinking patterns.

Beverage Alcohol Marketing

The beverage alcohol industry can trace its origins back many hundreds of years, but as competition grew and brands emerged, it has increasingly relied on quality standards to prosper. In markets that are either over- or underregulated, the informal sector may be thriving along-side the formal market (Adelekan, Razvodovsky, Liyanage, & Ndetei, 2008; Haworth & Simpson, 2004; see also Chapter 3). The producers of beverage alcohol can therefore be divided into two broad groups: the regulated and recorded and the unregulated and unrecorded.

The Regulated Producers In developed economies, the market for beverage alcohol is mature. The WHO (2004a) data on alcohol consumption, measured in liters of pure alcohol per capita, show a general decline in drinking between 1980 and 1988 and a flat trend with minor fluctuations between 1989 and 2000 (see also World Advertising Research Center, 2005). Figures published by Euromonitor International (2008) indicate low-volume growth between 2002 and 2007.

In mature markets where sales are flat, most marketing strategies would include those designed to increase consumption. This can be done by encouraging greater frequency of consumption among existing customers or by attracting new customers. As noted, the latter is a costly strategy; even if it were a viable commercial option, marketers of alcohol brands would be constricted in their ability to employ the approach because of the legal frameworks under which they operate and the voluntary codes that oversee their marketing activities. Government statutes that protect consumers and codes of responsible practice, developed and adopted by industry members in many countries, stand between the public and unacceptable marketing excesses. In some countries, self-regulation (in which an industry imposes its own strictures) is the primary control mechanism. In most countries, however, self-regulation works in conjunction with government regulation (co-regulation); this combination retains an overarching government authority but relieves the officials of the need to set up monitoring bodies and initiate expensive and drawn-out court cases. That unwieldy and crude approach is replaced with a timely, cost-effective process of review and imposition of targeted corrective steps.

A number of countries have self- or co-regulatory organizations that oversee the marketing activities of the alcohol industry. Although individual self-regulatory codes differ to meet national or regional market needs, they are often based on the *Advertising and Marketing*

Communication Practice: Consolidated ICC Code (International Chamber of Commerce [ICC], n.d.) and its basic principles that

> All marketing communication should be legal, decent, honest and truthful.
>
> All marketing communication should be prepared with a due sense of social and professional responsibility and should conform to the principles of fair competition, as generally accepted in business. (p. 13)

Table 4.1 lists main provisions of codes of responsible marketing for which there is broad consensus among industry members. Producers in many countries observe these extracompany codes and, in many cases, have a statutory obligation to do so. In addition, the International Center for Alcohol Policies (ICAP) sponsors have internal company codes whose detailed provisions go beyond the requirements listed in Table 4.1 and include, for example, bans on associating drinking with illegal activity, negative portrayal of abstinence, and brand identification on products (such as clothing, toys, and games) for people below the legal drinking age. Website age verification is also a widely used provision.

Industry leaders openly state in the narrative parts of their annual reports that, while they wish to maintain their positions in the developed countries and seek increases in market share, they are also actively involved in the emerging markets that offer growth opportunities. It is important to note that ICAP sponsor companies are as committed to observing the provisions of their codes in developing countries as they are in their established markets.

The Unregulated Producers   The term *unregulated* is used to describe the informal markets where alcohol is produced illicitly or sold through unregulated premises. By definition, the fact that these markets are unregulated means that they are unaffected by restrictions or bans on advertising and other forms of marketing. Also, they do not contribute to government revenues through excise duties. It is probably accurate to say that most markets where the production, sale, and marketing of alcohol are unregulated are found in the economies described as developing or emerging, although it is not true to say that all emerging

Table 4.1 Codes of Responsible Marketing: Main Provisions by Some Industry Organizations

PROVISIONS AGAINST	INDUSTRY ORGANIZATIONS										
	AUSTRALIAN ALCOHOL BEVERAGES ADVERTISING CODE (ABAC)	THE BEER INSTITUTE (USA)	BREWERS OF EUROPE	DISTILLED SPIRITS COUNCIL OF THE UNITED STATES (DISCUS)	THE INDUSTRY ASSOCIATION FOR RESPONSIBLE ALCOHOL USE (SOUTH AFRICA)	MATURE ENJOYMENT OF ALCOHOL IN SOCIETY (IRELAND)	PORTMAN GROUP (U.K.)	EUROPEAN FORUM ON RESPONSIBLE DRINKING	THE WINE INSTITUTE (USA)	ADVERTISING STANDARDS AUTHORITY (U.K.)	JAPAN LIQUOR INDUSTRY COUNCIL
Encouragement of immoderate/excessive drinking	✓	✓	✓	✓	✓	✓	✓	✓	✓	✓	✓
Appeal to the underage	✓	✓	✓	✓	✓	✓	✓	✓	✓	✓	✓
Placement at events where significant portion of audience is underage		✓	✓	✓	✓	✓	✓	✓	✓	✓	✓
Subjects in advertisements under 25 years of age	✓	✓		✓	✓	✓	✓	✓	✓	✓	✓[a]
Implication of enhanced ability (physical)	✓	✓		✓	✓	✓	✓	✓	✓	✓	✓
Implication of enhanced ability (sexual)	✓	✓	✓	✓	✓	✓	✓	✓	✓	✓	
Implication of enhanced ability (social)	✓	✓	✓	✓	✓	✓	✓	✓	✓	✓	
Depiction of unsafe conditions (driving)	✓	✓	✓	✓	✓	✓	✓	✓	✓	✓	
Depiction of intoxication	✓	✓	✓		✓	✓	✓	✓	✓	✓	
Association with violence	✓		✓			✓	✓	✓	✓	✓	✓
Claiming unsubstantiated medical and/or therapeutic benefits	✓					✓			✓	✓	✓
Emphasis of high alcohol content	✓		✓[b]	✓	✓		✓	✓	✓	✓	

[a] Underage models cannot be used in advertisements for beverage alcohol.

[b] Commercial communications should not present high alcoholic strength in itself as a positive quality of the brand or as a reason for choosing it. On the other hand, messages may not imply that consuming beer of low alcohol content will avoid misuse.

or developing markets are unregulated (e.g., Grant, 1998; Haworth & Simpson, 2004).[3]

There are probably fewer than 30 mature economies in the world that could be called *developed*.[4] Many countries that were in the European Eastern Bloc, most countries in South America, all of Africa, and a great deal of Asia would fit the description of developing countries. The major beverage alcohol companies are placing most of their growth attention on these emerging markets, although they are by no means limited to these regions. For example, India is a giant market in which the import of alcohol has relatively recently been partially liberalized. In this country, as in many new markets, "parallel with the international and more expensive alcohol beverages, there exist the local, cheap, potent brews, both legal and illicit" (Assunta, 2001, p. 2; see also Chapter 3).

Marketing and Young People

There is a shared recognition between the health profession and the beverage alcohol industry that young people may be at risk as they learn to drink alcohol, especially if their drinking occasions are unsupervised. This understanding extends to the commitment on the part of the industry not to target its marketing activities at those under the legal drinking age.

Drinking Prototypes in Adolescents   Available research, conducted mainly in the United States (U.S.), indicates that by the time adolescents have become adults, their drinking habits are largely formed. Thus, if drinking patterns are to be shaped, it is during these formative years that this will occur. To that end, Spijkerman, Van den Eijnden,

---

[3] In this section, the terms *emerging* and *developing* economies are used interchangeably. These are mainly used to describe economies in countries that have undergone major sociopolitical change marked by their move from centrally planned to free market economies. The World Bank would class them as "middle-" to "low-income" countries (Grant, 1998).

[4] The WHO (2004a) *Global Status Report on Alcohol* illustrates a difference between developed and developing countries in its analysis of unrecorded alcohol consumption. Unrecorded consumption in developing countries is on average almost three times greater than in developed economies.

Overbeek, and Engels (2007) proposed that adolescents create drinker prototypes. These are images they hold in memory of what a peer drinker looks like. Often, these drinker prototypes are quite negative and do not represent the adolescent's goal state; such prototypes can be sufficiently powerful to ensure that abstainers continue to abstain (Spijkerman et al., 2007, p. 9). Meanwhile, those who choose to try alcohol might take this decision because it conforms to their drinker prototype and seems the "cool" thing to do (Brown et al., 2007).

Spijkerman and colleagues (2007) argued that drinker prototypes are formed at an early age by reference to the behaviors, attitudes, and norms of parents and peers. Brown et al. (2007) found that even the majority of adolescents who disapprove of underage drinking believed that those who drink do so because they think it is an acceptable peer behavior. Exposure to negative peer pressure may result in children having their first taste of alcohol as early as 13 years of age and younger. For some, one taste is enough; for others, the first sip "marks the initiation of a pattern of alcohol use" (Brown et al., 2007, p. 33).

According to Spijkerman et al. (2007), images in advertisements and the media that display the type of people who drink also contribute to adolescents' perception of alcohol-related norms. Movies and television are important influences, but young people are increasingly exposed to pressures from newer forms of image projection, such as viral marketing, cell phones, and video-sharing websites, as well as events and promotional activities at drinking venues. To minimize this exposure, all codes governing beverage alcohol marketing, including individual corporate codes, industrywide codes, and statutory codes, place strict prohibitions on message content and media coverage of youth under the legal drinking age.

The particular value of the drinker prototype research lies in its implications for interventions. An approach suggested by Spijkerman and colleagues (2007) is to use advertising to communicate positive images of responsible behavior and help create negative and "uncool" drinker prototypes, which at the very least would help delay the onset of alcohol experimentation.[5] Often referred to as "social marketing

---

[5] If advertising is used for this purpose, it is assumed that it would not be subject to industry codes that forbid appealing to those under the legal drinking age and portraying links between alcohol consumption and performance in sport and career, social acceptability, and sexual performance.

campaigns" or "public service advertising," such programs have been implemented in a range of contexts, with support from alcohol producers and other industry members.

SOCIAL MARKETING IN THE UNITED KINGDOM

Social marketing uses the theory and concept of marketing to bring about social change. It has been employed by governments, nongovernmental organizations (NGOs), and others, for example, to encourage the wearing of seat belts when driving, reducing the incidence of HIV/AIDS by changing both private behavior and public attitudes, preventing alcohol-impaired driving, and reducing smoking (Lannon, 2008; see also www.social-marketing.org).

In the United Kingdom (U.K.), the Department of Health launched a major social marketing campaign on alcohol and health in 2008. Called Alcohol, Know Your Limits, the campaign is designed to encourage safe and responsible drinking. It uses a comprehensive mix of marketing tools, including advertising and point-of-sale promotions, to educate the public about alcohol and its effects, drinking patterns, standard drink measures, and avoiding harm. Current drinkers are provided with tools to monitor, evaluate, and moderate their consumption.

The industry, meanwhile, has responded to a request by the British Prime Minister to use its marketing expertise to contribute to the reduction of harmful drinking. The initiative, Project-10, launched in 2009, is a sustained multimedia campaign, conservatively valued at over GBP 100 million for the first 5 years. Its primary targets are frequent excessive drinkers and young adults, aged between 18 and 34 years. Project-10 leverages industry insights into how to influence attitudes of these consumers—for example, talk *with* them not *at* them and highlight the benefits of responsible enjoyment. The media campaign will connect consumers with the core idea of Project-10 and then amplify the message through alcohol packaging and point-of-sale materials. The emphasis is on providing practical advice and promoting benefits of responsible drinking. The campaign's tagline is, "Why let good times go bad?"

Is Marketing to Blame?

It has been contended (e.g., Clark, 1988) that advertising in earlier decades sometimes targeted population sectors considered to be at heightened risk for harm, particularly young people below the legal drinking age, in ways that would be considered inappropriate in the 21st century. Today, there is a very real and tangible commitment by leading alcohol producers to help reduce harmful drinking patterns and the problems they might cause. This takes the form of codes that prohibit certain types of advertising claims or associations and require that the reach and coverage of media schedules be constructed to minimize the exposure to alcohol marketing of those underage.

Over the years, the impact of alcohol marketing on young people has been studied extensively. One approach has been to examine the relationship between marketing and young people's attitudes and expectancies about drinking (Austin & Chen, 2003; Austin, Chen, & Grube, 2006; Austin & Knaus, 2000; Chen, Grube, Bersamin, Waiters, & Keefe, 2005; Fleming, Thorson, & Atkin, 2004). The results of these studies vary: Some found a small impact on young people's beliefs about drinking and their intentions to drink (e.g., van Dalen & Kuunders, 2006), while others showed no such relationship (e.g., Austin et al., 2006). However, there is no evidence that marketing *causes* particular beliefs or intentions.

Econometric studies have also looked at the relationship using economic methods, such as marketing expenditure. The methodologies used varied significantly, but on balance, these studies failed to show a clear and causal relationship (for a review, see Saffer & Dave 2006). Some have argued that longitudinal studies are best suited to shed light on any putative relationship as they follow a particular group of individuals over time and examine exposure to marketing and its impact on drinking behavior. Two systematic reviews, by Anderson, de Bruijn, Angus, Gordon, and Hastings (2009) and Smith and Foxcroft (2009), have reported the following: "Longitudinal studies consistently suggest that exposure to media and commercial communications on alcohol is associated with the likelihood that adolescents will start to drink alcohol" (Anderson et al., p. 3). However, it should be noted that any effect seen in the individual studies, where it was observed, was very small.

The relationship between young people's drinking and the many factors that influence it is extremely complex; no individual factor can be singled out, and each is influenced by many others (Austin et al., 2006). The evidence also shows consistently that other factors play a more significant role in shaping young peoples' drinking than do advertising and other forms of marketing, including—as the drinker prototype research indicated—family environment and parent and sibling behavior (Epstein, Griffin, & Botvin, 2008; Fowler et al., 2007; Mogro-Wilson, 2008; Trim, Leuthe, & Chassin, 2006; van der Vorst, Engels, Meeus, Dekovic, & van Leeuwe, 2007; van der Zwaluw et al., 2008); peer behavior (Chuang, Ennett, Bauman, & Foshee, 2005; Scholte, Poelen, Willemsen, Boomsma, & Engels, 2008; van der Zwaluw et al., 2008); and socioeconomic status (Arvanitidou, Tirodimos, Kyriakidis, Tsinaslanidou, & Seretopoulos, 2007; Chuang et al., 2005; Hoffmann, 2006). These are factors that can never be completely controlled for in any study.

Research conclusions may vary, but it is clearly important for the alcohol industry to err on the side of caution and avoid contributing to attitudes and drinking patterns that may encourage underage drinking and may result in harm. It is for this reason that the industry has imposed strict conditions on the nature of what it calls "message content" and audience coverage. Furthermore, producers must conform to the various requirements of the law and to regulations as well as abide by self-regulatory codes of practice.

Reducing Harmful Drinking: The Industry's Response

Self- and Co-regulation

In 1933, immediately after the prohibition on the production and sale of alcohol was lifted in the United States, the beverage alcohol industry adopted codes of practice regulating the way it sold and marketed its products (e.g., Distilled Spirits Council of the United States, 2009). In one form or another, self-regulation has been in place ever since. It is not recorded why the industry took this action, but one can surmise that it was part of an arrangement with government: Either the industry itself would place limitations on the way alcohol was to be marketed or the government would do it for the industry. A spokesperson for the Global Alcohol Producers Group, presenting at a WHO consultation with economic operators in November 2008, summed up the dilemma and solution as follows:

> [Beverage alcohol companies] can see to it that their marketing activities are in line with the [WHO] public health goals. . . . First, through a commitment to comply with all existing laws and regulations regarding alcohol marketing. . . . But there are limitations as to how much can be achieved through regulation and legislation. So, while this commitment is necessary, it is not sufficient on its own. The second way is to ensure that industry self-regulation, or co-regulation, is robust, effective, and culturally sensitive. (Pedlow, 2009, p. 55)

Self-regulation requires that a code of conduct be adopted by an industry grouping to which all members subscribe. It is often developed in acknowledgment of the importance of maintaining consumer trust and confidence. The advertising industry, for example, has responded to accusations of using unethical methods by devising and imposing codes of practice on all advertisers and their agencies. In many countries, these requirements are underpinned by a legal framework and administered by independent bodies, such as the Advertising Standards Authority (ASA) in the United Kingdom or the Better Business Bureau (BBB) in the United States. Some take the view that codes are still adopted as a way to ward off government interference in industry affairs (see, e.g., Belch & Belch, 1998).

The Australian government defined the regulatory options in the following terms: "a spectrum ranging from self-regulation where there is little or no government involvement, through co-regulation which refers to a range of rules, instruments or standards that government expects businesses to comply with, to explicit and prescriptive government regulation or legislation" (Commonwealth of Australia, 2000, para. 3). It is generally agreed that self-regulation is more flexible and less costly than direct government involvement (Curtis, 2005). A robust self-regulatory code allows an industry to act quickly and flexibly to remove noncompliant messages or campaigns. For ease of explanation, the available models for overseeing alcohol marketing can be split into four categories: company codes, voluntary self-regulation, co-regulation, and government legislation. These are not mutually exclusive and often complement each other (Belch & Belch, 1998, pp. 655–682; Curtis, 2005; ICAP, 2002, 2004, 2006a, 2006b, 2006c, 2007).

Company Codes Companies devise and impose their own internal codes of practice, called "codes of responsible marketing" in the alcohol field. All ICAP members have comprehensive codes that are applied to company offices and agencies worldwide (e.g., ICAP, 2004). Critical to the success of this system is the need for continuous training and review of compliance. This applies to all levels of marketing management within the firm and the secondary services they employ.

COMPANY CODES OF RESPONSIBLE MARKETING

The major beverage alcohol companies have devised codes of responsible marketing, which are applied with varying levels of rigor in their businesses. The two examples here indicate the manner in which the codes are applied and enforced.

- **Diageo:** The company has developed online e-learning courses on code content and processes; these courses are available to staff both internally and externally. Code compliance is mandatory; to facilitate it, Diageo provides an online approval tool, Smart Approve. Some 5,600 marketing projects have passed through Smart Approve, which permits regular review by staff in a range of departments, gives visibility to comments, allows for tracking of the project status, and leaves an audit trail. Senior managers have to complete a compliance certificate annually to signify their adherence to the code.
- **SABMiller:** SABMiller's policy on commercial communication provides content and placement standards for commercial communication in addition to local legislation.

The policy is applied and enforced with help of several key mechanisms: an internal compliance committee; a comprehensive education program about the policy for employees; the incorporation of alcohol responsibility into the SABMiller Marketing Way process to help embed responsibility at every stage of commercial communication development—not just the end; and the internal auditing of performance. As result of these mechanisms, for example, Miller Brands U.K.'s Sales and Marketing Responsibility Committee (SMRC) removed an image of house keys from a commercial communication to avoid any association with automobile keys and drinking and driving. SMRC also requires that age verification be added to external retail websites as a prerequisite for getting approval of online programs.

Voluntary Self-regulation   Under the voluntary self-regulation model, industry develops a common code, and industry members agree to be bound by its provisions. For a self-regulatory code to be effective, it must have the full support of all industry members. This implies that there is a strong body of industry, which is why codes are not operating in all developing markets. Finally, the code must be accompanied by meaningful sanctions. In cases of noncompliance, the transgressor can be embarrassed by public naming, be prevented from placing any advertising for a period of time, or be forced to submit all planned advertising to a regulatory body or a trade association for approval before exposure.

DEFINING BEST PRACTICE IN SELF-REGULATION

The Global Alcohol Producers Group, an industry coalition representing leading international beer, wine, and spirits companies, has set out what it believes to be the best practice principles on which self-regulatory systems should be based (Pedlow, 2009, p. 56). They should

- be inclusive of all industry players
- cover all media
- address both content and placement of messages
- set clear standards that are well publicized
- require training for brand and agency staff
- require preplacement review, whether internal or external, of marketing initiatives
- enable independent monitoring through regular publication of findings
- incorporate an independent complaints resolution process
- require timely removal of noncompliant marketing

Co-regulation   In the system of co-regulation, government and industry collaborate on setting the rules for industry activities: The legislature passes an enabling framework (the act), and industry develops regulations in conformity with the framework; industry then administers the code of conduct, usually through the establishment of an independent self-regulatory organization (SRO), but government always has the option of intervening to the extent permitted by the enabling act. From the government point of view, this route is preferred over self-regulation because it requires, by law, that all industry members subscribe to the code without the choice to "opt out."

Government Legislation   Under the government legislation model, a legislature passes an act that sets out the law applicable to the subject matter. In most jurisdictions, the law sets a framework; regulations within this framework may then be modified or changed by a minister or agency in the government. Transgressing the law constitutes a criminal or civil offense, incurring penalties prescribed by the act. Apart from the severity of the sanction, the process involves the police, public prosecutors, lawyers, and the courts. The transgression may result in fines or imprisonment; litigation typically stretches over a long period of time.

Does Self-regulation Work?

A number of public health advocates hold strong opinions on the effectiveness of self-regulation by the beverage alcohol industry, which they believe fails to prevent underage youth from being influenced by marketing techniques. They recommend that governments create statutory agencies to monitor and regulate the actions of alcohol marketers. For example, the Institute of Alcohol Studies (2008) reflected the views of most opponents of self-regulation by concluding that the approaches taken by contemporary alcohol marketers are analogous with the tobacco advertisers when they were under attack: "Voluntary self-regulatory codes . . . are treated cynically, the advertising agencies playing cat and mouse with the regulatory bodies, pushing to the limits and avoiding the rules whenever possible" (p. 4). In this context, imposing a complete ban on alcohol advertising is often offered as a promising way forward to reduce harm.

However, Nelson and Young (2001) posited that "advertising bans do not have a large impact on drinking patterns" (p. 293). The basis for this conclusion was a study of 17 member states of the Organisation for Economic Co-operation and Development (OECD) in the period between 1977 and 1995. Data on per capita alcohol consumption, road traffic mortality, and liver cirrhosis mortality were correlated with the use of broadcast advertising as a communication medium. The authors found no reduction in harmful drinking where there were advertising bans. These results are consistent with the theory that advertising of alcohol is persuasive to the extent that it produces effects on perceived product differentiation and price competition. Where advertising is banned, there is a move toward nonbanned media.

Before continuing our discussion of self-regulation and its effectiveness, several common myths about it need to be acknowledged:

First, there is the misperception that self-regulation can "fix" all the problems associated with harmful drinking—it cannot. While self-regulation is an essential part of the attempts to minimize harmful drinking, it is not sufficient on its own.

Second, there is the myth that self-regulation is just the industry sitting in judgment on itself. It is not—and should not be, as external bodies are created to administer the codes, review compliance, and update code provisions with input from other stakeholders, including governments and the public.

Third, there is the belief that codes of practice do not address public health concerns; in reality, the provisions of most codes are aligned with public health goals and apply at all stages of product development, packaging, and sale [see Chapter 2].

Fourth, there is the claim that self-regulation is incapable of removing noncompliant advertisements or products in a timely way. In fact, self-regulation can move much faster than a system that relies on legislation or using the courts to rule on complaints about marketing practices. A self-regulatory code can also be updated quickly, whereas making changes to existing legislation or pursuing cases before courts can be a long and complicated process.

Finally, there may be those who believe that the major drinks producers are opposed to working with governments and other stakeholders to extend and improve self-regulatory systems in parts of the world where they are inadequate or do not exist. That is not the case [as this book demonstrates]. (Pedlow, 2009, p. 56)

Few countries have the institutional capacity of the United States; therefore, it is not easy to generalize conclusions about self-regulation in the United States to the rest of the world. Nonetheless, considering the size of the U.S. market, the results of government examination of self-regulation in the alcohol industry have implications beyond the domestic market (Federal Trade Commission [FTC], 2008). What makes the review especially important is that the 12 leading alcohol suppliers receiving "special instructions" from the FTC to cooperate with the investigation—identified by public sources as "the top spenders on alcohol advertising in 'measured media' (television, radio, print, and outdoor advertising)"—are all companies that are involved in global markets both large and small, developed and developing (FTC, 2008, p. 3).[6]

---

[6] According to the FTC report (2008, p. 3), these 12 suppliers together represented about 73% of the U.S. alcohol supplier sales by volume in 2005: Absolut Spirits Company, Anheuser-Busch, Bacardi USA, Beam Global Spirits & Wine, Brown-Forman Corporation, Constellation Brands, Diageo North America, Heineken USA, InBev USA, Miller Brewing Company, Molson Coors Brewing Company, and Pernod Ricard USA.

The analysis of the data provided by the suppliers and their agencies indicated a high level of compliance to the various code requirements.[7] The FTC made a further point that, even where self-regulatory codes did not expressly apply, companies were mindful of the provisions of the codes. Again, considering the limited resources and capacity likely to be available in many markets that might be prompted to introduce formal statutory controls on the sale and marketing of alcohol, it is instructive to consider the conclusions of the FTC (2008): "A well constructed self-regulatory regime has advantages over government regulation. It conserves limited government resources and is more prompt and flexible than government regulation" (p. 25). This view is also reflected in ICAP's (2002) *Self-regulation and Alcohol: A Toolkit for Emerging Markets and the Developing World*:

> If bad advertising—dishonest, misleading, and offensive—is allowed to go unchecked, even though it may account for only a small percentage of the whole, it will gradually undermine consumers' confidence and all advertising will suffer. So it is in the interests of the advertising industry itself to ensure that advertising is properly regulated. (p. 2)

Independent reviews, such as that carried out by the FTC, are not limited to the United States. In Europe, the European Advertising Standards Alliance (EASA) produces annual reports that assess the levels of compliance of alcohol advertising with the various national codes of practice or relevant legislation. EASA's findings are reviewed by an independent expert panel. In 2008, the monitoring exercise was widened to include 19 countries, 4 more than in 2007. The report found that 94% of all advertisements for beer, wine, and spirits on television and in printed publications complied with both national advertising codes and applicable laws (EASA, 2008). In June 2008, EASA established a new international council to foster exchange of best practice in self-regulation outside Europe. In addition, ICAP has and will

---

[7] The FTC found a high degree of compliance, particularly with the rule that forbids alcohol advertising when at least 30% of the audience is underage (21 years of age in the United States). The FTC has proposed ways of strengthening the codes and hopes the industry will continue to cooperate on its more stringent suggestions; similar FTC surveys were conducted in the past, and these results are consistent with previous findings (FTC, 2008).

convene regional workshops and working groups on self-regulation and responsible marketing practices, as it has done to date in Africa, Asia-Pacific, and Latin America (ICAP, 2006b, 2006c, 2007).

THE PORTMAN GROUP'S *CODE OF PRACTICE*

The Portman Group is an industry-funded organization in the United Kingdom that works with producers to raise standards of alcohol marketing. It introduced the *Code of Practice on the Naming, Packaging and Promotion of Alcoholic Drinks* in 1996, now in its fourth edition (Portman Group, 2008). The code has been expanded to cover point-of-sale advertising, brand websites, sponsorship, branded merchandise, advertorials, press releases, and product sampling. One of the unique features of the way the code is implemented is the use of a *Retailer Alert Bulletin*, asking retailers not to stock products that have been found to be in breach of the code. As most of the United Kingdom's major retailers are code signatories, this means that offending products are, in effect, removed from sale. Complaints are ruled on by an independent complaints panel. A review of alcohol promotional activities in the United Kingdom, commissioned by the Home Office's Alcohol Strategy Unit, found that the Portman Group code was "binding and tightly regulated" (KPMG, 2008, p. 13; for a discussion on how the code applies to new product development and packaging, see Chapter 2).

Going Forward

As noted in Chapter 1, ICAP submitted six position papers to WHO in November 2008, one of which was titled "Alcohol Marketing" (Sinclair, 2009)[8] and contained several substantive proposals.

Global Survey

To complement the data collection by WHO from Member States on advertising laws and regulation, the industry could initiate an

---

[8] A referenced version of this paper is available at http://www.icap.org/Portals/0/download/all_pdfs/WHO/Marketing%20-%20REFERENCED.pdf

international survey of company and industrywide self-regulatory codes to establish where such practices do and do not exist. Where self-regulatory mechanisms cannot be found, the industry will use its best endeavors (ideally, in conjunction with WHO Member States) to persuade companies operating in those regions to initiate and commit themselves to a self-regulatory regime. To that end, the industry has given its commitment "to [work] with government and other stakeholders to extend and improve self-regulatory systems in parts of the world where they are inadequate or do not exist" (Pedlow, 2009, p. 56).

Best Practice

Many countries have company and consumer laws that require marketing communications to conform to basic requirements of truthfulness and accuracy (WHO, 2004b). In this context, governments are invited to (and often do) provide input into the voluntary code provisions. Member States that have worked with industry in developing self-regulatory systems can help others by compiling a best practice database on implementing codes and supporting them with appropriate policies.

Channel Commitment

The SROs are most effective when they can rely on proper policy framework and involve all members of related industry—that is, the producers, related agencies, the media, and retailers. Commitment by these channel members provides the SROs with powerful response options from warnings to removal of advertising from the media and the withdrawal of product from the shelves. Alcohol producers can, to the best of their ability, encourage such commitment by all channel participants.

Social Marketing

The skill, knowledge, and creativity that alcohol marketers employ in promoting their brands can be harnessed to promote the responsible use of their products and to combat misuse. Industry members can continue to build on their existing social marketing campaigns, particularly as they target specific consumer groups, for example, young adults or pregnant women (see also Chapter 7).

New Media

In marketing, the collection of vehicles employed to promote the continued use of brands to consumers is called *integrated marketing communications* (IMC). IMC ranges from the use of mass media (e.g., radio, television, and print) to in-store promotions, public relations, product placements, and the many opportunities associated with digital and electronic communications. A constant watch needs to be focused on this area to identify new marketing approaches and technology. There are bodies that monitor this, mainly for the advertising industry. Such bodies could be employed to identify the new means by which alcohol brands are being promoted to ensure comprehensive coverage in codes of practice.

Media Help

The world's media groupings, such as Time Warner, News Group, and Bertelsmann, rely on advertising for a large part of their income. The alcohol industry is a contributor to this. An approach to the major world media players by a joint group representing the main concerned parties in the campaign against harmful drinking could encourage the media industry to participate in this process in the form of free health promotion space. The opportunity could also be used to encourage media owners to adopt codes of responsible marketing practice, such as those in place with major alcohol producers, and apply these to all advertisers of beverage alcohol brands.

Expanding Self-regulation

The industry offers its expertise, network of branches, and offices to assist governments to introduce self-regulatory bodies and codes where none exist or where they are poorly applied. The major companies in the formal beverage alcohol sector are represented in a large proportion of Member States.

Education

WHO can establish a multi-stakeholder working group—consisting of NGOs, family psychologists, governments, alcohol marketers, and others—to strengthen existing awareness campaigns about the influence parents and peers have in preventing underage drinking, the dangers of extreme or "binge" drinking, and alcohol-impaired driving.

Concluding Remarks

A very common misperception is that advertising is marketing. Modern marketers do not see advertising in isolation. Marketing strategy is designed to communicate with consumers using a combination of promotional vehicles, of which advertising is one. The idea is that consumers are exposed to a variety of message channels and do not separate the sources of commercial information that they process and absorb. Marketers therefore choose an appropriate mix of advertising types (e.g., television, print, or radio) and merge this with other methods of reaching the consumer (e.g., in-store promotion, product placement, the Internet, cell phones, and sponsorship). For this reason, it is essential that marketing codes of practice cover all forms of marketing communication—not just advertising.

A decade ago, traditional advertising was the predominant element, accounting for as much as 60% of marketing expenditure. Changes in retailer power and influence, the emergence of more informed and questioning consumers—who, among other things, may be cynical about claims made in advertising—the availability of an increasing variety of promotional vehicles, and the advent of the Internet have changed this (Kotler & Keller, 2006, p. 585).

Not only has traditional advertising been given less prominence by marketers themselves in favor of other means of communication, but also the approaches they prefer, by definition, lack the broad coverage that advertising is able to achieve. Whereas advertising reaches a wide audience of product users and non-users, promotion tends to take place within the retail environment. Even in product placement and sponsorship, the very best marketers can hope for is brand awareness, with minimal scope for persuasion through message argument.

For over 50 years, the beverage alcohol industry has adopted codes of practice and, in more recent decades, corporate codes of responsible marketing. Self-regulation does not stand still, however. It must continue to evolve to reflect changes in society and marketing communications. Work will always be needed to ensure that codes of practice are up to date and sufficiently broad in their scope. More attention needs to be paid to countries where codes are poorly applied or are nonexistent. Here, the industry offers its assistance to work with authorities and local businesses to encourage both the passing of legal frameworks by governments and the development of SROs by industry.

Consumers select and prefer a brand because it provides them with guaranteed quality, consistency, and familiarity. This requires producers to ensure quality control and innovation to maintain brand freshness. Marketing is the tool businesses use to learn about consumer wants and needs, communicate with consumers, and ensure that their products and services are constantly available both geographically and over time. Responsible consumption of high-quality beverage alcohol requires an industry that not only is sophisticated, well structured, and regulated but also able to communicate freely and responsibly with its consuming market. The dangers associated with alcohol are well known, and it is in the best interest of the population at large if industry, governments, and health professionals work together to limit the excesses that cause harmful effects.

References

Adelekan, M., Razvodovsky, Yu., Liyanage, U., & Ndetei, D. (2008). *Noncommercial alcohol in three regions* (ICAP Review 3). Washington, DC: International Center for Alcohol Policies.

Anderson, P., de Bruijn, A., Angus, K., Gordon, R., & Hastings, G. (2009). Impact of alcohol advertising and media exposure on adolescent alcohol use: A systematic review of longitudinal studies. *Alcohol and Alcoholism, 44,* 229–243.

Arvanitidou, M., Tirodimos, I., Kyriakidis, I., Tsinaslanidou, Z., & Seretopoulos, D. (2007). Decreasing prevalence of alcohol consumption among Greek adolescents. *American Journal of Drug and Alcohol Abuse, 33,* 411–417.

Assunta, M. (2001). Impact of alcohol on Asia. *The Globe, 4,* 4–8.

Austin, E. W., & Chen, Y. J. (2003). The relationship of parental reinforcement media messages to college students' alcohol-related behaviors. *Journal of Health Communication, 8,* 157–169.

Austin, E. W., Chen, M. J., & Grube, J. W. (2006). How does alcohol advertising influence underage drinking? The role of desirability, identification and scepticism. *Journal of Adolescent Health, 38,* 376–384.

Austin, E. W., & Knaus, C. (2000). Predicting the potential for risky behavior among those "too young" to drink as the result of appealing advertising. *Journal of Health Communication, 5,* 13–27.

Belch, G. E., & Belch, M. A. (1998). *Advertising and promotion: An integrated marketing communications perspective* (4th ed.). Boston: Irwin/McGraw-Hill.

Brealey, R. A., & Myers, S. C. (1996). *Principles of corporate finance.* New York: McGraw-Hill.

Brown, S. L., Teufel, J. A., Birch, D. A., Raj, S., Izenberg, N., Lyness, N. D., et al. (2007). Reported alcohol use and perception of use among early adolescents. *American Journal of Health Studies, 22,* 33–41.

Chen, M. J., Grube, J. W., Bersamin, M., Waiters, E., & Keefe, D. B. (2005). Alcohol advertising: What makes it attractive to youth? *Journal of Health Communication, 10,* 553–565.

Chuang, Y. C., Ennett, S. T., Bauman, K. E., & Foshee, V. A. (2005). Neighborhood influences on adolescent cigarette and alcohol use: Mediating effects through parent and peer behaviors. *Journal of Health and Social Behavior, 46,* 187–204.

Clark, E. (1988). *The want makers.* London: Hodder & Stoughton.

Commonwealth of Australia. (2000, August). Executive summary. In *Industry self-regulation in consumer markets: Report prepared by the Taskforce on Industry Self-Regulation.* Retrieved March 7, 2009, from http://www.treasury.gov.au/documents/1131/HTML/docshell.asp?URL=01_executive_summary.asp

Curtis, K. (2005). *The importance of self-regulation in the implementation of data protection principles: The Australian private sector experience.* Paper presented at the 27th International Conference of Data Protection and Privacy Commissioners, Montreux, Switzerland.

Dickerson, S., & Dorsett, J. (2004). Advertising and alcohol consumption in the U.K. *International Journal of Advertising, 23,* 149–171.

Distilled Spirits Council of the United States (DISCUS). (2009). *Code of responsible practices for beverage alcohol advertising and marketing.* Retrieved March 8, 2009, from http://www.discus.org/responsibility/code.asp

Epstein, J. A., Griffin, K. W., & Botvin, G. J. (2008). A social influence model of alcohol use for inner-city adolescents: Family drinking, perceived drinking norms, and perceived social benefits of drinking. *Journal of Studies on Alcohol and Drugs, 69,* 397–405.

Euromonitor International. (2008). *Euromonitor database.* Retrieved March 8, 2009, from http://www.euromonitor.com/contact.aspx

European Advertising Standards Alliance (EASA). (2008). *Alcohol advertising monitoring report.* Retrieved March 8, 2009, from http://www.easa-alliance.org/page.aspx/357

Federal Trade Commission (FTC). (2008). *Self-regulation in the alcohol industry: Report of the Federal Trade Commission.* Retrieved March 8, 2009, from http://www.ftc.gov/os/2008/06/080626alcoholreport.pdf

Financial Accounting Standards Board (FASB). (2001). *Summary of statement 141 (revised 2007).* Retrieved March 8, 2009, from http://www.fasb.org/st/summary/stsum141r.shtml

Fleming, K., Thorson, E., & Atkin, C. K. (2004). Alcohol advertising exposure and perceptions: Links with alcohol expectancies and intentions to drink or drinking in underaged youth and young adults. *Journal of Health Communication, 9,* 3–29.

Fowler, T., Shelton, K., Lifford, K., Rice, F., McBride, A., Nikolov, I., et al. (2007). Genetic and environmental influences on the relationship between peer alcohol use and own alcohol use in adolescents. *Addiction, 102,* 894–903.

Grant, M. (Ed.). (1998). *Alcohol and emerging markets: Pattern, problems and responses.* Philadelphia: Brunner/Mazel.

Grube, J. W. (2003). Alcohol and the media: Drinking portrayals, alcohol advertising, and alcohol consumption among youth. In Institute of Medicine, *Reducing underage drinking* (pp. 597–624). Washington, DC: National Academies Press.

Harris, R., & Seldon, A. (1959). *Advertising in a free society.* London: Institute of Economic Affairs.

Haworth, A., & Simpson, R. (Eds.). (2004). *Moonshine markets: Issues in unrecorded alcohol beverage production and consumption.* New York: Brunner-Routledge.

Henriksen, L., Feighery, E. C., Schleicher, N. C., & Fortmann, S. P. (2008). Receptivity to alcohol marketing predicts initiation of alcohol use. *Journal of Adolescent Health, 42,* 28–35.

Hoffmann, J. P. (2006). Extracurricular activities, athletic participation, and adolescent alcohol use: Gender-differentiated and school-contextual effects. *Journal of Health and Social Behavior, 47,* 275–290.

Houghton, E., & Roche, A. M. (Eds.). (2001). *Learning about drinking.* Philadelphia: Brunner-Routledge.

Institute of Alcohol Studies (IAS). (2008). *Alcohol and advertising* (IAS Fact Sheet). St. Ives, U.K.: Author.

International Center for Alcohol Policies (ICAP). (2002). *Self-regulation and alcohol: A toolkit for emerging markets and the developing world.* Washington, DC: Author.

International Center for Alcohol Policies (ICAP). (2004). *Sharing best practice in self-regulation: An international workshop. London, United Kingdom.* Washington, DC: Author.

International Center for Alcohol Policies (ICAP). (2006a). *Responsible drinks marketing: Shared rights and responsibilities. Report of an ICAP Expert Committee.* Washington, DC: Author.

International Center for Alcohol Policies (ICAP). (2006b). *A workshop on self-regulation: Africa Region. Meeting report*. Washington, DC: Author.

International Center for Alcohol Policies (ICAP). (2006c). *A workshop on self-regulation: Asia-Pacific Region. Meeting report*. Washington, DC: Author.

International Center for Alcohol Policies (ICAP). (2007). *A workshop on self-regulation: Latin America Region. Meeting report*. Washington, DC: Author.

International Chamber of Commerce (ICC). (n.d.). *Advertising and marketing communication practice: Consolidated ICC code*. Paris: Author.

Keller, K. L. (2008). *Strategic brand management: Building, measuring, and managing brand equity* (3rd ed.). Upper Saddle River, NJ: Prentice Hall.

Kotler, P., & Keller, K. L. (2006). *Marketing management* (12th ed.). Upper Saddle River, NJ: Pearson Prentice Hall.

KPMG. (2008). *Review of the social responsibility standards for the production and sale of alcoholic drinks: Volume 1*. Retrieved March 8, 2009, from http://drugs.homeoffice.gov.uk/

Lannon, J. (2008). *How public service advertising works*. London: Central Office of Information (COI) & Institute of Practitioners in Advertising (IPA).

Lipsitz, A., Brake, G., Vincent, E. J., & Winters, M. (2003). Another round for the brewers: Television ads and children's alcohol expectancies. *Journal of Applied Social Psychology, 23*, 439–450.

Mogro-Wilson, C. (2008). The influence of parental warmth and control on Latino adolescent alcohol use. *Hispanic Journal of Behavioral Sciences, 30*, 89–105.

National Institute on Alcohol Abuse and Alcoholism (NIAAA). (2000). *Tenth special report to the U.S. Congress on alcohol and health*. Washington, DC: U.S. Department of Health and Human Services.

Nelson, J. P., & Young, D. J. (2001). Do advertising bans work? An international comparison. *International Journal of Advertising, 20*, 273–296.

Pedlow, G. (2009). Statement on behalf of the Global Alcohol Producers Group. In World Health Organization, *Report from a roundtable meeting with economic operators on harmful use of alcohol* (pp. 55–56). Retrieved March 8, 2009, from http://www.who.int/substance_abuse/activities/msbeoreport.pdf

Portman Group. (2008). *The code of practice on the naming, packaging and promotion of alcoholic drinks* (4th ed.). Retrieved February 28, 2009, from http://portman-group.org.uk/?pid=18&level=2

Reichheld, R. F. (1996). *The loyalty effect: The hidden force behind growth, profits and lasting value*. Boston: Harvard Business School Press.

Ringold, D. J. (2008). Responsibility and brand advertising in the alcoholic beverage market: The modeling of normative drinking behavior. *Journal of Advertising, 37*, 127–141.

Saffer, H., & Dave, D. (2006). Alcohol advertising and alcohol consumption by adolescents. *Health Economics, 15*, 617–637.

Scholte, R. H. J., Poelen, E. A., Willemsen, G., Boomsma, D. I., & Engels, R. C. (2008). Relative risks of adolescent and young adult alcohol use: The role of drinking fathers, mothers, siblings, and friends. *Addictive Behaviors, 33*, 1–14.

Sinclair, R. (2009). Alcohol marketing. In World Health Organization, *WHO public hearing on harmful use of alcohol. Volume IV: Received contributions from individuals* (p. 175). Retrieved March 8, 2009, from http://www.who.int/substance_abuse/activities/6individuals.pdf

Smith, L. A., & Foxcroft, D. R. (2009). The effect of alcohol advertising, marketing and portrayal on drinking behaviour in young people: Systematic review of prospective cohort studies. *BMC Public Health, 9*. Retrieved March 8, 2009, from http://www.biomedcentral.com/1471-2458/9/51/abstract

Spijkerman, R. J., Van den Eijnden, R. J. M., Overbeek, G., & Engels, M. J. (2007). The impact of peer and parental norms and behavior on adolescent drinking: The role of drinker prototypes. *Psychology & Health, 22*, 7–29.

Trim, R. S., Leuthe, E., & Chassin, L. (2006). Sibling influence on alcohol use in a young adult, high-risk sample. *Journal of Studies on Alcohol, 67*, 391–398.

van Dalen, W., & Kuunders, M. (2006). Alcohol marketing and young people: An analysis of the current debate on regulation. *Nordic Studies on Alcohol and Drugs, 23*, 415–426.

van der Vorst, H., Engels, R. C. M. E., Meeus, W., Dekovic, M., & van Leeuwe, J. (2007). Similarities and bi-directional influences regarding alcohol consumption in adolescent sibling pairs. *Addictive Behaviors, 32*, 1814–1825.

van der Zwaluw, C. S., Scholte, R. H., Vermulst, A. A., Buitelaar, J. K., Verkes, R. J., & Engels, R. C. (2008). Parental problem drinking, parenting, and adolescent alcohol use. *Journal of Behavioral Medicine, 31*, 189–200.

World Advertising Research Center (WARC). (2005). *World drink trends 2005: Containing data to 2003*. Henley-on-Thames, U.K.: Author.

World Advertising Research Center (WARC). (2008). *Find case study*. Retrieved March 7, 2009, from http://www.warc.com/Search/CaseStudies/Default2.asp

World Health Organization (WHO). (2004a). *Global status report on alcohol*. Geneva, Switzerland: Author.

World Health Organization (WHO). (2004b). *Global status report: Alcohol policy*. Geneva, Switzerland: Author.

World Health Organization Expert Committee on Problems Related to Alcohol Consumption. (2007). *Second report* (WHO Technical Report Series 944). Geneva, Switzerland: World Health Organization.

5

PRICING BEVERAGE ALCOHOL

GODFREY ROBSON

Introduction

In economic theory, the relationship between price and demand is simple. If price rises, then (other things being equal) demand falls. Some consumers are priced out of the market, decide not to pay the higher price, or choose to buy less of the product. So, when we come to address public policy on alcohol-related problems, do we really need to make things as complicated as we do? Why not just raise prices? This is the fundamental question addressed in this chapter.

It is an important question. If the answer is "Yes, just get on with it," it would make policy-makers' job a lot easier. It would also mark the end of the unproductive and sometimes ill-tempered exchange—calling it dialogue would be misleading—among academic commentators. Unfortunately, as this chapter will show, things are not that simple. Pricing has, obviously, a role to play in devising any policy to tackle harmful drinking, but there are a few reasons why it cannot be the whole answer—or even a substantial part of it. These include the openness of international markets generally, the intricacies of consumer markets for alcohol beverages, a range of cultural issues, and, not least, the relative deafness of problem drinkers to price signals.

All of this is explored here in the light of a substantial literature. It seems appropriate also to consider in some detail a number of policy approaches based on pricing that have been tried or proposed but do not appear to be helpful or are helpful only to a limited degree. None of this should really be surprising. The modern world is complex, and those charged with social policy face a particularly difficult task, not least arising from those most complex of phenomena—people.

Some Initial Ground Clearing

The practical issue examined in this chapter is how, if at all, the price of alcohol beverages can be used or manipulated as a tool of public policy. Public policy is concerned with harmful drinking. The question is not how we might reduce overall alcohol consumption in the population, although it is acknowledged that harmful drinking arises for reasons, and these might arguably include too ready access to the product in the first place.[1] Rather, this chapter is about the use or manipulation of price through the agency of government or related public bodies, with the intention of influencing consumer behavior, for public health reasons. It also provides the perspectives of producers on costs, profit requirements, and market pricing strategies, as well as the commercial decisions of other economic players in the supply chain. Alcohol producers have surprisingly little influence on the final price the consumer pays for their product—compared, that is, with the influence of governments (which set tax rates and excise duties), retailers (which are often in a strong position to extract tight terms from producers but have much leeway in their own pricing decisions), or hospitality sectors (which enjoy significant pricing freedom but, of course, also face their own distinctive cost structures).

Two caveats must be acknowledged. First, most of the research reviewed here refers to developed markets. It is recognized that different considerations may apply in the developing world, although some of the evidence—for example, in relation to product substitution—is known to apply. Second, while there is a substantial literature in this field (albeit dealing mainly with developed economies), there is also a wide variety of research approaches as well as much room for technical debate on method. On the other hand, there is a fair consistency of outcome, and two of the more recent meta-analyses, featured in the

---

[1] This begs the question, however, why the whole population, with such ready access, does not succumb to harmful drinking.

discussion here (Gallet, 2007; Wagenaar, Salois, & Komro, 2009), are well respected in the field and have provided a review and reanalysis of a wide range of earlier work.

Two important pieces of background information must also be mentioned. The first concerns antitrust/competition law, which normally prevents any collaboration (or collusion) among market players in the commercial determination of price. As we review, some commentators see competition law as a potential weapon for tackling harmful drinking. It is worth being clear about its purpose: protecting consumers from unfair practices by manufacturers or suppliers that lead to higher prices than would apply in a properly competitive market. This derives from the economic theory that, in a perfectly competitive market, profit (and so prices) of all market players will fall to an equilibrium level at the lowest price sustainable by an efficient producer. The wider picture is that, if competition is maintained throughout the economy, this will result in the most efficient allocation of capital resources, and hence the whole economy will operate and grow in the most efficient way.

This is all simply stated and, of course, refers to a theoretical construct that is never fully achievable in the real world. But, it explains why economic policy-makers will resist giving their competition authorities wider social remits. In practice, competition authorities usually concentrate their efforts on maintaining competition at a macrolevel—for example, by imposing rules to prevent takeovers or breaking up existing quasi-monopolies where these threaten the competitiveness of the market—and on combating anticompetitive behavior by market participants, such as collusion on prices or agreements not to compete. Competition authorities generally report to governments or, at the very least, are statutory creations of government. Therefore, it is up to government to act in circumstances when the regular operation of the rules produces results deemed to be against the public interest. This is normally thought more appropriate than giving the competition authorities themselves wider social remits, which they would have difficulty (and, perhaps, lack legitimacy) in balancing with their main role.

The second piece of background worth covering at this stage is how the price of an alcohol beverage is determined or, at least, how the price at the final point of sale is reached. This is important for understanding how price can be adjusted—or not—for public policy purposes. Although the cost structure of the product will obviously vary by the beverage type, a producer's regular management accounts will look much like those of any other business, starting with income from sales minus direct costs (including for raw materials and labor) and indirect costs (for buildings and plant, administration, marketing, and financing costs, including cost of capital and provision for tax on profits). At the point of product distribution, excise duty or other taxes will be added but will just pass straight through the accounts. The end figure, at least for a successful product, will be net profit, and the producer's first consideration in setting price will be to recover the costs of production, including a proper return on capital employed.

The producers then have to consider the marketing strategy for the product and the competition. Marketing strategy is critical. A key question here is where the product is to be situated in the marketplace, for example, as an "economy" product, a "premium" product, or as part of a particular niche, often defined by relationship to competing products. This decision will determine the scale of production and design—and, perhaps, cost—of marketing (advertising, packaging, promotional activities, and much else, as discussed in Chapter 4). It will also determine the end price the producer wants to achieve for the product. An economy product—for example, a mainstream, nonpremium beer or a spirits beverage sold under a supermarket brand—will typically yield low profit margins and so require high-volume sales and good cash flow. Price competition and substitutability of product will be greatest in this part of the market as the scope for creating product differentiation is limited. A premium product will cost more to produce and probably more to market but will have the potential to achieve higher profit margins.

Marketing strategy has to take account of—or be buffeted by—competition in the marketplace. This is complex. First, the consumer has all sorts of potential trade-offs among competing brands or products in the same product categories. In practice, much market elasticity is elasticity of choice among products, not elasticity of the market as a whole. In other words, consumers are choosing among brands of products rather than choosing to drink more. Thus, producers' desired end price relates not only to recovering costs and making a decent return but also to what market signals the price gives. For example, in the case of a new beverage, the producer may want to use price to position the product somewhere between other competing brands. Price, among other influences, will help to create the product's image or market signal.[2] Whether this desired end price can be achieved is another matter. It should be noted that this works both ways: Producers may want to maintain a high price to achieve the intended image and market niche; however, if externalities (e.g., a new competitor, a repricing of a competitive good, or a tax increase) threaten the established niche, they may choose to reduce their profit margin to maintain the price and market position. So, the challenge is to design and market successfully a premium product (or otherwise establish a market niche) and produce high profit margin, but the complexity of the marketplace and its competitiveness make this difficult.

The operation of the market can keep price and profit margin under control. The competition is, of course, not only with similar products but also inherent in the routes to market. For producers, this process is usually indirect and involves large-scale retailers and distributors. This is exacerbated as retailers, unlike producers, are selling a wide range of products, including some that, for commercial reasons, are sold below cost (meaning, at prices less than manufacturing or purchasing costs of a product). In some markets, certainly including the United Kingdom (U.K.), the retail sector is dominated by a small number of powerful supermarket and wine shop chains; these chains wield enormous influence over the price they pay to producers. For example, they may require large bulk discounts, contributions to their own advertising and marketing costs, and "rent" for prominent display space. This power is particularly pronounced for some products—the most obvious in the United Kingdom is Scotch whisky, whose annual sales tend to be concentrated within a very short period around the end of the year and whose producers are therefore especially vulnerable to retailers' stocking and marketing decisions around that period.

---

[2] This is perhaps especially likely to apply in the beer market, where price of raw materials can fluctuate and where time to market is more critical than for other alcohol products.

Finally, regardless of the producers' preference on retail price, their real capacity to influence that price is limited by consumer protection and other regulation. Producers may be able to make suggestions to retailers and distributors, but they cannot insist or, for example, refuse to supply discounters.

Thus, alcohol producers are in many cases effectively price-takers, and it is those nearer to the final consumer who are the price-makers. It is interesting to note that the financial performance of major quoted alcohol producers does not tend to exceed that in other market segments, including, to be fair, that of retailers. It is also important to realize that a publicly imposed price increase, in the form of a tax hike, does not necessarily feed through fully to the final price. Both producers and retailers have scope to absorb additional costs and adjust their margins if they see commercial benefit in so doing. They may judge that, in certain circumstances, competitive pressures leave them no option.

Price Sensitivity of Beverage Alcohol

Price sensitivity is the measure of how demand for a product is influenced by price. Specifically, it measures the comparison between a change in price and the resulting change in consumption. If a price increase of X% results in an X% reduction in consumption, the price elasticity is –1. Generally, for a wide range of products, responsiveness to price changes is lower, falling somewhere in the range between –1 and 0. The key point is that price and demand are usually in some kind of inverse relationship.

We would expect that, in principle, the normal relationship between demand and supply would apply in the market for alcohol, as for most other products. So it proves.[3] Many studies have been undertaken to confirm the normally inverse relationship of price and demand in the alcohol market. These include some major and groundbreaking historical studies from the 19th and early 20th centuries in England and Sweden, now old but still referenced (e.g., Malmquist, 1948;

---

[3] There are exceptions, as noted, for example, a luxury product whose premium is on exclusivity, with higher prices actually making the product more attractive.

Niskanen, 1960; Prest, 1949; Stone, 1951). The use of historical data series does, of course, present problems, including those of properly identifying and controlling for exogenous factors. Nevertheless, the relative consistency of results of a large number of studies confirms the basic hypothesis.

There have also been some "controlled experiments," in which significant shifts in pricing have happened suddenly and afforded the opportunity to measure the consequences. These also support the general point that price and demand are inversely related. For example, one study (Simon, 1966) was able to compare United States (U.S.) state alcohol sales shortly before and shortly after price (tax) increases in circumstances for which there were sufficient data to standardize for other possible factors, such as changes in consumer tastes and relative changes in income, and comparison could be made with states where prices had not changed. Areas with high informal trade in illicitly produced alcohol were excluded. The elasticity calculated was consistent with the earlier findings. Another U.S. study, based on data from 1982 to 1989 and covering 50 states, again confirmed the basic price-consumption correlation, but with some interesting additional points (Trolldal & Ponicki, 2005). The principal of these was that the relevant consideration for consumers was what the authors referred to as the "full price" of the product. This included not just the nominal cash price over the counter but also the "transaction costs," the trouble to which the consumer had to go to make the purchase. In practice, the difference arose mainly between states with closely regulated alcohol markets and more economically liberal states. In the former, there were nonprice transaction costs, such as longer journeys to sales outlets, restricted sales hours, and other hurdles that the consumers had to face.

We will return to the effectiveness of market regulation of this kind, which, in principle, allows for the possibility of greater central control on price (the wider issue of alcohol monopolies is dealt with in Chapter 6). The interesting point here is simply the relevance of indirect, as well as direct, costs in determining consumer behavior. The general conclusion, so far as it goes, is that demand for beverage alcohol is certainly price sensitive, but up to a point. "Up to a point" is an important qualification. In almost all the studies referred to so far, the estimate of price elasticity has been less than –1. In other words, the product is technically price elastic, but not very, in the sense that a given percentage price increase produces a less-than-proportionate decrease in consumption. This point was confirmed internationally (Babor et al., 2003) and appears to apply similarly when prices, measured in real terms, are dropping (e.g., see data for the period from 1997 to 2006 in Brinner, Brinner, & Zislin, 2007).

The study of price elasticity is a continuing one, perhaps destined to be never-ending. The work of Wagenaar and colleagues (2009) is especially worth reading as a detailed and admirable—even valiant— attempt to bottom out the issue through a new meta-analysis of previous research data. This study bears careful attention, but the main revelations are the huge uncertainty of the results and the evident other-worldliness of statistical research. The study's first conclusion, that "beverage alcohol prices and taxes are related inversely to drinking" (p. 179), can best be described as indisputable (and therefore not disputed). But, it does not take us any further forward.

The issue of what price elasticity means in practice, in the context of harmful drinking, is not a nit-picking point but an important issue of interpretation. The conclusion of an interim report by academics from the University of Sheffield (Booth et al., 2008), undertaking a review of the effects of alcohol pricing and promotion for the English Health Department—"There is strong and consistent evidence to suggest that price increases and taxation … have a significant effect in reducing demand for alcohol" (p. 5)—really just begs the question, "What is meant by 'significant'?" It does not mean "decisive" or "conclusive." Depending on the policy intention (if the increase is government imposed), it might not even mean "adequate." It all depends. And, quite apart from the question of how much effect price increases have on harmful drinking, there is the whole other question of how long that effect lasts.

Price Sensitivity in Practice

It has to be said that the classic supply-demand curve model is a simple one and rather theoretical. As with many products, the real market for alcohol is not simple. We therefore need to examine and deconstruct the evidence more closely. The key issue in market complexity is, of course, the existence of a wide variety of different types of product—beer, wine, and spirits—and, within each type, of many product variations, for example, by quality, brand image (shaped by marketing), alcohol content, and price. According to Gallet (2007), demand for beer is more inelastic than for other alcohol beverages. This is not further investigated, although we may reasonably take into account the nature of the customer base, beer's well-entrenched position in certain national markets, its social function in bars, and the fact that customers buying in bars are anyway accustomed to pay higher prices than in off-premise venues.

For wines and spirits, there are many more product variations than for beer. Spirits may be marketed as high-quality and exclusive luxury goods sold in airports and specialist outlets, premium-quality brand leaders, middle-market products, or low-end cheaper beverages (e.g., supermarket-owned brands). The wine market, with its immense range of brands, grape types, blends, national provenances, and quality, lends itself to particular price opacity, even if connoisseurs think they know how to identify the best products. There are examples of low-end wines, such as cask wine, often linked to heavy drinking in Australia: The beverage can be sold cheaper than other drinks because wine is taxed on value, while beer, spirits, and ready-to-drink (RTD) beverages are taxed on alcohol content.

Consumer flexibility up and down the scale is well known, at least to marketers. Economic recession and exchange rate turbulence may dent alcohol markets, but this is likely to be met by new promotion and pricing strategies by producers and retailers. The wide range of existing products has proved difficult for researchers to take into account in estimating demand responsiveness, but some conclusions emerge. First, as income rises, consumers tend to spend more on drinking in on-premise establishments (such as bars and restaurants).[4] Second, controlling for income, as consumers drink more, they are more inclined to buy from off-premise venues and drink elsewhere.

---

[4] In this book, the term *on-premise establishments* is used to refer to venues where alcohol is sold to be consumed on the premises, as in bars, pubs, and restaurants; the term *off-premise establishments* is used to refer to venues where alcohol is sold to be consumed elsewhere, as in alcohol shops, supermarkets, and state-owned alcohol outlets.

Venue substitution also applies as affordability declines, with consumers moving from bars to home drinking. The wide range of product and price variation allows consumers to "regulate costs by substituting one form of consumption for another" (Gruenewald, Ponicki, Holder, & Romelsjö, 2006, p. 97)—for example, by switching drinking venues or moving from a high-quality/high-image brand to less-costly options. It should be noted that, in turn, there may be different consequences for consumers who are already buying the low-cost products; we will return to this.

Notwithstanding the ability on the part of consumers to meet rising costs by purchasing strategy, it should be noted that, as income rises, so does expenditure on alcohol (this is not surprising since rising income boosts discretionary spending). However, as income continues to rise, there comes a point at which the appetite for further increase in alcohol consumption declines, although this may be substituted for by buying more expensive products (Brinner et al., 2007).

There is little direct research on price sensitivity and socioeconomic groupings, although a number of studies touched on the matter indirectly, allowing some reasonably confident inferences. For example, a study of alcohol consumption in Alaska examined the determinants of prices charged for alcohol drinks in on- and off-premise establishments, addressing particularly issues of competition, as measured by proxy of outlet density and costs to vendors (Treno, Gruenewald, Wood, & Ponicki, 2006). The conclusion was that competition did not make much difference for price, but vendor distribution costs did; demographic and economic variables within a community were significant determining factors. This finding was supported by Harwood and colleagues (2003), who observed that off-premise beer prices varied with urbanity (higher in urban areas, lower in suburbs) and median income of a given area.

As regards young people, there is a lot of anecdotal information but not a great deal of hard research evidence on price sensitivity. Intuitively, one might expect that this group would be more sensitive to price, and a number of studies showed that this is the case with tobacco consumption. On alcohol, Chaloupka and Wechsler (1996) seemed to bear this out, as did Gallet (2007), although only by some passing references and assertions (see also Martinic & Measham,

2008). Studies of the short-term effect of the 1999 reduction in spirits taxation in Switzerland indicated particularly increased consumption by the young (Heeb, Gmel, Zurbrugg, Kuo, & Rehm, 2003; Kuo, Heeb, Gmel, & Rehm, 2003).

On the other hand, a fair amount of recent evidence, not all of it anecdotal (e.g., Measham, 2006), points to the price sensitivity among young drinkers being addressed not by reduced consumption but by substitute behavior, such as drinking at home before going out. This phenomenon, variously referred to as "tanking up," "predrinking," or "preloading," has become increasingly common—and increasingly worrying—as an almost ritualized prelude to an evening's entertainment for many young people, often involving harmful drinking (Wells, Graham, & Purcell, 2009). Notably, early drinking by adolescents happens outside the marketplace, in the sense that they are introduced to alcohol by family or peers. In addition, many young people, who may well be of legal drinking age, typically have the capacity for relatively high discretionary expenditure (if, for example, they do not yet have liabilities for houses and families).

For chronic problem drinkers, we would expect intuitively that price elasticity would be low—in other words, the more alcohol dependent an individual is, the more prepared he or she will be to find the means to pay for drinks rather than reduce consumption. For example, Brinner and colleagues (2007), referring to a number of studies carried out since 1980, concluded: "Abusive behavior would not be diminished by price changes to the same degree that responsible consumers react," noting that, "Empirical analyses indicate that light and moderate drinkers are the most price sensitive" (p. 10).

It is worth mentioning that there have been at least two recent natural experiments in reducing alcohol prices. These offer the chance to look at price sensitivity through the other end of the telescope. The first took place in Finland in 2004 as a consequence of joining the European Union (EU) and in parallel with a policy decision to reduce taxation in the interest of economic competition with neighboring countries (the overall price changes were wider than might have been needed just to keep within the new legal framework). The excise duty reduction was 33% overall, including a 44% reduction for spirits. The market response was an increase in total domestic sales of 8%, with spirits sales rising by 19% (Alavaikko

& Österberg, 2000; for a study that did not find a short-term change in consumption, see Mäkelä, Bloomfield, Gustafsson, Huhtanen, & Room, 2008). The authors postulated that much of this increase in consumption could have been accounted for by substitution of domestic purchases for imports—in other words, recorded consumption of domestically purchased alcohol beverages was substituting for earlier unrecorded imports. On the other hand, it is hardly credible to think that such a large reduction in prices would not have led to some increase in demand. It was also concluded that the price reduction correlated with a rise in drink-related sudden deaths (Koski, Sirén, Vuori, & Poikolainen, 2007), pointing to an increase in consumption at least among some groups in the population. The Finnish experience clearly needs further study, and Mäkelä and Österberg (2009) have helpfully stated this.

EFFECT OF ALCOHOL PRICE REDUCTIONS IN FINLAND

In 1995, Finland joined the EU. The immediate effect of the EU membership was to allow travelers to import higher quantities of alcohol beverages for personal consumption, bought at lower prices elsewhere in Europe. Finland was, however, given until December 2003 to align its import regime (other than personal imports) with EU rules. An import quota system was gradually phased out, with full freedom to import from elsewhere in the EU from January 2004. In March 2004, Finland also reduced substantially its consumption taxes on alcohol. This was in anticipation of neighboring Estonia (with much lower taxes) joining the EU in May 2004.

Koski and colleagues (2007) tested the outcomes of these policy changes against incidence of alcohol-related sudden deaths, reporting two main outcomes. First, the 1995 increase in travelers' allowances did not correlate with an increase in deaths. This is consistent with market evidence that the main consumer response in this case was to substitute imported for locally produced alcohol. However, the substantial price decrease in 2004 clearly did correlate with increased deaths. Again, this is consistent with market data indicating increased consumption.

The second natural experiment took place in 1999, when Switzerland substantially reduced its taxes on spirits. This was in accordance with the World Trade Organization's (WTO's) requirements, intended to remove discrimination against imported products. The retail price reduction on most imported spirits brands ranged from 30 to 50%. Taxes on wine and beer were unchanged. Two studies examined the Swiss experience and found that spirits consumption rose by 28.6% in the six months after the tax change, while consumption of beer and wine was not significantly affected (Heeb et al., 2003; Kuo et al., 2003). However, the biggest increases in spirits consumption were among moderate drinkers and the young. There are also recent examples of tax changes in the opposite direction: Alcohol taxes were raised in the Netherlands in 2007 and in the United Kingdom and the Russian Federation in 2008. It is too early to assess the consequences of these changes, which will merit further study.

The data from the Finnish and Swiss price reductions indicate price elasticity, but of an order consistent with the wider evidence. Finally, it is worth remembering that, as we noted, dominant power to determine price rests at the retail end of the market—not with producers.

Unintended Consequences

In examining pricing as a public health tool, we need to consider what effects higher prices might have beyond their effect (when this arises) in suppressing demand. Note that "unintended consequences" are not the same as "unforeseen consequences," and obviously we risk the latter as well. A consequence is *unintended* if it is a byproduct of a policy, not what the policy was intended to achieve. It may be an acceptable price to pay, or it may not. We just need to identify it and be able to make that judgment.

The first issue, as already referred to, is *substitution effect*, the ability of the consumer to respond to higher prices through strategies other than reducing consumption, for example, by switching to different beverage types or cheaper brands or by drinking more at home. This is well attested by the evidence. Thus, at best, a price increase may be relatively ineffectual. In these circumstances, would it be worth doing anyway in the hope of achieving some effect? Such a calculation might be difficult to make given different price elasticities for different alcohol products.

The main counterargument, also difficult to evaluate, would be the potential damage done to problem drinkers (and their families) if their response is simply to devote more of their budget to alcohol. There is also added health risk (additional to the prior overconsumption) of turning to low-cost and, perhaps, low-quality substitute products. Several studies, including research by Manning, Blumberg, and Moulton (1995), indicated clearly that heavy and abusive drinkers demonstrate little or no price sensitivity.

In their book *Drinking in Context: Patterns, Interventions, and Partnerships*, Stimson, Grant, Choquet, and Garrison (2007) gave examples of harmful consumption of illicit alcohol or other ethanol-based products in India and the former Soviet Union. This is also a problem in parts of Africa and elsewhere, made worse by the use of toxic ingredients (see Chapter 3). A graphic commentary on the failure of policy to curb harmful drinking in the former Soviet Union, Kenya, and Truk in Micronesia, precisely because of the substitution effect, was offered by Partanen (1993).

A second issue is that higher prices do have a distributional effect within the population. Thus, as Brinner et al. (2007) noted, "[The fact that] the consumer can move freely to a lower quality serving or a higher alcohol concentration . . . reduces the price elasticity of servings for modest, responsible customers" (p. 10). But, evidence (e.g., Manning et al., 1995) shows that light and moderate drinkers are the most price sensitive. The fact of being a light or moderate drinker says nothing, of course, about a person's means and ability to pay. But, the category of what we might refer to as "non-problem drinkers" will also include people on modest incomes, on whom price increases will have a hard impact. It adds insult to injury if the price increase is in fact aimed at curbing the drinking of others.

An important consideration in liberal economic markets is the difficulty of making tax-based price increases stick. The higher the overall retail price (however constructed), the more incentive and scope there will be for market players to seek larger market share through price competition. U.K. supermarkets have increasingly been discounting alcohol prices and, indeed, using alcohol products as loss leaders. The evidence for this is clear and attested, for example, in the U.K. Competition Commission's provisional report of 2007. The commission was not recommending a remedy to this on the basis of its limited statutory remit, which is to consider competition issues, not health issues. The investigation arose from complaints by small retailers of unfair competition. The important point here is that, in a competitive market, tax increases do not necessarily carry straight through to retail prices. This kind of response in the off-premise retail market does, of course, have its own substitution effect, encouraging consumers (particularly the young, as mentioned) to do more home drinking, based on cheap alcohol purchased in off-premise establishments, in preparation for a night out. The on-premise trade in turn responds with cheap offers during designated "happy hours."

Another important issue for governments is tax revenue consequences. In effect, governments in developed countries typically, although not always, tax alcohol at relatively high levels. This is partly explained, on occasion, by reference to public health considerations but is mainly done because alcohol provides a good and reliable base, over the economic cycle, to raise revenue. As a result, many governments are, in practice, locked into a revenue dependence on alcohol sales. Proportionately, with the advent of ad valorem taxes, the dependence is less than, say, 50 years ago, but it is still significant—for example, in the United Kingdom it raises (using 2003 figures) 4.5% of total tax revenue, amounting to GBP 13,477 million. Governments therefore look carefully at the risk of raising taxes beyond the point at which total revenue will fall. Obviously, our evidence so far indicates that this is not especially likely for modest tax increases, but, for example, in 2003 the U.K. government's own HM Revenue and Customs estimated the price elasticity for spirits at –1.31. Based on similar calculations, the Scotch Whisky Association was able to persuade the U.K. government against tax increases for many years. This period ended with a 9.2% tax increase on spirits in 2008 and the promise of further inflation-related increases to come.

Finally, in considering increases to tax levels, governments must look at the industrial and employment implications. As with tax consequences discussed, these are unlikely to be significant for a modest tax increase. However, for example, the U.K. alcohol producers employ many thousands of people and the licensed retail and related businesses 1.47 million. In the United Kingdom, as well as in France and Spain, bar owners are already claiming significant losses in customers following recent smoking bans.

All this draws a complex picture. The main conclusions poking through so far from all the detail seem to be as follows: At a whole-population level, alcohol consumption can certainly be reduced by increasing price—however, the effect of price increases is significantly qualified by the relative inelasticity of demand in many cases. An increase in price generally gives rise to a less-than-proportionate reduction in consumption. In a liberal economic market, competition makes it hard for price increases to stick. Moreover, higher "official" prices encourage and make more profitable illicit production and imports, which bring their own health risks. The effect of price increases will fall most heavily on moderate and unproblematic drinkers. By contrast, problem drinkers will be least affected. This seems to include young problem drinkers, although in this case there is conflicting evidence. This raises issues of both equity (in relation to non-problem drinkers) and efficiency (in relation to problem drinkers). There are other public policy issues at stake. Governments balance public health considerations with others, such as security of tax revenue and employment (not to mention risks of unpopularity). They are concerned not to reduce revenue or seriously jeopardize jobs in alcohol-related industries.

Pricing Options Under Discussion

It would seem from all this that, while price has obviously some role to play in addressing harmful drinking, that role is likely to be limited. We now consider some particular possibilities that have been suggested or tried in different countries.

Alcohol Products and International Trade Agreements?

It has been suggested by some commentators that there should be some kind of general agreement that control by individual jurisdictions of their internal alcohol markets is to be exempted from international trade agreements. This is based on the assertion (see, e.g., Babor et al., 2003; Zeigler, 2009) that the now-extensive internationalization of trade—and, in particular, the relevant international treaties that underpin it—have reduced or inhibited in some way individual governments' ability to regulate alcohol properly in the interests of national health.

Zeigler's article (2009) merits attention as a particularly egregious example of overstatement and conspiracy theorizing. It starts with the surprisingly sweeping assertion, "Liberalization of alcohol trade [sic] increases availability and access, lowers prices through reduced taxation and tariffs, and increases promotion and advertising of alcohol" (p. 13). The article then tries to demonstrate this in a lengthy but highly confused muddling of WTO and the EU, as the argument drifts from alcohol control to tobacco and even to online gambling. In the course of his journey, the author uncovers some astonishing revelations, such as that the alcohol industry is consulted by WTO—yes, its charter requires that, and it also consults nongovernmental organizations, over 1,500 times (according to WTO data)—and that WTO dispute panels are peopled by "trade experts" (and not by public health analysts). What next? Will the Pope turn out to be a Catholic?

This kind of approach is not uncommon among academic commentators. There are four key points to make in response. First, as a matter of fact, most alcohol beverages are not traded internationally but are produced and consumed within single national frontiers, even with existing trade agreements (see Chapter 2). Second, WHO estimates levels of unrecorded alcohol consumption (mainly homemade or illegally traded drinks that are outside control of treaty mechanisms) to be at levels comparable to official internationally traded amounts in some regions. Third, what treaties like the one supporting WTO actually do is prohibit rules or tariffs that are discriminatory between locally produced and imported products. WTO members are otherwise free to apply excise and other taxes on alcohol as they see fit. Finally, all international treaties are, of course, freely entered into by participating countries, which are equally free to seek ad hoc amendments to the treaties as and when they wish. Therefore, there seems no need, or purpose, likely to be served by some overarching provision to exempt alcohol products, as a class, from trade agreements, quite apart from the precedent this would create in relation to other products, such as pharmaceuticals.

Tax Equalization?

It is sometimes suggested that beer, wine, and spirits should be taxed (and regulated) in the same way, with a uniform tax rate calculated on the basis of alcohol concentration measured by volume (ABV). There are different points of view. Where different products are taxed at different rates per volume of pure ethanol, excise taxes are often considerably higher on distilled spirits. For example, the excise taxes on spirits in the United States are almost three times the rate of tax on still wine and over two times the rate on beer. The variation in excise rates is often justified on the basis that different beverages are served in different ways, and that the pattern in which they are consumed varies as well. Distillers suggest that this is discriminatory as ethanol is common to all these beverages. The WHO (2004) *Global Status Report: Alcohol Policy* notes that one of the factors explaining the higher tax rates on spirits is that "production costs per litre of pure alcohol are higher for making wine and beer than distilled spirits" (p. 41). Furthermore, WHO noted that in some countries it is "official policy of the pricing system to steer people towards a particular type of low-alcohol or non-alcoholic beverage, in order to substantially reduce [sic] risky or high blood alcohol levels" (p. 41). The alcohol producers have no agreed view on this matter.

Regular Tax Revalorization?

In jurisdictions where tax and duty form a high proportion of retail price for alcohol, there is a case for reviewing tax levels regularly with a view to keeping the retail price of the product constant in real terms (provided that the tax increase follows through into the final price). This potentially addresses total population consumption rather than problem drinkers, but it has potential advantages for government and for the industry in avoiding periodic more substantial price hikes, with risk of market disruption, as happened in some countries in 2008. The alcohol producers do not have an agreed view on this topic.

Ban Below-cost Selling?

We noted that the U.K. Competition Commission (2007) declined to ban below-cost selling in supermarkets, albeit on the ground that it had no power to do so. However, the commission also observed that there would be considerable practical difficulties in enforcement. This would be no surprise to a cost accountant familiar with the many legitimate ways, in a major business, to allocate costs. There is certainly a long history of difficulty in the implementation of antitrust law as it is hard to demonstrate in practice whether an offer price is or is not below cost. This does not seem a fruitful road to follow.

Restrict Reduced-price Promotions?

Clearly, some price and price-related promotions of alcohol are irresponsible and lead to harmful drinking. The most common are discount bar offers to increase consumption, such as happy hours, two-for-one offers, or standard entrance charges for "as much as you can drink." On the other hand, price promotions designed, for example, to promote a new product, encourage consumers to stock up in advance of a celebratory event (such as a party or Christmas), or take advantage of a good price for a favorite brand seem to fall into a different category in the sense that they are designed to achieve product substitution or affect timing of purchase rather than increase consumption overall. Such strategies may be regarded as legitimate marketing devices. So, a blanket ban on reduced-price offers would seem unjustified and a step too far. But, there is a strong case for encouraging codes of practice in the industry—including producers, retailers, and hospitality sectors—to regulate price promotions.

**CODE OF CONDUCT ON PRICING
PROMOTIONS IN SOUTH AFRICA**

The Industry Association for Responsible Alcohol Use (ARA) has promoted a *Code of Commercial Communication* in South Africa. The code reminds ARA members that "responsible, moderate consumption by those not at risk can be compatible with a balanced

and healthy lifestyle" but sets out rules to avoid "excessive or irresponsible consumption [leading to] negative personal, social or
health consequences" (ARA, 2004, p. 1). The code provides guidance on advertising, packaging, promotion, merchandising, and
sponsorship with detailed and regular monitoring of compliance,
an enforcement procedure with penalties, and a complaints procedure. As regards promotional events, use of price (price promotion) is allowed for on-premise promotion but only provided that
it is linked to the trial of a specific brand or product; promotions
that encourage increased consumption over a limited period (such
as two-for-one offers) are specifically prohibited.

Impose Minimum Prices?

The idea of a government-imposed minimum price regime is not
straightforward. From the point of view of economic theory, the over-
ruling of market pricing mechanisms would, over the longer term,
distort the market by encouraging overproduction and reducing efficiency. From a practical point of view, imposing a minimum retail
price and a minimum profit margin—these are the two main options
commonly advanced—poses significant problems of definition and
enforcement. A minimum price per unit of alcohol content (with different minima for on- and off-premise sales), as examined by Booth et
al. (2008), is simpler and potentially more practicable in concept, but
it is not clear that (as claimed) it would have most impact on problem
drinkers or dissuade them simply from allocating more of their budget to maintaining their level of consumption.

It is easier to think of a minimum price regime (or simply directly
regulated prices) working if alcohol sales were subject to state monopoly and control. This subject is dealt with in Chapter 6. However, in
practice, monopoly regimes are as much about controlling access and
availability as about price, and they still have to operate in a world of
ever-more-porous borders. Of course, state monopoly arrangements
do not deal any better than others with the key issue of harmful
drinking. However, if we focus more narrowly on chronic harmful

drinking, a minimum price option could be useful in particular and focused circumstances. One option being made legally available to local licensing authorities in Scotland is to ban special-price promotions. It will be interesting to see how the practicalities of this are worked through and what difference such arrangements can make. For other governments adopting this idea, it will be important to ensure that antitrust/competition legislation is adapted accordingly (uncertainty about this held up progress in Scotland for some time—the law has not been changed, but, presumably, some appropriate assurance has been given).

Another option is to impose a minimum retail price on particular categories of beverage alcohol that are thought problematic. For example, in Canada, this is done with beers over a prescribed alcohol strength. Sweden addresses the same issue through graduated tax levels on beer (and also increasing regulatory constraints on purchase), rising with alcohol content. The alcohol companies would have to think about their own views on a proposal of this kind but might well feel that, provided it is tailored to address specific problems in particular markets, it could be worth trying and might not necessarily be deleterious to the bottom line.

Suggestions

This analysis was undertaken at the request of the beverage alcohol producers in an attempt to identify how they can better help to address alcohol-related harm. The evidence seems reasonably clear that, while the seriousness of these problems is acknowledged, price is not necessarily a key factor in addressing them. Price, however, is clearly far from being irrelevant, and there are some options worth further thought, albeit that the initiative will largely be with other parties. First, while the industry will have differing views on the issue, there could be a case for governments being less cautious in indexing alcohol duties to inflation. Second, while minimum-price schemes applied nationally and to all alcohol beverages seem unrealistic and impractical (quite apart from whether they could be justified), there may be room for more focused price regulation—for example, in relation to problems identified in local areas or in relation to particular classes of beverages. Third, more widespread codes of conduct on price promotions in retail establishments would help. Finally, where local initiatives seem appropriate, legal frameworks (e.g., in relation to antitrust/competition law) should be adjusted to accommodate them.

References

Alavaikko, M., & Österberg, E. (2000). The influence of economic interests on alcohol control policy: A case study from Finland. *Addiction, 95*(Suppl. 4), S565–S579.

Babor, T., Caetano, R., Casswell, S., Edwards, G., Giesbrecht, N., Graham, K., et al. (2003). *Alcohol: No ordinary commodity.* Oxford, U.K.: Oxford University Press.

Booth, A., Brennan, A., Meier, P. S., O'Reilly, D. T., Purshouse, R., Stockwell, T., et al. (2008). *The independent review of the effects of alcohol pricing and promotion. Summary of evidence to accompany report on phase 1: Systematic reviews.* Sheffield, U.K.: University of Sheffield.

Brinner, R. E., Brinner, J. Y., & Zislin, J. (2007). *Global patterns in alcoholic beverage consumption: Understanding the roles of key drivers as guides for public policy.* Unpublished paper.

Chaloupka, F. J., & Wechsler, H. (1996). Binge drinking in college: The impact of price, availability, and alcohol control policies. *Contemporary Economic Policy, 14,* 112–124.

Gallet, C. A. (2007). The demand for alcohol: A meta-analysis of elasticities. *Australian Journal of Agricultural and Resource Economics, 51,* 121–135.

Gruenewald, P. J., Ponicki, W. R., Holder, H. D., & Romelsjö, A. (2006). Alcohol prices, beverage quality and the demand for alcohol: Quality substitutions and price elasticities. *Alcoholism: Clinical and Experimental Research, 30,* 96–105.

Harwood, E. M., Erickson, D. J., Fabian, L. E., Jones-Webb, R., Slater, S., & Chaloupka, F. J. (2003). Effects of communities, neighborhoods and stores on retail pricing and promotion of beer. *Journal of Studies on Alcohol, 64,* 720–726.

Heeb, J. L., Gmel, G., Zurbrugg, C., Kuo, M., & Rehm, J. (2003). Changes in alcohol consumption following a reduction in the price of spirits: A natural experiment in Switzerland. *Addiction, 98,* 1433–1446.

Industry Association for Responsible Alcohol Use (ARA). (2004). *ARA code of commercial communication.* Retrieved March 8, 2009, from http://ara.co.za/self-regulation/

Koski, A., Sirén, R., Vuori, E., & Poikolainen, K. (2007). Alcohol tax cuts and increases in alcohol-positive sudden deaths—a time-series intervention analysis. *Addiction, 102,* 362–368.

Kuo, M., Heeb, J. L., Gmel, G., & Rehm, J. (2003). Does price matter? The effect of decreased price on spirits consumption in Switzerland. *Alcoholism: Clinical and Experimental Research, 27,* 720–725.

Mäkelä, P., Bloomfield, K., Gustafsson, N.-K., Huhtanen, P., & Room, R. (2008). Changes in volume of drinking after changes in alcohol taxes and travellers' allowances: Results from a panel study. *Addiction, 103,* 181–191.

Mäkelä, P., & Österberg, E. (2009). Weakening of one more alcohol control pillar: A review of the effects of the alcohol tax cuts in Finland in 2004. *Addiction, 104,* 554–563.

Malmquist, S. (1948). *A statistical analysis of the demand for liquor in Sweden.* Uppsala, Sweden: Uppsala University.

Manning, W., Blumberg, L., & Moulton, M. (1995). The demand for alcohol: The differential response to price. *Journal of Health Economics, 14,* 123–148.

Martinic, M., & Measham, F. (Eds.). (2008). *Swimming with crocodiles: The culture of extreme drinking.* New York: Routledge.

Measham, F. (2006). The new policy mix: Alcohol, harm minimisation and determined drunkenness in contemporary society. *International Journal of Drug Policy, 17,* 258–268.

Niskanen, W. A. (1960). *Taxation and the demand for alcoholic beverages.* Santa Monica, CA: Rand.

Partanen, J. (1993). Failure in alcohol policy: Lessons from Russia, Kenya, Truk and history. *Addiction, 88*(Suppl. 1), S129–S134.

Prest, A. R. (1949). Some experiments in demand analysis. *Review of Economics and Statistics, 21,* 33–49.

Simon, J. (1966). The price elasticity of liquor in the U.S. and a simple method of determination. *Econometrics, 34,* 193–205.

Stimson, G., Grant, M., Choquet, M., & Garrison, P. (2007). *Drinking in context: Patterns, interventions, and partnerships.* New York: Routledge.

Stone, R. (1951). *The role of measurement in economics.* Cambridge, U.K.: Cambridge University Press.

Treno, A. J., Gruenewald, P. J., Wood, D. S., & Ponicki, W. R. (2006). The price of alcohol: A consideration of contextual factors. *Alcoholism: Clinical and Experimental Research, 30,* 1734–1742.

Trolldal, B., & Ponicki, W. (2005). Alcohol price elasticities in control and license states in the U.S., 1982–99. *Addiction, 100,* 1158–1165.

U.K. Competition Commission. (2007). *Groceries market investigation.* Retrieved March 8, 2009, from http://www.competition-commission.org.uk/inquiries/ref2006/grocery/provisional_findings.htm

Wagenaar, A. C., Salois, M. J., & Komro, K. A. (2009). Effects of beverage alcohol price and tax levels on drinking: A meta-analysis of 1003 estimates from 112 studies. *Addiction, 104,* 179–190.

Wells, S., Graham, K., & Purcell, J. (2009). Policy implications of the widespread practice of "pre-drinking" or "pre-gaming" before going to public drinking establishments—are current prevention strategies backfiring? *Addiction, 104,* 4–9.

World Health Organization (WHO). (2004). *Global status report: Alcohol policy.*
    Geneva, Switzerland: Author.
Zeigler, D. (2009). The alcohol industry and trade agreements: A preliminary
    assessment. *Addiction, 104*(Suppl. 1), 13–26.

6

SELLING AND SERVING BEVERAGE ALCOHOL

GRAEME WILLERSDORF

Introduction

The young Chinese man consuming multiple drinks at a dinner with his boss and the young Brazilian woman drinking with her friends at a *balada*[1] might on some level be engaging in the same behavior. Yet, while both are consuming alcohol, the meaning of this behavior differs widely within each context. The Chinese man drinks every glass his boss pours to demonstrate respect for superiors. The Brazilian woman drinks to signal her inclusion in a specific subculture, involving particular types of music and dance. It is unlikely that either of these two people would see their drinking context as similar, apart from the fact that alcohol is consumed on both occasions.[2]

These two examples illustrate why the role of alcohol in society cannot be understood without also understanding the environment that surrounds drinkers. The sale and service of alcohol are the final stages in the process of alcohol production and distribution, providing an interface among consumers, producers, and retailers. These stages are the focus of many policies and interventions that seek to reduce harmful drinking and related problems.

A large portion of alcohol consumption occurs within the retail sector, which includes both on-premise establishments (such as pubs, bars,

---

[1] Brazilian slang used to denote any kind of party, for instance, a rave, a bar outing, or any other collective amusement.

[2] These examples are based on focus groups described in the book *Swimming with Crocodiles: The Culture of Extreme Drinking* (Martinic & Measham, 2008, pp. 79–159).

and restaurants, where alcohol is sold to be consumed on site) and off-premise venues (such as alcohol shops, supermarkets, kiosks, and state-owned outlets, where alcohol is sold to be consumed elsewhere). The relationship between the drinkers and the physical and social environments that surround them shapes the patterns of drinking and their potential outcomes. Significant variations exist across societies and groups in the cultural norms and practices associated with drinking. They need to be considered both when assessing the overall impact that alcohol consumption may have on a community and when evaluating interventions to minimize harm. Thus, a strategy that works within a young male cohort in urban Australia is unlikely to be effective if implemented in a remote Bolivian village during the fiesta season.

It is also important to remember that, like all public policies, strategies to change prevailing alcohol sale and service patterns can have both intended and unintended consequences. Evaluations of strategies that focus solely on the intended consequences may miss important aspects of their impact on the community. A comprehensive assessment of initiatives must balance their positive and negative outcomes, whether intended or unintended. For example, stringent enforcement of rules in the retail environment may have a negative overall impact if it simply displaces consumption to high-risk unregulated settings, as discussed in this chapter (e.g., Galloway, Forsyth, & Shewan, 2007). Clearly, selling and serving alcohol do not occur in isolation, and the success or failure of interventions often relies on cooperation and support from other sectors, such as government, law enforcement, and the broader community.

Broad Social Influences on Drinking

Before discussing programs and policies implemented at the retail level, it is worth exploring other influences that may have an impact on the way consumers drink, always the result of a complex interaction between individual and environmental factors. This requires much more than a simple analysis of consumption data. Although it may seem obvious that communities with high levels of alcohol consumption also experience high rates of alcohol-related harm, the situation is more complex in practice (see discussion in Stimson, Grant, Choquet, & Garrison, 2007). This is because aggregate alcohol consumption data across an entire population tell us little about the individual and environmental factors that influence the impact of that consumption on drinkers and community.

A common way of describing drinking behavior in a country is per capita consumption. This figure reports the total amount of alcohol intake in the population, as recorded by official statistics, divided by the number of adults of legal drinking age in a given country. While this figure is useful in certain contexts, it does not reveal anything about individual drinkers, prevalent drinking occasions, and outcomes. Two communities may have the same per capita figure but differ in almost every other aspect, including the common drinking patterns and associated risks for harm. The case study next reviews some of the common influences on drinking as they relate to populations, drinking contexts, and behaviors around alcohol.

POPULATIONS, DRINKING CONTEXTS, AND BEHAVIORS

POPULATIONS

A range of factors should be taken into account when looking at the drinking patterns within a population, including age, gender, socioeconomic status, education, and individual health and genetic issues.

One of the most important of these factors is gender. In addition to the physiological differences between men and women in alcohol metabolism and effects, most societies have marked cultural proscriptions on male and female drinking. Nevertheless, as gender roles evolve, drinking patterns become realigned in a number of countries. For example, in India, alcohol has traditionally been associated with male culture and male activities. However, in recent years, as women have entered the workforce in increasing numbers and adopted many aspects of male culture, the rate of alcohol consumption—and harmful drinking—among Indian women has increased (Benegal, Nayak, Murthy, Chandra, & Gururaj, 2005).

Age is another important factor. Most people change their drinking patterns during the course of their lives. Young people are a particular target group for many harm reduction efforts because—although they do not consume more alcohol than other age groups in terms of volume—their drinking patterns are more likely to involve risk-taking and excess. Other population groups, including older adults and pregnant women, also face specific risks of alcohol-related problems and are often targeted through harm reduction programs (for discussion, see International Center for Alcohol Policies [ICAP], 2005–ongoing; see also Chapter 7).

DRINKING CONTEXTS

The context and the culture within which alcohol is consumed are equally important to consider when assessing the role of drinking within a society. Simpura (2001), among others, divided drinking cultures into three broad categories: wine cultures (e.g., the Mediterranean countries); beer cultures (found throughout Europe, Africa, and Latin America); and spirits cultures (including many eastern European, Scandinavian, and Asian countries). However, there has been considerable overlap across categories in recent years, spurred by globalization. Within individual countries, there is also a range of different cultural patterns of alcohol consumption. For example, in many multicultural countries (including Australia, the United Kingdom [U.K.], and the United States [U.S.]), Caucasians typically drink more than black and Asian groups.

The physical and social contexts around drinkers certainly play a role in defining the meanings, goals, and outcomes of drinking occasions. While alcohol can be consumed in almost any environment, typical settings include private homes; bars, hotels, restaurants, and other retail establishments; sporting and other public events; and group or community celebrations. In some countries, drinking is associated with specific cultural practices—for example, in Sweden and Finland, it is common for men to share a drink with friends in communal baths and saunas (Heath, 2000). In other countries, there may be taboos around drinking in specific locations; thus, the Navajo of North America traditionally do not consume alcohol near living quarters (Heath, 2000).

The importance of context for drinking behavior has been highlighted by recent research into the practice of "predrinking," also referred to as "pregaming" and "preloading," planned, often heavy drinking prior to going out to a public drinking venue, reported to be increasingly common among young people (Wells, Graham, & Purcell, 2009). Motivations for this behavior include wanting to avoid paying a high price for drinks at on-premise venues and looking to establish a sense of camaraderie before the night out, particularly among groups of young men. There is some evidence that this practice is associated with a high risk of alcohol-related harm. According to Wells and colleagues (2009), strategies designed to reduce drinking in licensed premises may have the unintended consequence of encouraging predrinking in unregulated private settings. They concluded that, "Effective policy and prevention for drinking in licensed premises requires a comprehensive approach that takes into account the entire drinking occasion (not just drinking that occurs in the licensed environment), as well as the 'determined drunkenness' goal of some young people" (Wells et al., 2009, p. 4).

BEHAVIORS

Like any social and cultural practice, alcohol consumption accompanies a range of other behaviors and activities. These differ from society to society and from context to context but form an important part of the overall picture of alcohol consumption in each setting. One of the most important associations is between drinking and leisure. In many societies, consuming alcohol is linked to social and pleasurable activities. Drinking is often used to mark the boundary between "work and play," as demonstrated by the tradition of "Friday night drinks" in many countries, used to signal the end of the working week. Another important association is between celebrations and drinking. From marking individual milestones, such as birthdays, graduations, and marriages, to celebrating important community events, such as festivals, historical dates, and public successes, alcohol has a place in many different celebratory settings.

Drinking may also be associated with risk-taking behaviors, such as unsafe sex, driving, and fighting. Understanding the complex pattern of risk-taking that may surround alcohol consumption is important when attempting to reduce the overall problems. The role of different stakeholders needs to be seen within the broader context of the complex individual, social, and environmental factors that contribute to risky behaviors, including harmful drinking.

At least four key issues should be considered as we review policies and programs in the retail environment:

1. Significant cultural variations exist in the place of alcohol in society and predominant drinking practices.
2. Like all public policies, regulations in the retail environment can have both intended and unintended outcomes; a comprehensive assessment of a given measure must consider both.
3. Most retailer-focused policies to reduce harm target all consumers, including the responsibly drinking majority.
4. Alcohol distribution does not occur in a vacuum; the success or failure of interventions at this level often relies on the broader legal framework and support from all stakeholders, including industry members, governments, law enforcement, and the community.

Licensed drinking environments are just one channel for accessing drinkers and having an impact on their choices (see also Chapters 7 and 8). Retail practices can help reduce the incidence of alcohol-related harm in the community, but as discussed, their contribution cannot be seen in isolation from other factors. A range of strategies involving retailers is commonly introduced to address alcohol-related harms at the point of purchase, including

- licensing restrictions on when, where, how, and what alcohol can be sold (e.g., outlet density in a community and rules on point-of-sale promotions)
- broad health promotion and consumer education activities as well as efforts to enforce local laws (e.g., displaying alcohol and health information in retail outlets and programs to prevent alcohol sale to minors)
- voluntary retailer efforts to promote responsible sale and service of alcohol through codes of practice, physical modifications to drinking environments, and education and training of sellers, servers, and other staff (e.g., server training programs)

There is good evidence to support the involvement of the retail sector in strategies to reduce alcohol-related harm (Stimson et al., 2007, pp. 125–137). Most countries incorporate a focus on alcohol distribution practices within their broad policy approach. However, a range of factors can influence the outcome of these efforts, including the prevailing political and social climate (Craplet, 2007), support from other stakeholders, and consistency in implementation and enforcement. This makes it difficult to generalize about the effectiveness of any individual strategy.

Licensing Restrictions

Licensing restrictions for retail outlets are a common way for governments to limit the availability and accessibility of alcohol. In a World Health Organization (WHO) (2004b) survey, only 11% of 109 countries reviewed had no licensing restrictions. These can cover a number of different aspects of the retail environment, including *when* alcohol can be sold (the days and times), *where* it can be sold (the number of venues able to sell alcohol in a particular area), *how* it can be sold (the physical environment and hospitality practices), and *what* alcohol can be sold (beer, wine, spirits, or premixed drinks). Typical conditions required to obtain an alcohol retail license in most jurisdictions include the prospective proprietor's age and lack of criminal record, payment of a fee, and lack of objections from local community or law enforcement (see Stimson et al., 2007, pp. 125–137). The aims of specific licensing restrictions vary; however, most such measures intend to reduce antisocial behavior, violence, and crime (e.g., Her Majesty's Stationery Office, 2005). In general, they try to achieve this through limiting the overall volume of alcohol consumed, although some licensing restrictions target specific groups of problem drinkers.

Of course, not all alcohol sales occur in licensed premises. In fact, in many countries a significant portion of them takes place in the unregulated informal sector (see Chapter 3; Haworth & Simpson, 2004). Webb and Block (2008) provided an example of such consumption in Mexico. Their study focused on three types of illicit alcohol sales: counterfeit products that simulate genuine beverages; genuine products that evade taxation through smuggling, unregistered import, or under-reporting of production by registered local producers; and adulterated products that evade quality standards and may at times be harmful to health. The authors concluded that the "illicit alcohol market is prevalent in Mexico, and presents a serious public policy challenge" (p. 1) but were unable to quantify this statement because of the methodological weaknesses in existing studies (these generally place the share of illicit alcohol at 30 to 40% of all alcohol intake). In South Africa, around 70% of total alcohol sales occur in unlicensed premises, principally *shebeens*, small bars that serve alcohol and food, often located in people's homes. An estimated 200,000 shebeens exist throughout the country, compared to 50,000 licensed premises. Many other countries have a high level of unrecorded drinking—for instance, Hungary (22.7%), Poland (27.1%), and Croatia (26.9%) (WHO, 2004a; see Chapter 3).

In this context, licensing policies have an effect on both licensed and nonlicensed venues. There is evidence that, in some cases, licensing restrictions can boost the informal sector, with resultant increases in alcohol-related health and social harm. For example, if licensing conditions are so stringent that legal retailers are unable to meet consumer demand, this demand may shift to the black market. Thus, restrictive alcohol policies implemented in Poland and the Soviet Union in the 1980s resulted in an increase in unrecorded alcohol production and consumption (Moskalewicz & Simpura, 2000; for a review, see Razvodovsky, 2008). In western Europe, the level of unrecorded drinking is relatively high in countries with strict alcohol policies and high taxation (Leifman, 2002). In addition, where neighboring jurisdictions impose different licensing and other restrictions, demand—and problems—may shift across borders (Nordlund & Österberg, 2002), with additional risks of unrecorded alcohol consumption, harmful drinking, and alcohol-impaired driving (e.g., Clapp, Voas, & Lange, 2001).

The evidence in support of the intended outcomes of licensing restrictions is mixed. Some studies have found that extending opening hours and days of alcohol establishments has resulted in an increase in drink-related problems (Chikritzhs & Stockwell, 2006), while others report little or no increase in harm (Norström & Skog, 2005; U.K. Department for Culture, Media and Sport, 2008). Research from several countries has linked the density of retail outlets with some alcohol-related social problems (Reid, Hughey, & Peterson, 2003; Stevenson, Lind, & Weatherburn, 1999; Wechsler, Lee, Hall, Wagenaar, & Lee, 2002; Zhu, Gorman, & Horel, 2004), but this relationship depends on location, context, and drinking culture. The literature on the impact of restrictions on the type of alcohol being sold at venues is limited, although there is some evidence that selling alcohol in open plastic containers (as opposed to closed cans or bottles) at large public events reduces both overall consumption and alcohol-related injuries (Cusens & Shepherd, 2005). Finally, the box next discusses restrictions on point-of-sale advertising imposed in some jurisdictions. While evidence is, again, mixed, such measures may have a positive impact on behavior, particularly among high-risk groups like young people and problem drinkers; they can also help raise awareness. This is an example of an area where the retailers and producers can contribute beyond simple compliance with licensing requirements.

RESTRICTIONS ON POINT-OF-SALE ADVERTISING

Advertising occurring in conjunction with the purchase of alcohol is generally called "point-of-sale" or "point-of-purchase" advertising. A visible marketing strategy, this can include brand information and discount offers. In most jurisdictions, point-of-sale advertising is less stringently regulated than other forms of alcohol marketing because it communicates with consumers who are already in the process of making a decision to drink (Howard, Flora, Schleicher, & Gonzalez, 2004).

There is no clear evidence linking point-of-sale advertising with increased alcohol consumption, although some studies indicated that this may be the case (Jones & Lynch, 2007). In particular, there is some evidence to suggest that point-of-sale advertising affects the overall consumption pattern of groups at specific risk of alcohol-related harm, such as young people (Hurtz, Henriksen, Wang, Feighery, & Fortmann, 2007) and problem drinkers (Booth et al., 2008). However, other evidence suggests that alcohol advertising generally has little overall impact on level or pattern of drinking, although it may affect the choice of brands consumed (for discussion, see Sinclair, 2009;[1] see also Chapter 4). One review of a number of studies of alcohol advertising bans concluded the following:

> In summary, seven studies have examined the effects of state-level advertising bans on alcohol consumption and abuse, including billboard bans and bans of other visible displays. . . . In a few instances, a significant effect was found, but these results are small in magnitude or statistically fragile. . . . The policy issue is whether or not there is a robust negative relationship between bans and drinking, but the evidence clearly speaks against this outcome. None of these studies produced results that support the null hypothesis that advertising bans will materially reduce alcohol consumption or alcohol abuse. (Nelson, 2001)

Research about the influences on young people generally reports that factors other than advertising—parents and peers, in particular—take the lead in shaping adolescent alcohol debut and drinking behavior. When examining this issue in the United

---

[1] A referenced version of this paper is available at http://www.icap.org/Portals/0/download/all_pdfs/WHO/Marketing%20-%20REFERENCED.pdf

Kingdom, research commissioned by the Alcohol Education and Research Council (2008) concluded the following:

> Exposure to alcohol advertising can raise familiarity with brands among young people, but whether it has a direct link to the onset of drinking is a more debatable point. Any effects that do occur as a result of exposure to advertising might be indirect rather than direct.... Parental and peer group influences emerged more often than did advertising as significant predictors of young people's reported overall frequency or amount of alcohol consumption. Advertising did not feature at all as a predictor of frequency of drinking. Exposure to cinema advertising was a negative predictor of frequency of getting drunk. This finding implied that regular cinema-goers are less likely to get drunk even though they experience higher levels of exposure to cinema-based alcohol advertising. (pp. 2, 3)

Point of sale can serve as a useful channel for delivering health promotion messages, particularly for at-risk individuals. Thus, U.S. studies have found that requiring retailers to display point-of-sale messages about fetal alcohol syndrome helped raise awareness of this condition among pregnant women, although this may not necessarily translate into a reduction in alcohol consumption (Nelson, 2001). Alcohol producers can support such activities by supplying appropriate point-of-sale materials to retailers and working with government and the local community on backing them with education and interventions for at-risk groups.

It should be noted that licensing systems in some countries have resulted in discriminatory practices toward populations seen as at risk for alcohol-related harm, particularly when laws led to a virtual monopoly by licensees in specific areas (on remote areas in Australia, see Gray et al., 1995). Addressing this issue requires greater community involvement in the regulation and administration of licenses and an increased focus on skills training and culturally appropriate harm reduction practices.

To function successfully, any licensing arrangement must rely on the support of the local population, law enforcement, and retailers. State-run monopolies on alcohol distribution and retail have been vibrant in a number of jurisdictions—for example, in most provinces of Canada, some states and counties in the United States, and some European countries—where their stated purpose appears to be broadly supported by the public. The statement from the Utah Department of Alcoholic Beverage Control (2009) in the United States provides some of the reasons behind such arrangements:

> The purpose of control is to make liquor available to those adults who choose to drink responsibly—but not to promote the sale of liquor. By keeping liquor out of the private marketplace, no economic incentives are created to maximize sales, open more liquor stores or sell to under-age persons. Instead, all policy incentives to promote moderation and to enforce existing liquor laws is [sic] enhanced. (para. 3)

While this is appropriate for some communities, many WHO member states have found such government control unappealing. As noted, where a neighboring jurisdiction has cheaper or more widely available alcohol, a state-owned monopoly that restricts availability may shift demand across the border. It is also important to remember that restrictions on availability and price limit choice and utility for all consumers, not just those with alcohol-related problems. Overall, promising licensing strategies are those that are sensitive to the cultural context around alcohol consumption.

Implementation of minimum legal drinking age legislation in the retail environment has effectively brought together a control-based approach, founded in legislation and enforceable through the law, with targeted interventions aimed at young people in particular. When supported by retailer efforts, this approach has shown promise in reducing the incidence of harm among young people resulting from excessive and risky drinking patterns (Wagenaar & Toomey, 2002).

Preventing Underage Drinking at the Retail Level

The implementation of minimum drinking age sets a formal threshold at which the consumption of alcohol is deemed appropriate in a particular society and provides a legally enforceable tool in preventing alcohol access by those under a certain age. The primary rationale behind imposing a minimum age limit is that young people may be neither physically nor emotionally ready to consume alcohol and thus do not yet possess the necessary internal controls needed to minimize harm to themselves and others (ICAP, 2004). Such limits are therefore intended to prevent access and exposure to alcohol and to delay the age at which young people begin to drink.

Drinking age laws have two distinct components: the threshold at which alcohol can be consumed and the threshold at which it can be purchased on- and off-premise. Legislation in some countries addresses both of these components, while in others the focus is solely on either minimum purchase age or consumption. Where such provisions exist, the minimum age to buy alcohol off-premise may be lower than for obtaining drinks on-premise. In addition, exemptions may apply where parents are present or when drinking occurs within the home (WHO, 2004b), although stringent hosting laws, as in many states of the United States, can criminalize any provision of alcohol to minors, including by parents serving alcohol at home. Legal age limits may also be different in some jurisdictions, depending on alcohol content or the type of beverage. For example, a higher age limit may be set for spirits than for beer or wine (Österberg & Karlsson, 2003; see also ICAP, 2009).

Given the strong cultural influences around drinking, there is no international consensus on the age at which alcohol consumption becomes appropriate, and the legal age at which individuals may consume or purchase alcohol beverage products varies around the world. In some, drinking age may correspond to the age of legal majority; in others, the legislated age is different. As a result, where they exist, legal age limits range from 16 to 21 years and above (ICAP, 2009; WHO, 2004b). The most commonly applied drinking age, however, is 18 years.

Despite drinking age laws, in some cultures young people are permitted (or even encouraged) to consume a small quantity of alcohol with family members at times of cultural or religious rituals and family events. The degree to which young people are exposed to alcohol depends on cultural views on the substance and its role within a given society (e.g., Araoz, 2004; Heath, 2000). These differences in societal values are clearly reflected in the rules imposed to govern legal access to alcohol.

With increasing globalization and demands to harmonize policy approaches, consideration in some regions may be given to a uniform drinking age across geographical boundaries. For example, there has been discussion of harmonizing alcohol policies within the European Union (Österberg & Karlsson, 2003). The rationale for a standardized approach is in part provided by the problems that can arise when drinking ages are different in neighboring jurisdictions, as discussed. Young people below the drinking age under one set of laws may have easy access to alcohol in a nearby jurisdiction with lower age limits, leading to cross-border movement and increase in harm (e.g., Baker & Ramirez, 2000; Clapp et al., 2001; Shelley, 2001).

In addition, studies indicated that the majority of underage drinkers obtain alcohol from so-called social sources—peers, families, and other adults of legal drinking age (Harrison, Fulkerson, & Park, 2000; King, Taylor, & Carroll, 2005; Williams & Mulhall, 2007). Thus, according to a 2008 survey by the U.S. Substance Abuse and Mental Health Services Administration (SAMHSA, 2008), 90% of underage drinkers were either given alcohol for free or had someone else purchase it for them; a quarter of underage drinkers reported getting alcohol from an adult who was not related to them; 1 in 12 said they got it from an adult family member other than a parent or a guardian; and 1 in 16 said they got it from a parent. Because beverages are easily accessible through social sources, prevention policies directed only at retail outlets may not have the desired effect of reducing underage drinking. Greater attention to reducing underage access to all substances from social sources is needed (Harrison et al., 2000).

Although they are not the main source, retail venues do play a significant role in supplying alcohol to young people and can therefore be an effective channel for prevention. Drinking age laws are generally concerned with public activities and, as such, present an opportunity for enforcement. Although evidence exists that visible and consistent enforcement of drinking age laws is the key to the success of legislation (Houghton & Roche, 2001; Huckle, Greenway, Broughton, & Conway, 2007; Wagenaar et al., 2000; Wagenaar, Toomey, & Erickson, 2005), it has been lacking or insufficient in many countries.

There are different approaches to enforcing drinking age laws. The police, of course, are central to ensuring compliance with legislation and can, for example, be involved in monitoring licensed premises, sometimes undercover (e.g., Dedel Johnson, 2004; Levy, Stewart, & Wilbur, 1999; National Alcohol Beverage Control Association, 1997). Enforcement may also include fines or revocation of serving licenses for establishments and sellers in breach of existing laws, as well as fines, community service, or referrals to mandatory treatment and education programs for underage drinkers (Dedel Johnson, 2004; Hafemeister & Jackson, 2004). In the United States, some states delay, revoke, or suspend driver's licenses as a penalty for underage drinking even if offenders were not caught operating a motor vehicle (Hafemeister & Jackson, 2004; Ulmer, Shabanova, & Preusser, 2001).

Personnel in serving establishments need to be trained to identify minors and effectively enforce minimum age limits. Strategies that rely solely on the ability of servers to estimate the age of the purchaser are less successful than those emphasizing the need to actually check the age of all customers who could potentially be underage. Some jurisdictions mandate proof-of-age identification that must be presented for service or purchase, while in others, like the United Kingdom, this can be done voluntarily by the industry—for example, the Portman Group in the United Kingdom has developed and circulated proof-of-age cards that retailers can use to confirm age of customers (see also Chapter 7).

Much time, effort, and resources have been allocated by the industry to train both on- and off-premise staff to enforce laws; in-store awareness campaigns emphasizing the fact that proof-of-age documents will be requested have been widely funded by many major alcohol producers.

RESPECT 21 RESPONSIBLE RETAILING PROGRAM, USA

In partnership with Brandeis University and the Responsible Retailing Forum (RRF), MillerCoors conducted the Respect 21™ Responsible Retailing program in the New York City area to help the National Supermarket Association's (NSA's) beverage

alcohol licensees and their staff improve their ID-checking procedures and refusal to sell alcohol to underage customers. Forty-
two participating NSA grocery stores were provided with tools
and assistance through point-of-sale materials and the H.E.L.P.
Guide for Retailers™, developed in cooperation with Brandeis
University and derived from government-recognized best practices on responsible retailing.

An important element of the Respect 21 program is reports
on the actual performance of cashiers when young, legal-age
"mystery shoppers" ask to purchase alcohol. "Green Cards" were
issued when clerks correctly asked for IDs, and "Red Cards"
were given when clerks failed to ask for an ID or offered to sell
without an ID. Follow-up reports were sent by mail to store
managers. During the program's run in the area, age verification increased from 67% correct ID checking in the first quarter
of 2008 to 70% in the second quarter. And, in July 2008, the
final month of the Respect 21 program, correct age verification
rose to 89%.

As an additional evaluation tool, RRF selected 10 grocery
stores and conducted five unreported inspections by different
mystery shoppers at each location before Respect 21 began.
Following Respect 21, those same stores were visited five times
by different mystery shoppers. At baseline, the pass rate was
48%; at posttest, the rate was 60%—an improvement of 25% or
12 percentage points.

Simply controlling access to beverage alcohol, however, is not sufficient for prevention. A number of interventions have been carried
out by law enforcement, retailers and producers of beverage alcohol,
educators, and local community actors to target the social influences
on young people's drinking beyond the immediate retail environment,
including parents and peers, and employ a range of new channels to
disseminate messages.

EXAMPLES OF INITIATIVES AGAINST UNDERAGE DRINKING

- We Don't Serve Teens is a national campaign in the United States to reduce underage drinking. An associated website, www.DontServeTeens.gov, was prepared and is being maintained by the U.S. Federal Trade Commission (FTC) in English and Spanish. In addition to the Century Council, a social aspects organization sponsored by distillers, and the FTC, other organizations involved in the campaign are the U.S. Department of the Treasury Alcohol and Tobacco Tax and Trade Bureau, the National Alcohol Beverage Control Association, the National Consumers League, Students Against Destructive Decisions, the Responsible Retailing Forum, the National Liquor Law Enforcement Association, the National Association of State Alcohol and Drug Abuse Directors, and the American Beverage Licensees. In September 2007, one of the largest-ever public service campaigns was developed to provide adults with tools and education about restricting underage access to alcohol through We Don't Serve Teens. This partnership accomplished 1.1 billion media impressions, with a market value of USD 9 million through advertising in newspapers, magazines, billboards, sports stadiums, public transportation, television, and other venues. The campaign has received national recognition and governmental awards.
- The Brewers Association of Japan (BAJ) has been conducting the project Stop! Underage Drinking since 2005. The project is led by BAJ and its five member companies: Asahi, Kirin, Orion, Sapporo, and Suntory. Organizations, individuals, stores, and supermarkets that agree with the project's objectives are welcome to

participate by using the STOP! Underage Drinking logo and various supporting materials, such as badges and point-of-purchase materials, and displaying them in the store. To enhance the project's effectiveness, this exercise has been carefully synchronized with supporting advertising programs. BAJ sponsors a series of advertisements against underage drinking in various papers and on transport; these advertisements are aimed at adults and minors. Moreover, all television commercials and advertising for alcohol beverages are required to bear the STOP! Underage Drinking symbol. To check the performance of the campaign, BAJ conducts consumer surveys twice a year. Public awareness about the project has increased steadily. According to BAJ's research conducted in April 2008, 87% of underage persons (the drinking age is 19 in Japan) were familiar with the STOP! Underage Drinking symbol, compared to 49% in 2005, and 88% of those underage acknowledged that underage drinking is wrong and illegal, compared to 76% in 2005. In addition, 88% of surveyed adults (N = 600) reported a feeling of guilt about allowing underage drinking, compared to 79% in 2005.

- Using technology and focusing on parents, Anheuser-Busch launched Positive Parenting Connection on MySpace, a popular social networking website. This online resource offers parents advice from authorities on how to help prevent underage drinking. It includes materials, tips, and links to expert-designed resources to help parents use their positive influence to communicate with children about making smart and responsible choices.
- The Drinkaware Trust in the United Kingdom developed www.truthaboutbooze.com, a website to reduce underage drinking, following surveys with young people under the U.K. drinking age of 18 years. The research showed that under-18s believe the antidrink message is

being diluted by the official approach and patronizing slogans. What they want is real information and facts on the effects of drinking, but without being patronized. The website's approach draws heavily on the social networking and blog phenomena associated with such sites as Bebo, Facebook, MySpace, and YouTube.

Retailer Responsibility

Apart from compliance with laws, internal codes of practice and other self-regulatory mechanisms can help engage retailers and other stakeholders in harm reduction activities. However, to be effective, they need to be backed by ongoing monitoring and incentives for compliance (Jones & Lynch, 2007). Partnerships between producers and retailers have been developed in a number of countries to address specific aspects of alcohol sale and service (e.g., Portman Group, 2008). Some partnerships also involve governments, local community, and other stakeholders—as Pubwatch, a voluntary organization developing best practice in the retail environment, does in the United Kingdom (www.pubwatch.co.uk). In addition, community "accords," formal or informal agreements involving a range of local stakeholders (usually, community organizations, the police, and retailers) have been implemented in a number of areas to complement responsible service of alcohol and enforcement of laws (for an overview, see Australian Department of Gaming and Racing, 2004; see also Homel, Carvolth, Mauritz, McIlwain, & Teague, 2004; Stimson et al., 2007).

It is difficult to generalize about the impact of such partnerships as the research on this issue is mixed (Baggott, 2006). Those strategies that are well supported, solidly researched, and backed by complementary activities in other areas (such as consumer education and law enforcement) are generally more successful than those occurring in isolation without a supportive policy context. Building on successes of existing joint initiatives is important so that future efforts can be focused on the strategies most likely to succeed. The key initiative in this area is server training. Such measures aim to directly influence consumer behavior around alcohol at the point of purchase.

Server Training

A range of programs exists to train staff in retail establishments in the responsible service of alcohol (for an example of one such program, Training for Intervention Procedures [TIPS], see Chapter 8). Many programs aim to educate and train sellers and staff at alcohol-serving establishments about standard drink sizes, proper identification checking, recognition of inebriation, not overserving, and dealing (in non-confrontational ways) with individuals who have consumed too much alcohol. In addition to sellers and servers, security personnel are often trained to recognize potential conflicts before they occur and to deal with problems constructively rather than aggressively. The main emphasis of these efforts is to avoid serving alcohol to minors and intoxicated patrons, thereby reducing the incidence of alcohol-related problems, specifically violence, antisocial behavior, and alcohol-impaired driving (ICAP, 2005–ongoing; for an example, see Buka & Birdthistle, 1999). These programs can also reduce liability for the retailers.

In addition to training staff, retailers can act to minimize the incidence of alcohol-related problems in or around their venues by affecting certain physical characteristics of the drinking environment. Such initiatives attempt to reduce those cues in the environment that may lead to disruptive behaviors and aim to discourage intoxication, which exacerbates reactions to the cues when they are present (Deehan, 1999; Leonard et al., 2008; Plant, Single, & Stockwell, 1997). The efforts include having clean, attractive, and well-maintained premises and restrooms; providing live entertainment; and creating a physical space that allows easy access to the bar or provides sitting areas without causing crowding (Arnold & Laidler, 1994; Deehan, 1999; Portman Group, 2000). Certain serving practices, such as using safety glass, providing affordable or free non-alcohol options, and offering food may further reduce the incidence of harmful drinking. In addition, promotional materials (such as beer mats on tables or posters in bathrooms) can be used to impart advice about safety, moderate drinking, or testing for drugs that may have been added to drinks.

Several issues need to be resolved to predict the effectiveness of server training and initiatives that support it. These include

- comparative evaluations of server training programs to assess which are the most effective (Graham, 2000)
- research into how often programs need to be delivered for maximum impact (Saltz, 1989)
- research into the optimum level and type of law enforcement to support server initiatives (Stockwell, 2001)

As with other harm reduction strategies, it is also important to assess whether server training programs result in alcohol consumption shifting from retail to other settings, such as secluded street corners and public places that may be less safe. This is particularly important for high-risk groups, such as young people.

There are a number of additional actions that governments and community organizations could undertake to strengthen the role of server training programs, for example:

- making it a licensing requirement that all staff involved in the serving of alcohol at venues undertake server training on a regular basis
- developing national standards for server training programs (Toomey et al., 1998) and accrediting individual programs
- directing law enforcement agencies to monitor breaches of legislation governing the serving of alcohol and to impose sanctions
- supporting retailers to provide training for their staff (which can be costly because of high staff turnover)

Retailers could also play a greater role through developing self-regulatory codes of practice covering server training programs, increasing manager training (Gehan, Toomey, Jones-Webb, Rothstein, & Wagenaar, 1999), and working more closely with the police and local transportation authorities to ensure the appropriate enforcement of regulations.

Conclusion

Alcohol sale and service practices help influence the overall impact of alcohol consumption in the community. The retail sector plays an important role in developing and implementing alcohol distribution strategies, along with other stakeholders such as producers, governments, and the community. There is a wide range of evidence to support the effectiveness of specific policies in reducing alcohol-related harms. However, the effectiveness of these policies and strategies often relies on the context in which they are implemented, including the cultural appropriateness of the specific strategy and the support provided by relevant stakeholders. Additional research is required to determine the most effective strategies and to assess which external factors are the most important in influencing their success. Most policies and programs that seek to influence alcohol sale and service patterns can have both positive and negative outcomes (in some cases unintended), and these must be balanced in any evaluation of their overall impact on the community.

References

Alcohol Education and Research Council (AERC). (2008, February). The representation and reception of meaning in alcohol: Advertising and young people's drinking. *Alcohol Insight 55*. Retrieved March 8, 2009, from http://www.aerc.org.uk/documents/pdfs/insights/AERC_AlcoholInsight_0055.pdf

Araoz, G. (2004). Cultural considerations. In International Center for Alcohol Policies (ICAP), *What drives underage drinking: An international analysis* (pp. 39–47). Washington, DC: International Center for Alcohol Policies.

Arnold, M. J., & Laidler, T. J. (1994). *Alcohol misuse and violence: Situational and environmental factors in alcohol-related violence*. Canberra, Australia: Commonwealth of Australia.

Australian Department of Gaming and Racing. (2004). *Liquor accords: Local solutions for local problems*. Sydney, Australia: Author.

Baggott, R. (2006). *Alcohol strategy and the drinks industry: A partnership for prevention*. York, U.K.: Joseph Rowntree Foundation.

Baker, J., & Ramirez, A. (2000). Binational alcohol policies: USA and Mexico. In A. Varley (Ed.), *Towards a global alcohol policy: Proceedings of the Global Alcohol Policy Conference, Syracuse, New York, USA, August 2000* (pp. 79–80). London: Institute of Alcohol Studies.

Benegal, V., Nayak, M., Murthy, P., Chandra, P., & Gururaj, G. (2005). Women and alcohol in India. In I. Obot & R. Room (Eds.), *Alcohol, gender and drinking problems: Perspectives from low and middle income countries* (pp. 89–123). Geneva, Switzerland: World Health Organization.

Booth, A., Brennan, A., Meier, P. S., O'Reilly, D. T., Purshouse, R., Stockwell, T., et al. (2008). *The independent review of the effects of alcohol pricing and promotion. Summary of evidence to accompany report on phase 1: Systematic reviews*. Sheffield, U.K.: University of Sheffield.

Buka, S. L., & Birdthistle, I. J. (1999). Long-term effects of a community-wide alcohol server training intervention. *Journal of Studies on Alcohol, 60*, 27–36.

Chikritzhs, T., & Stockwell, T. (2006). The impact of later trading hours for hotels on levels of impaired driver road crashes and driver breath alcohol levels. *Addiction, 101*, 1254–1264.

Clapp, J., Voas, R., & Lange, J. (2001). Cross-border college drinking. *Journal of Safety Research, 32*, 299–307.

Craplet, M. (2007). Prevention of alcohol- and tobacco-related harms: Education or control—must we choose? *Nordisk Alkohol- & Narkotikatidskrift, 24*, 299–319.

Cusens, B., & Shepherd, J. (2005). Prevention of alcohol-related assault and injury. *Hospital Medicine, 66*, 346–348.

Dedel Johnson, K. (2004). *Underage drinking. Problem-oriented guides for police* (Problem-specific Guides Series No. 27). Washington, DC: Office of Community Oriented Policing Services (COPS).

Deehan, A. (1999). *Alcohol and crime: Taking stock* (Crime Reduction Research Series Paper 3). London: Research, Development and Statistics Directorate, Home Office.

Galloway, J., Forsyth, A., & Shewan, D. (2007). *Young people's street drinking behaviour: Investigating the influence of marketing and subculture*. London: Alcohol Education Research Council.

Gehan, J. P., Toomey, T. L., Jones-Webb, R., Rothstein, C., & Wagenaar, A. C. (1999). Alcohol outlet workers and managers: Focus groups on responsible service practices. *Journal of Alcohol and Drug Education, 44*, 60–71.

Graham, K. (2000). Preventive interventions for on-premise drinking: A promising but under-researched area of prevention. *Contemporary Drug Problems, 27*, 593–668.

Gray, D., Drandich, M., Moore, L., Wilkes, T., Riley, S., & Davies, S. (1995). Aboriginal wellbeing and liquor licensing legislation in Western Australia. *Australian Journal of Public Health, 19*, 177–185.

Hafemeister, T. L., & Jackson, S. L. (2004). Effectiveness of sanctions and law enforcement practices targeted at underage drinking not involving operation of a motor vehicle. In National Research Council and Institute of Medicine, *Reducing underage drinking: A collective responsibility, background papers. [CD-ROM]. Committee on Developing a Strategy to Reduce and Prevent Underage Drinking, Division of Behavioral and Social Sciences and Education*. Washington, DC: National Academies Press.

Harrison, P.A., Fulkerson, J. A., & Park, E. (2000). The relative importance of social versus commercial sources in youth access to tobacco, alcohol, and other drugs. *Preventive Medicine, 31*, 39–48.

Haworth, A., & Simpson, R. (Eds.). (2004). *Moonshine markets: Issues in unrecorded alcohol beverage production and consumption.* New York: Brunner-Routledge.

Heath, D. B. (2000). *Drinking occasions: Comparative perspectives on alcohol and culture.* Philadelphia: Brunner/Mazel.

Her Majesty's Stationery Office (HMSO). (2005). *Licensing (Scotland) Act 2005.* Retrieved on March 1, 2009, from http://www.opsi.gov.uk/legislation/scotland/acts2005/20050016.htm

Homel, R., Carvolth, R., Hauritz, M., McIlwain, G., & Teague, R. (2004). Making licensed venues safer for patrons: What environmental factors should be the focus of interventions? *Drug and Alcohol Review, 23,* 19–29.

Houghton, E., & Roche, A. M. (Eds.). (2001). *Learning about drinking.* New York: Brunner-Routledge.

Howard, K. A., Flora, J. A., Schleicher, N. C., & Gonzalez, E. M. C. (2004). Alcohol point-of-purchase advertising and promotions: Prevalence, content, and targeting. *Contemporary Drug Problems, 31,* 318–321.

Huckle, T., Greenaway, S., Broughton, D., & Conway, K. (2007). The use of an evidence-based community action intervention to improve age verification practices for alcohol purchase. *Substance Use and Misuse, 42,* 1899–1914.

Hurtz, S., Henriksen, L., Wang, Y., Feighery, E., & Fortmann, S. (2007). The relationship between exposure to alcohol advertising in stores, owning alcohol promotional items, and adolescent alcohol use. *Alcohol and Alcoholism, 42,* 143–149.

International Center for Alcohol Policies (ICAP). (2004). *What drives underage drinking: An international analysis.* Washington, DC: Author.

International Center for Alcohol Policies (ICAP). (2005–ongoing). *ICAP Blue Book: Practical guides for alcohol policy and prevention approaches.* Washington, DC: Author.

International Center for Alcohol Policies (ICAP). (2009). *Policy table: Minimum age limits.* Retrieved on March 8, 2009, from http://www.icap.org/Table/MinimumAgeLimitsWorldwide

Jones, S., & Lynch, M. (2007). A pilot study investigating of the nature of point-of-sale alcohol promotions in bottle shops in a large Australian regional city. *Australian and New Zealand Journal of Public Health, 31,* 318–321.

King, E., Taylor, J., & Carroll, T. (2005). *Alcohol consumption patterns among Australian 15- to 17-year-olds from 2000 to 2004.* Sydney, Australia: Department of Health and Ageing.

Leifman, H. (2002). Trends in population drinking. In T. Norström (Ed.), *Alcohol in postwar Europe: Consumption, drinking patterns, consequences and policy responses in 15 European countries* (pp. 11–48). Stockholm: Almqvist & Wicksell International.

Leonard, K. E., Fox, A., O'Connor, C. M., Dickson, C., Asare, J., et al. (2008). *Alcohol and violence: Exploring patterns and responses.* Washington, DC: International Center for Alcohol Policies.

Levy, D. T., Stewart, K., & Wilbur, P. M. (1999). *Costs of underage drinking.* Rockville, MD: Pacific Institute for Research and Evaluation.

Martinic, M., & Measham, F. (Eds.). (2008). *Swimming with crocodiles: The culture of extreme drinking.* New York: Routledge.

Moskalewicz, J., & Simpura, J. (2000). The supply of alcoholic beverages in transitional conditions: The case of Central and Eastern Europe. *Addiction,* 95(Suppl. 4), S505–S522.

National Alcohol Beverage Control Association (NABCA). (1997). *Retail oriented best practices for underage drinking prevention: An exemplary selection of retail oriented programs and practices aimed at reducing underage drinking and related drinking and driving.* Washington, DC: Author.

Nelson, J. P. (2001). Alcohol advertising and advertising bans: A survey of research methods, results, and policy implications. In M. R. Baye & J. P. Nelson (Eds.), *Advances in applied microeconomics: Advertising and differentiated products* (pp. 235–295). Amsterdam: JAI & Elsevier Science.

Nordlund, S., & Österberg, E. (2002). Unrecorded alcohol consumption: Its economics and its effects on alcohol control in the Nordic countries. *Addiction,* 95(Suppl. 4), S551–S564.

Norström, T., & Skog, O. (2005). Saturday opening of alcohol retail shops in Sweden: An experiment in two phases. *Addiction, 100,* 767–776.

Österberg, E., & Karlsson, T. (2003). *Alcohol policies in EU Member States and Norway. A collection of country reports.* Helsinki, Finland: National Research and Development Centre for Welfare and Health (STAKES).

Plant, M. A., Single, E., & Stockwell, T. (Eds.). (1997). *Alcohol: Minimizing the harm. What works?* London: Free Association Books.

Portman Group. (2000). *Keeping the peace: A guide to the prevention of alcohol-related disorder.* Retrieved February 28, 2009, from http://www.portmangroup.org.uk/uploaded_files/documents/35_49_KeepingthePeace.pdf

Portman Group. (2008). *The code of practice on the naming, packaging and promotion of alcoholic drinks* (4th ed.). Retrieved February 28, 2009, from http://portman-group.org.uk/?pid=18&level=2

Razvodovsky, Yu. E. (2008). Noncommercial alcohol in eastern and central Europe. In Adelekan, M., Razvodovsky, Yu. E., Liyanage, U., & Ndetei, D. M., *Noncommercial alcohol in three regions* (ICAP Review 3, pp. 17–23). Washington, DC: International Center for Alcohol Policies.

Reid, R. J., Hughey, J, & Peterson, N. A. (2003). Generalizing the alcohol outlet-assaultive violence link: Evidence from a U.S. Midwestern city. *Substance Use and Misuse, 38,* 1971–1982.

Saltz, R. F. (1989). Research needs and opportunities in server intervention programs. *Health Education Quarterly, 16,* 429–438.

Shelley, S. J. (2001). Border crossing, club hopping, and underage "possession" of alcohol: An analysis of the law enforcement response to the problem of cross-border underage drinking in Southern Arizona. *Arizona Law Review, 43,* 709–735.

Simpura, J. (2001). Trends in alcohol consumption and drinking patters: Sociological and economic explanations and alcohol policies. *Nordisk Alkohol- & Narkotikatidskrift, 18*(Suppl.), 3–13.

Sinclair, R. (2009). Alcohol marketing. In World Health Organization, *WHO public hearing on harmful use of alcohol. Volume IV: Received contributions from individuals* (p. 175). Retrieved March 8, 2009, from http://www.who.int/substance_abuse/activities/6individuals.pdf

Stevenson, R. J., Lind, B., & Weatherburn, D. (1999). Property damage and public disorder: Their relationship with sales of alcohol in New South Wales, Australia. *Drug and Alcohol Dependence, 54,* 163–170.

Stimson, G., Grant, M., Choquet, M., & Garrison, P. (Eds.). (2007). *Drinking in context: Patterns, interventions, and partnerships.* New York: Routledge.

Stockwell, T. (2001). Responsible alcohol service: Lessons from evaluations of servers training and policing initiatives. *Drug and Alcohol Review, 20,* 257–265.

Toomey, T. L., Kilian, G. R., Gehan, J. P., Perry, C. L., Jones-Webb, R., & Wagenaar, A. C. (1998). Qualitative assessment of training programs for alcohol servers and establishment managers. *Public Health Reports, 113,* 162–169.

U.K. Department for Culture, Media and Sport. (2008). *Evaluation of the impact of the Licensing Act 2003.* Retrieved March 8, 2009, from http://www.culture.gov.uk/images/publications/licensingevaluation.pdf

Ulmer, R. G., Shabanova, V. J., & Preusser, D. F. (2001). *Evaluation of use and lose laws.* Washington, DC: U.S. Department of Transportation, National Highway Traffic Safety Administration.

U.S. Substance Abuse and Mental Health Services Administration (SAMHSA). (2008). *Underage alcohol use: Findings from the 2002–2006 National Surveys on Drug Use and Health.* Retrieved March 8, 2009, from http://www.oas.samhsa.gov/underage2k8/toc.htm

Utah Department of Alcoholic Beverage Control (UDABC). (2009). *About UDABC: Origin and purpose.* Retrieved March 8, 2009, from http://www.alcbev.state.ut.us/Background/origin_purpose.html

Wagenaar, A. C., Murray, D. M., Gehan, J. P., Wolfson, M., Forster, J. L., Toomey, T. L., et al. (2000). Communities mobilizing for change on alcohol: Outcomes from a randomized community trial. *Journal of Studies on Alcohol, 61,* 85–94.

Wagenaar, A. C., & Toomey, T. L. (2002). Effects of minimum drinking age laws: Review and analyses of the literature from 1960 to 2000. *Journal of Alcohol Studies,* (Suppl. 14), 206–225.

Wagenaar, A. C., Toomey, T. L., & Erickson, D. J. (2005). Complying with the minimum drinking age: Effects of enforcement and training interventions. *Alcoholism: Clinical and Experimental Research, 29,* 255–262.

Webb, P., & Block, S. (2008). *Illicit alcohol in Mexico: A pilot study of what we know and what we need to know.* Unpublished paper prepared for Steven Block Economic Consulting.

Wechsler, H., Lee, J. E., Hall, J., Wagenaar, A. C., & Lee, H. (2002). Secondhand effects of student alcohol use reported by neighbors of colleges: The role of alcohol outlets. *Social Science and Medicine, 55,* 425–435.

Wells, S., Graham, K., & Purcell, J. (2009). Policy implications of the widespread practice of "pre-drinking" or "pre-gaming" before going to public drinking establishments—are current prevention strategies backfiring? *Addiction, 104,* 4–9.

Williams, S., & Mulhall, P. (2007). Where public school students in Illinois get cigarettes and alcohol: Characteristics of minors who use different sources. *Prevention Science, 6,* 47–57.

World Health Organization (WHO). (2004a). *Global status report on alcohol.* Geneva, Switzerland: Author.

World Health Organization (WHO). (2004b). *Global status report: Alcohol policy.* Geneva, Switzerland: Author.

Zhu, L., Gorman, D. M., & Horel, S. (2004). Alcohol outlet density and violence: A geospatial analysis. *Alcohol and Alcoholism, 39,* 369–375.

7

MAKING RESPONSIBLE CHOICES

MARJANA MARTINIC

Introduction

From a broad public health perspective, alcohol policies serve at least three purposes: to establish appropriate, realistic, and sustainable approaches to reduce harmful drinking and related problems; to promote safer drinking practices; and to enhance the positive aspects of alcohol consumption (International Center for Alcohol Policies [ICAP], 2005b–ongoing; Stimson, Grant, Choquet, & Garrison, 2007). The challenge is to create an approach broad enough in scope and emphasis to meet the needs of those who drink and those who do not, flexible enough to apply to a range of conditions, and specific enough to directly target harm where it is likely to occur.

Reaching both current drinkers and abstainers is a major objective for sustainable alcohol policies. This includes the prerequisite of a robust regulatory framework around the production, sale, and marketing of beverage alcohol. There is no doubt that a major role in these efforts falls under the remit of government. Regulatory measures are the backbone of any attempt to address harmful drinking. Yet, experience shows that regulatory measures alone are insufficient. A more nuanced and targeted approach is also required that can respond to the many variations in drinking patterns that exist around the world (Grant & Litvak, 1998; Stimson et al., 2007; Thom & Bayley, 2007). Such an approach offers opportunities to engage a wide range of stakeholders—including civil society and nongovernmental organizations, the public health community, educators, and those who produce, sell, and serve beverage alcohol—each with unique expertise, experience, and resources.

143

Without entering into a largely fruitless philosophical discussion on whether the duty for making responsible choices about drinking (or any other human activity) rests with the individual or with society at large, it should be acknowledged that individual choice does play a significant role. At the same time, there is a shared societal responsibility to help equip individuals with the skills necessary to make informed decisions, encouraging those who consume alcohol to do so safely and without endangering others and ensuring that one's choice to drink—or not to drink—is respected.

It is argued here that reducing harmful drinking can be achieved most usefully by addressing three areas: providing the skills that can help consumers make responsible choices, encouraging positive behaviors and discouraging risky and potentially harmful practices, and making drinking environments safer. This chapter focuses on consumers, with an emphasis on drinking patterns and their relationship with outcomes, both good and bad. Understanding this relationship can help determine which interventions are likely to be most appropriate, specific, and feasible (Plant, Single, & Stockwell, 1997; Stimson et al., 2007). In keeping with the broader theme of this book, this chapter highlights the areas in which producers and retailers in their different roles can help promote safer drinking and minimize harm.

Empowering Responsible Choices

Reducing harmful drinking begins with equipping those individuals who choose to drink with the appropriate tools to make informed decisions. Alcohol education at its broadest offers the foundation on which other prevention measures and interventions can build. There is considerable debate about the efficacy and effectiveness of alcohol education, particularly its ability to change attitudes and, ultimately, behavior (Babor et al., 2003; Foxcroft, Ireland, Lister-Sharp, Lowe, & Breen, 2003; Foxcroft, Ireland, Lowe, & Breen, 2002; Giesbrecht, 2007). The view against relying on education in the alcohol field is supported by the lack of rigorous evaluation of many programs and interventions and a lack of agreement on what is being measured. This notwithstanding, even the most ardent critics are likely to agree that there is merit in at least informing the public about alcohol, making available the basic facts about drinking and its relationship with potential outcomes, and attempting to encourage responsible drinking as a normative behavior for those adults who choose to drink.

Beverage alcohol producers and their various trade associations and social aspects organizations (SAOs) have invested considerable resources in programs aimed at empowering informed consumer choices (European Forum for Responsible Drinking [EFRD], 2008; ICAP, 2005a–ongoing; Worldwide Brewing Alliance, 2007). Yet, these initiatives have been repeatedly criticized as window dressing by an industry that, for reasons that remain unclear, chooses to invest its resources into efforts known to be ineffective. While the effectiveness of certain types of educational programs has been questioned, several approaches show considerable promise, at a minimum, for changing attitudes and norms. It would seem, therefore, that joint initiatives between industry and public health experts to help determine which programs are most likely to be effective and how such effectiveness could be measured are a constructive way forward.

Creating an Informed Consumer

Just the Facts   The most basic education about alcohol consists of providing the facts about beverages, their alcohol content, particular ingredients, or provenance. This offers adult consumers of legal drinking age the information they can use when choosing a drink, although, in most cases, the decision is also guided by taste and personal preference. While little research has been done to date on the relationship between consumer choices and the provision of factual information about specific products, there is some indication that consumers find the availability of these facts helpful (Kypri et al., 2007).

Among the most important information to be conveyed is the alcohol content in drinks. Generally provided in terms of alcohol by volume (ABV), it is expressed as the percentage of the total volume in a given container (a bottle or a can). In some cases, alcohol content may also be expressed in terms of weight, as grams of absolute ethanol per unit volume. Making such information available can help consumers understand the strength of drinks and relate it to their own alcohol consumption as well as to their choices about other behaviors that may accompany drinking, such as driving, operating machinery, or taking medications.

Making consumers aware of the ingredients in beverages is another important tool for facilitating safer choices, particularly when ingredients may be harmful to some drinkers. For instance, informing individuals with allergies that a product may contain sulfites, gluten, barley, albumin from eggs, casein from milk, or artificial sweeteners like aspartame and acesulfame potassium allows them to avoid potential health problems and adverse reactions. For many consumers, nutritional information about caloric content or the presence of carbohydrates, minerals, salts, sugars, or fiber can also play a role in making a choice about which beverages to drink or even whether to do so at all.

Other factual information that can be provided to consumers includes the date of production or bottling and, depending on the beverage type, the country and the region of production. Such information serves several purposes. It may help ensure the integrity and quality of a product: For example, information about the sell-by date and optimal storage conditions may be helpful to both those who consume and those who sell and serve alcohol. Information on recycling of containers can help influence sound decisions about the environment and sustainability. Where counterfeit or illicit products are prevalent, certain factual information can help safeguard the authenticity of commercial drinks and keep consumers safe.

The provision of factual information about beverage alcohol is required by law in a number of countries. In most cases, the requirement is for on-product information, visible and accessible to consumers. Where mandated, this includes, at a minimum, details about the type of beverage, the producer or importer, and food safety information (such as expiration dates and storage guidelines). There is, however, a significant disparity in the scope and complexity of labeling requirements among countries (ICAP, 2008). It is also important to note that policies apply as much to what should be included on labels as what should not. Most regulations require listing the "common name" of the product, especially its local language name where it is available. Common names are universally recognized product names like "rum" or "beer" and do not include brand names. In France, it is forbidden to use foreign names when a comparable French word exists (Alcohol and Tobacco Tax and Trade Bureau, 2007).

There is also room for voluntary measures to be taken by producers where official labeling requirements are absent. Examples of this are discussed in this chapter and focus on drink/unit sizes, responsible drinking messages, and warnings for pregnant women, all of which have been displayed on container labels. The Internet is another useful medium through which producers can share simple and straightforward consumer information. Websites exist for virtually every branded beverage and include facts about the products themselves, descriptions of the production process, and other related information (ICAP, 2008).

Drinking Guidelines   On its own, factual information about alcohol is of limited use unless consumers are able to relate it to their actual drinking practices. To provide this context, government bodies or quasi-governmental organizations in numerous countries offer drinking guidelines (ICAP, 2009d). These guidelines are intended to help consumers relate the quantity and frequency of their drinking to possible health outcomes and to define what are variously called "sensible" or "low-risk" and "hazardous" or "harmful" drinking patterns.

Given the differences between men and women in their ability to metabolize alcohol, drinking guidelines, where they exist, provide gender-specific risk information. Age, health status, and other factors also influence the effect alcohol is likely to have. As a result, some guidelines include specific recommendations that relate not only to men and women in general but also to pregnant women, older individuals, and those with particular health issues or alcohol dependence (ICAP, 2003, 2009d). It should be noted that the details of drinking guidelines, the specificity of information they offer, and the recommendations tailored to particular groups vary considerably. In addition, whereas some guidelines relate advice and discussions of outcomes only to daily intake levels, others offer more nuanced recommendations by addressing both daily and weekly amounts consumed.

Official guidelines and recommendations may be complemented by definitions of "standard drinks" or "units" (ICAP, 1998). As with drinking guidelines, standard measures vary among countries, as well as in the scientific literature (Brick, 2006; Dawson, 2003; Kerr,

Greenfield, Tujague, & Brown, 2005; Stockwell & Single, 1997). Many countries do not use a standard definition for drinks; where serving sizes are defined, they generally depend on local customs and a given beverage type—spirits, wine, or beer (Dufour, 1999; ICAP, 1998, 2003). Alcohol content can differ considerably from one definition to the next and has bearing on how such information can be operationalized. Together with drinking guidelines, standard measures can help consumers gauge their alcohol intake and relate it to other areas, such as blood alcohol concentrations (BACs) legally permissible for driving (Gill & Donaghy, 2004; Stockwell, Blaze-Temple, & Walker, 1991).

While guidelines are best issued through official channels and need to be based on the best available research, the beverage alcohol industry—producers and retailers alike—can help promote this type of information among consumers. As noted, there is a requirement in some countries to provide information on labels about the alcohol content of a particular beverage, relating this information to standard drinks. Some companies, however, have chosen to provide on-product information about standard units and servings on a voluntary basis. Information may be given regarding the number of standard measures in a particular bottle or a can, and a reference may be made to the official drinking guidelines. The voluntary provision of such information has been implemented by producers in a number of markets. Most information is provided on a country-by-country basis, largely because of local variations in definitions and guidelines, as no global standard currently exists.

For example, in 1999, six major producers in the United Kingdom (U.K.)—Allied Domecq, Bacardi-Martini, Diageo, Matthew Clark, Seagram & Sons, and Whitbread—began voluntary inclusion of unit information on their product packaging. Other companies have followed suit and now include Brown-Forman, Carlsberg, Coors, Heineken, Anheuser-Busch InBev, Moet Hennessy, Pernod Ricard, and Scottish & Newcastle. In addition, advice about drinking during pregnancy (expressed by a logo or a statement), "know-your-limits" recommendations, and reference to the U.K. Sensible Drinking guidelines, as well as to the Drinkaware Trust—a national charity providing consumer education—are found on containers of beer, wine, and spirits (Campden and Chorleywood Food Research Association Group, 2008). Similar voluntary information is also found in other countries, and some company policies apply across the European Union (EU) or, in certain cases, worldwide.

Various other channels lend themselves to reminding the public about standard measures, official guidelines, and recommendations. For example, the workplace has been used to provide information, at least to employees of a particular company or organization. In the case of the alcohol industry, employees are educated about the relationship between drinking and outcomes, drinking guidelines, standard measures, and other facts. The distribution and sales staff in alcohol companies can also be involved in sharing information and responsible practices with the retailers who make up their clients, allowing for an education chain that closely follows the supply chain.

Retailers can then further share this information with customers. Points of sale offer direct contact with consumers and can be used to disseminate information (see Chapter 6). Many consumers may have little direct contact with beverage alcohol labels as they may drink primarily in on-premise establishments, where drink sizes can be anything but "standard" (Kerr, Patterson, Koenen, & Greenfield, 2008). As such venues offer direct access to key target audiences, it is important that servers be well versed in information about alcohol content, beverage strength, and the relationship with standard measures and guidelines. Not only can this help ensure that serving sizes in pubs, bars, and restaurants are relatively uniform and consistent with standard definitions, but also it can create opportunities to prevent excessive consumption and other harmful drinking patterns.

Finally, the Internet provides a useful way of communicating information to a large audience and reaching consumers directly. Company websites often include information that can facilitate consumer choices. Some producers have dedicated websites, separate from corporate and product sites, that are explicitly devoted to consumer education. Included on such sites are facts about alcohol and information about drinking guidelines, standard drinks, drinking patterns, possible outcomes, and specialized resources for those seeking additional information or assistance with particular issues, such as intervention and treatment for problem drinkers.

It is worth noting that the usefulness of standard drink labeling and drinking guidelines is limited to those beverages whose
strengths are known or that are served in standard containers (Graves
& Kaskutas, 2002). In practice, this means that such information is
available only for commercially produced beverage alcohol or those
traditional home-produced drinks whose strengths are defined.
However, a significant proportion of all alcohol consumed around
the world is "noncommercial"—home produced, illicit, or otherwise
unrecorded (World Health Organization [WHO], 2004; see Chapter
3). In most cases, the alcohol content of such beverages is hard to
determine (Nayak, Kerr, Greenfield, & Pillai, 2008; Paine & Davan,
2001; Papas et al., 2008), rendering the application of definitions and
guidelines impracticable. In addition, in many developing countries,
homebrews are traditionally consumed from communal vessels, com-
plicating drinkers' ability to monitor their alcohol intake. Therefore,
while drinking guidelines and other related information may be useful in countries where beverage alcohol is largely within the reach of
government regulation and oversight, the utility of such measures in
other parts of the world is considerably more limited.

Preventing Risky Behaviors

As valuable as factual information about alcohol, drinking guidelines,
and standard measures might be, it is of little use unless it can be
applied to modifying behavior. Certain drinking patterns, including
heavy drinking, whether occasional or chronic, are linked to various
health and social problems—and so are other behaviors and activities
that may accompany drinking.

Directional Information

Factual information about alcohol is often supplemented by so-
called directional information, intended to alert consumers to practices that may be harmful, point them toward behaviors that are
part of a healthy lifestyle, and help them apply concepts like alcohol
content to their own drinking. Directional information can relate
drinking levels to intoxication or blood alcohol limits for operating

motor vehicles, allowing direct application to lifestyles and making informed choices.

Directional information is certainly included in some drinking guidelines, but it is usually provided in the form of campaigns and messaging that encourage consumers to act responsibly. For example, in some countries, health warning labels are mandated by law to alert the public to potential risks. They offer reminders about moderate drinking and, in some instances, warn about specific risks inherent in drinking before driving, operating machinery, and taking medications as well as drinking during pregnancy.

There has been a concerted voluntary effort by producers in this area. Industry responsibility campaigns are widespread. They include messaging in advertising and other commercial communications about drinking responsibly or moderately and about not drinking and driving. They also include campaigns aimed specifically at changing consumer behavior and, in some cases, the voluntary inclusion of warnings on packaging and product labels.

There is considerable debate about the immediate impact of campaigns and related efforts, such as public service announcements and responsibility messages, in changing behaviors around drinking (Babor et al., 2003). As with many other educational measures, the impact of directional information has not been evaluated with consistency and rigor. However, there is evidence that messages and campaigns applied alongside other initiatives can effectively change norms and, in the long run, affect consumer conduct. The provision of directional information, like any other measure, cannot be implemented in isolation, and its impact should not be examined outside a broader context of comprehensive action to change behavior.

Supporting Road Traffic Safety

Perhaps the most salient example of attempts to change consumer behavior is in the area of drinking and driving. Certainly, government and law enforcement have been central in raising awareness about allowable BAC limits and likely penalties for infractions. Backed by rigorous enforcement through breath testing and random sobriety checkpoints, this work has served to change perceptions in many countries about respecting limits and the relative (un)acceptability of alcohol-impaired driving (Global Road Safety Partnership, 2007). However, such measures are just some components of a broader societal effort that includes other stakeholders.

Producers of beverage alcohol, as well as those who own and operate retail establishments, have played a part in helping to reduce alcohol-related road traffic crashes and other incidents (see Chapter 8). Initiatives against alcohol-impaired driving range from mass media campaigns and responsibility messages to offers of safe transportation, dial-a-cab programs, and confiscating car keys from intoxicated patrons. Such measures have contributed to raising awareness and changing culture and attitudes about drinking and driving (DeJong & Winsten, 1999; Elder et al., 2004; Homel, 1988; McCammon, 2001; Stimson et al., 2007, pp. 105–123). Attitudinal changes have been observed among those who frequent licensed premises and those who serve them, as well as among young people generally, a group particularly likely to drink and drive. These types of measures are being implemented in both developed and developing countries.

As noted, premises that sell or serve alcohol offer convenient venues for initiatives aimed at minimizing risk for harm (see Chapter 6). They lend themselves well to sharing information about mandated BAC limits and raising awareness of penalties for noncompliance. Coupled with designated driver schemes and other measures, these efforts can help reduce risk. They may also lower the legal liability of licensed premises, thereby providing additional and tangible incentives for retailers (Sloan, Stout, Whetten-Goldstein, & Liand, 2000). Other interventions at the retail level include, for example, offering free food or non-alcohol beverages to patrons willing to serve as designated drivers and making breathalyzers available in bars or pubs as a means of encouraging customers to monitor their BAC levels while drinking. Driving simulators, presented as entertainment and video games in bars, pubs, and other premises, could be used to help raise awareness among patrons about the degree to which their ability to drive after drinking is impaired.

In many countries, producers of beverage alcohol have joined forces with law enforcement to support screening checkpoints, awareness campaigns, or the introduction of interlock devices for repeat drink-driving offenders (Stimson et al., 2007, pp. 105–123). However, producers can also help by focusing on their own distribution chains, which rely heavily on road transportation. Drivers of distribution fleets can be targeted by company programs to reduce alcohol-impaired driving and related harm. Such efforts already exist in a number of countries around the world, including Brazil, India, and South Africa.

Targeting Those at Risk

For certain individuals, the consumption of beverage alcohol represents an elevated risk for harm. The reasons for this are several: heavy and otherwise high-risk drinking patterns, physical or psychological factors that influence the ability to metabolize alcohol or heighten its effects, socioeconomic considerations (e.g., social exclusion), age, and relative experience with alcohol. Such at-risk groups include pregnant women, young people, older adults, alcohol-dependent individuals, and those with particular health problems. Addressing harmful drinking among them requires targeted measures extending beyond approaches that blanket the general population. Specific, well-tailored prevention can help diminish the likelihood of harm; for current problem drinkers, interventions can be successfully aimed at reducing negative outcomes.

The ability to reach at-risk individuals relies on approaches that are targeted, appropriate, and realistic, employing messaging tailored to resonate with a given audience. Programs can be aimed directly at those at risk or indirectly through health and education professionals, parents, and other role models or authority figures. In both cases, producers and retailers of beverage alcohol can lend their resources and experience to the effort of reducing harmful drinking.

PERNOD RICARD AND RAISING AWARENESS AMONG PREGNANT WOMEN

Consuming alcohol during pregnancy can pose major risks to the unborn child. A serious consequence of prenatal alcohol exposure is fetal alcohol syndrome disorders (FASDs), a range of permanent birth defects that includes fetal alcohol syndrome (FAS), characterized by a range of physical, mental, and behavioral problems. On this issue, Pernod Ricard takes the same precautionary approach as recommended by many health authorities: abstain completely from alcohol consumption (see ICAP, 2009b). In this context, the company is committed to supporting and relaying health authorities' abstinence messages and informing women of the entirely avoidable risks associated with drinking during pregnancy.

In 2005, the French legislature approved an amendment that requires warning labels on alcohol products. A pictogram on bottle labels now alerts pregnant women to the dangers of alcohol consumption. Pernod Ricard applies this measure on a voluntary basis to reach as many consumers as possible—in 2007, the company extended the use of the label on its products sold throughout the European Union. Pernod Ricard also participates in public awareness campaigns to highlight the risks posed by prenatal exposure to alcohol.

Source: Pernod Ricard (2009, paras. 1–4)

Interventions for Young People

Young people are perhaps the most obvious at-risk group for whom specific measures have been developed. Physiological changes during early adolescence make young people particularly susceptible to the effects of alcohol (Masten, Faden, Zucker, & Spear, 2008; Spear, 2002; Spear & Varlinskaya, 2005; Varlinskaya & Spear, 2004; Windle et al., 2008), and their inexperience with drinking means that they are likely not to know with precision or to ignore their own limits. Overall, youth is a period of experimentation, of pushing limits—not of common sense and moderation.

Most countries around the world mandate a minimum age for the legal purchase of beverage alcohol in an effort to restrict access for young people (see Chapter 6; ICAP, 2009c). However, reality shows that drinking—whether occasional sampling or more regular consumption—often begins before the mandated purchase age (see, e.g., Andersson et al., 2007; Johnston, O'Malley, Bachman, & Schulenberg, 2008). Additional measures are clearly needed to supplement legal age limits and to address the issue through a multipronged approach to prevention.

The beverage alcohol industry—producers and retailers—can help prevent underage drinking. In countries where carrying some form of legal identification is mandatory, servers can check patrons for proof of age and refuse service to minors. Voluntary proof-of-age schemes have also been introduced in countries where carrying identification is not obligatory, as in the United Kingdom (Portman Group, 2009). In some cases, industry members have developed partnership approaches with law enforcement to ensure that legal age limits are respected, for example, through the use of undercover police in retail outlets (Century Council, 2009a). Shops and serving establishments are also convenient venues for educating the general public about the legally mandated drinking age and penalties for breaking the law. An effective strategy is to link retailer licenses to demonstrable compliance with minimum age legislation, imposing fines, and even license revocation on retailers who break the law. However, here, as in other areas, success also hinges on proper enforcement (see Chapter 6).

Preventing harmful drinking among young people is another issue of considerable international concern (Martinic & Measham, 2008). Various initiatives have been implemented, largely in educational settings (schools and universities), the workplace, and within the broader community (Gorgulho & Tamendarova, 2008; Martinic, Tamendarova, & Houghton, 2005). While the effectiveness of many such interventions has been questioned (Babor et al., 2003), some approaches, including those supported by the beverage alcohol industry, have shown promising results.

Parents and peers also play a significant, if not the most important, role in shaping youthful drinking. Programs have been developed to involve these two groups in changing drinking norms and reducing the potential for harm. Prevention efforts that focus on parents and the family have an impact on young people's perceptions and behaviors (Centre for Addiction and Mental Health, 1999; Kumpfer, Alvarado, Tait, & Turner, 2002; Kumpfer, Alvarado, & Whiteside, 2003). Some of these efforts—including the Strengthening Families

Program: For Parents and Youth 10–14 (SFP 10–14), implemented in the United States (U.S.) and adapted for other countries (Foxcroft et al., 2002, 2003)—have received support from producers, who can bring resources to bear in helping the development of measures that positively affect behavior change. This is discussed in greater detail in Chapter 8.

Similar initiatives have also been developed and implemented directly by industry-supported groups, notably the SAOs. Often resulting from collaborative efforts and partnerships, these programs may be aimed, for example, at teaching parents the skills they need to talk to their children about alcohol and to recognize and address potential problems. These are typified by such programs as the Century Council's campaign Parents, You're Not Done Yet in the United States (Century Council, 2009b) and Éduc'alcool's 2009 guide *Be Prepared to Talk to Your Children about Drinking* in Canada.

Focusing on the role of peers is the basis of the social norms marketing approach, designed to change young people's attitudes and perceived drinking norms (Mattern & Neighbors, 2004; Perkins, 2003; Perkins & Craig, 2002). Often implemented within a school or university setting, social norms programs may be directed at the general student population or specific groups of young people perceived to be at high risk for harmful drinking (e.g., first-year college students and student athletes). Such programs use a variety of formal and informal channels to provide accurate information about actual drinking patterns and norms in a given population, aiming to dispel misperceptions and thereby decrease risky behaviors. As with SFP 10–14 and other initiatives, the social norms approach has received industry funding; however, development, implementation, and evaluation have been left to those with expertise in these areas—independent researchers and practitioners.

Finally, when it comes to young people, a crucial area for industry involvement is the responsible marketing of beverage alcohol. Government regulations and voluntary industry codes include clear provisions against depictions of youth drinking and marketing that encourage underage or heavy consumption (see Chapter 4; ICAP, 2009a).

Screening and Brief Intervention

For those individuals for whom primary prevention comes too late and whose drinking is already problematic although not yet diagnosable as alcohol dependence, screening and brief interventions offer an opportunity for reducing harm (Babor, de la Fuente, Saunders, & Grant, 1989; Babor, Higgins-Biddle, Saunders, & Monteiro, 2001). Generally, this approach consists of brief diagnosis using instruments such as the Alcohol Use Disorders Identification Test (AUDIT) and similar questionnaires, followed by brief counseling and sessions aimed at modifying behavior. In some cases, brief follow-up sessions are also held. The evidence shows that this approach can be highly effective in modifying problematic drinking behavior and that its impact may endure over extended periods of time. Brief interventions can be applied in any number of settings and have been used in primary care facilities, pharmacies, hospital emergency departments, educational institutions, and the workplace (Anderson & Larimer, 2002; Chang et al., 2005; Cherpitel, 1995; D'Amico & Fromme, 2002; Marlatt, 1998; Saitz, Sullivan, & Samet, 2000; Zunino, Litvak, & Israel, 1998). The advantage of on-site interventions, such as in emergency rooms, is that they can directly reach individuals who have already experienced harm and act quickly to reduce future risk.

Screening and brief intervention can also be tailored to meet the needs of specific populations. For example, in efforts to prevent fetal alcohol spectrum disorders, screening for alcohol problems can be integrated into other, broader prenatal screening and included in antenatal care (Chang, 2004). Providing pregnant women with advice can help modify their behavior not only around drinking but also around other potentially harmful practices. Such advice may be usefully disseminated through primary care providers and clinics as well as by obstetricians and gynecologists. Screening for alcohol problems can also be integrated into efforts to detect other health issues, such as HIV/AIDS. There is evidence that the effectiveness of antiretroviral therapy for HIV-positive individuals may be compromised by heavy drinking (Bryant, 2006), and that heavy drinkers who are HIV positive (and often also socially marginalized) are less likely to comply with treatment regimens (Bryant, 2006; Cook et al., 2001; Semple,

Patterson, & Grant, 2003). In the case of HIV-positive individuals, modifying drinking patterns can help avoid both further alcohol-related problems and HIV/AIDS complications.

Specific brief intervention approaches have also been tailored to meet the needs and habits of young people (Burke, O'Sullivan, & Vaughan, 2005; Larimer, Cronce, Lee, & Kilmer, 2004; Lubman, Hides, Yucel, & Toumbourou, 2007; Saunders, Kypri, Walters, Laforge, & Larimer, 2004). Electronic screening tools, online advice, and brief interventions have shown considerable promise in modifying harmful drinking patterns, particularly among youth (Kypri, Langley, Saunders, Cashell-Smith, & Herbison, 2008; Kypri et al., 2005; Saitz et al., 2004). For the elderly, among whom problem drinking is not uncommon and often linked with the loss of social networks and loneliness, screening and brief interventions can be integrated into general geriatric care and services provided in long-term care facilities (Finfgeld-Connett, 2004; Sorocco & Ferrell, 2006).

There is evidence that those working in certain professions and industries may be at elevated risk for alcohol-related harm. As a result, they may be particularly suitable targets for interventions to help reduce harmful drinking and other behaviors, such as risky sexual practices. This may be of particular importance in those jobs where the safety of others is also at risk, such as in the transportation sector (road traffic, airline transport, rail, and shipping) or medical and healthcare professions. Workplace screening, brief interventions, and employee assistance programs (EAPs) are important tools for minimizing risk among particular groups (Cook & Schlenger, 2002; Roman & Blum, 2002).

Like other industries that take corporate responsibility seriously, producers of beverage alcohol have a long-standing track record of promoting workplace safety and the wellbeing of employees. All ICAP sponsor companies, for example, have codes regarding alcohol in the workplace. These codes vary from one market to another, in compliance with national laws, and may be guided by national regulations around privacy issues, the ability to conduct BAC testing on drivers, union rules, and other considerations. Individual provisions in the codes differ by company but range from responding to employee drink-driving and drinking in the workplace to providing counseling for alcohol problems and establishing EAPs.

Essential to the prevention of risk and to harm minimization is the availability of trained and knowledgeable professionals who are able to offer advice and assistance to those at risk. While the provision of such professional assistance is well beyond the purview of industry members, it nevertheless offers opportunities for engagement. Working in partnership with educational institutions (e.g., medical and nursing programs and schools for social workers and law enforcement personnel), industry can help to make available balanced and comprehensive information on alcohol and the relationship among drinking, health, and social issues. Access to such information can assist professionals with screening, identification, and treatment of problem drinkers. For example, the Distilled Spirits Council of the United States (DISCUS) has supported the development and distribution of an online continuing medical education course by the University of Florida Alcohol Education Center (AEC). Topics covered include, among others, alcohol metabolism, age and gender issues, BAC levels, standard drink information, health effects of moderate consumption, FAS, screening and brief intervention, alcohol abuse and dependence, treatment and relapse, and genetic and environmental risk and protective factors for developing alcohol problems. The course is part of an AEC free curriculum for healthcare professionals across the United States and is offered both online and in hard copy (more information about the course is available at http://webapps.health.ufl.edu/aec).

Making the Drinking Environments Safer

The third and final element of addressing harmful drinking discussed here has to do with those public and private venues where alcohol is sold, served, and consumed, ranging from cafés, restaurants, bars, *shebeens*, and beer gardens to open public spaces (Heath, 2000; Marshall, 1979). While measures aimed at the drinking environment do not directly target consumers, their behaviors, and choices, they help create safer drinking contexts by putting into place safeguards against potential harm. This area is one in which the role for industry participation is strong and results are proven.

Responsible Retail, Hospitality, and the Nighttime Economy

Some drinking contexts, by virtue of their location, design, type of clientele, or management practices, can pose a risk for harmful outcomes. As such, they are opportune venues for implementing measures for responsible hospitality and the safety of patrons as well as of the broader community. There is general agreement on the effectiveness of such measures (Babor et al., 2003; Burns, Nusbaumer, & Reiling, 2003; Sloan et al., 2000; Stimson et al., 2007, pp. 125–137; Stockwell, 2001).

Responsible hospitality is a basic element on which efforts to minimize alcohol-related harm rest. It includes training of sales and service staff and modifications to the physical drinking environment (see Chapters 6 and 8). It should be noted that, ironically, these interventions may at times be hindered by prevailing laws and regulations. In some countries, refusal to sell alcohol to a patron may be considered an infraction of the penal code. For example, in France and Germany, refusal to serve alcohol may not be permitted unless service constitutes breaking the law (as in selling to minors) or places the patron's safety directly at peril (e.g., serving an intoxicated customer who will be driving) (Boella, Legrand, Pagnon-Maudet, Sloan, & Baumann, 2006). While discrimination (on the basis of religion, gender, or ethnicity) must be proven in each case, such provisions can complicate the implementation of responsible service.

Responsible hospitality also includes awareness of how much patrons have consumed and whether they are likely to have reached a BAC limit at which they should not drive, as well as the ability to offer alternative transportation. Various programs have been developed and implemented for this purpose in many countries, relying on best practice (ICAP, 2005a–ongoing; ICAP & EFRD, 2008a, 2008b). For an example, see Chapter 8 for the discussion of the Training for Intervention Procedures (TIPS) program.

Modifications that enhance the safety of the physical drinking environment are a significant component of responsible hospitality. Thus, space management through partitions and seating arrangements can help reduce the likelihood of congestion and violent incidents; music and entertainment, as well as noise level and lighting, have an impact on how quickly and how much patrons are likely to drink (Homel, Carvolth, Hauritz, McIlwain, & Teague, 2004; see discussion in Chapter 6). Making food and snacks available can help consumers avoid rapid intoxication, as can the availability of non-alcohol beverages at reasonable cost. Some types of drinking establishments are focal points for sexual encounters and transactional sex (Go et al., 2007; Kalichman, Simbayi, Vermaak, Jooste, & Cain, 2008; Morojele et al., 2006; Weir et al., 2003). They offer those who own and operate them (and have a will to reduce potential for harm) opportunities for intervention—at the very least, by making available condom vending machines.

Overall, involvement by owners and managers of serving establishments is crucial to creating safer drinking environments and in ensuring appropriate training and attitudes among staff. This also includes avoiding those promotions that encourage heavy drinking practices, such as two-for-one promotions, comparably expensive non-alcohol beverages, or salty snacks. Notably, in most markets, producers have little leverage over retailers and owners of serving establishments. Despite these limitations, they have taken a prominent role in promoting responsible sale and service, often sponsoring drink-drive and server training programs by working with retailers, either directly as companies or through trade association and SAO initiatives (see Chapters 6 and 8).

Other measures in which the industry can play a prominent role include linking retail licenses with demonstrated implementation of responsible hospitality practices. Where responsible service and training are not required by law, incentives might be given by the industry itself; for example, seals of approval or publicly available safety ratings could be awarded to serving establishments with proven good practice. Such initiatives could be sponsored by retailers' trade associations or even by producer groups in an effort to encourage good practice.

Responsible hospitality measures are not exclusively confined to the interiors of licensed premises; they extend to the general environment within which these outlets are located. Urban areas are focal points for late-night entertainment, bringing with it economic advantages but also a burden on public services (Gruenewald et al., 1996; Reid, Hughey, & Peterson, 2003; Treno, Grube, & Martin, 2003;

Weitzman, Folkman, Folkman, & Wechsler, 2003). Safety in areas that depend on the nighttime economy is contingent in large measure on the participation of serving and retail venues. Accords, community policing efforts, and other measures allow many opportunities for voluntary involvement of licensed premises as good corporate citizens (see Chapter 6). Creative urban planning that involves input from retailers, law enforcement, public transportation authorities, and local communities can help with the development of viable management of the nighttime economy and allows the integration of safeguards for minimizing risk and keeping the consumer safe.

Concluding Remarks

The focus of this chapter has been on consumers, on reducing potential for alcohol-related harm by empowering responsible choices and behaviors, and on making the drinking environment safer. Targeted interventions aimed at providing information and changing behaviors and contexts offer an opportunity for the involvement of many stakeholders, particularly those who produce, sell, and serve alcohol. There is no doubt that regulatory measures and government involvement provide the backbone for solid alcohol policies. However, it is equally true that no one approach is effective on its own; targeted interventions are best implemented in conjunction with other measures, be they compliance or enforcement of regulations.

There can also be no discussion about targeted interventions, particularly those that are directed at consumer knowledge and awareness, without at least some mention of effectiveness. Critics of the targeted approach have maintained that educational measures, in particular, are ineffective. Yet, there is a sleight of hand in this argumentation. While many measures have not proven successful in effecting an immediate behavior change, they *are* able to inform and raise awareness. Changing drinking practices and norms, as with any attitudinal adjustment and behavioral modification, is a long-term effort; such changes do not occur overnight but take time and a broader culture shift that requires repeated and widespread application and reinforcement. It should also be acknowledged that, particularly in the field of alcohol education, it is not that many programs are ineffective, but rather that their effectiveness has not been measured and properly evaluated over the long term. In the spirit of intellectual honesty and transparency, this distinction is an important one: Lack of evidence about effectiveness is by no means the same as evidence of a lack of effectiveness.

A final word: The ultimate decision whether and how to drink rests with the individual, but it is futile to debate whether responsible practices are an individual or a societal domain. The answer likely lies somewhere in between, and the responsibility is a shared one. While there is a clear role for the individual, it is equally the responsibility of society (writ large) to help enable that individual to make choices that are as informed and responsible as possible. Included in this collective are certainly not only the efforts of government, the healthcare sector, and educational and other societal institutions but also those of industry. Each can play a part in helping to create an informed consumer, one capable of making an intelligent and educated choice, and who, it is hoped, will also opt to exercise it.

References

Alcohol and Tobacco Tax and Trade Bureau. (2007). France. In *International import/export requirements*. Retrieved March 11, 2009, from http://www.ttb.gov/itd/france.shtml

Anderson, B. K., & Larimer, M. E. (2002). Problem drinking and the workplace: An individualized approach to prevention. *Psychology of Addictive Behavior, 16*, 243–251.

Andersson, B., Hibell, B., Beck, F., Choquet, M., Kokkevi, A., Fotiou, A., et al. (2007). *Alcohol and drug use among European 17-18 year old students: Data from the ESPAD Project*. Stockholm: Swedish Council for Information on Alcohol and Other Drugs (CAN) and the Pompidou Group at the Council of Europe.

Babor, T. F., Caetano, R., Caswell, S., Edwards, G., Giesbrecht, N., Graham, K., et al. (2003). *Alcohol: No ordinary commodity. Research and public policy*. Oxford, U.K.: Oxford University Press.

Babor, T. F., de la Fuente, J. R., Saunders, J., & Grant, M. (1989). *AUDIT: The Alcohol Use Disorders Identification Test. Guidelines for use in primary health care*. Geneva, Switzerland: World Health Organization.

Babor, T. F., Higgins-Biddle, J., Saunders, J. B., & Monteiro, M. G. (2001). *AUDIT: The Alcohol Use Disorders Identification Test. Guidelines for use in primary care* (2nd ed.). Geneva, Switzerland: World Health Organization.

Boella, M. J., Legrand, W., Pagnon-Maudet, C., Sloan, P., & Baumann, A. (2006). Regulation of the sale and consumption of alcoholic drinks in France, England and Germany. *Hospitality Management, 25,* 398–413.

Brick, J. (2006). Standardization of alcohol calculations in research. *Alcoholism: Clinical and Experimental Research, 30,* 1276–1287.

Bryant, K. J. (2006). Expanding research on the role of alcohol consumption and related risks in the prevention and treatment of HIV/AIDS. *Substance Use and Misuse, 41,* 1465–1507.

Burke, P. J., O'Sullivan, J., & Vaughan, B. L. (2005). Adolescent substance use: Brief interventions by emergency care providers. *Pediatric Emergency Care, 21,* 770–776.

Burns, E. D., Nusbaumer, M. R., & Reiling, D. M. (2003). Think they're drunk? Alcohol servers and the identification of intoxication. *Journal of Drug Education, 33,* 177–186.

Campden and Chorleywood Food Research Association Group (CCFRA). (2008). *Monitoring implementation of alcohol labelling regime (including advice to women on alcohol and pregnancy).* Chipping Campden, U.K.: Author.

Centre for Addiction and Mental Health (CAMH). (1999). *Alcohol and drug prevention programs for youth: What works?* Toronto: Author.

Century Council. (2009a). *Cops in shops.* Retrieved March 11, 2009, from http://www.centurycouncil.org/

Century Council. (2009b). Parents, you're not done yet. Retrieved March 11, 2009, from http://www.centurycouncil.org/

Chang, G. (2004). Screening and brief intervention in prenatal care settings. *Alcohol Research and Health, 28,* 80–84.

Chang, G., McNamara, T. K., Orav, E. J., Koby, D., Lavigne, A., Ludman, B., et al. (2005). Brief intervention for prenatal alcohol use: A randomized trial. *Obstetrics and Gynecology, 105,* 991–998.

Cherpitel, C. J. (1995). Screening for alcohol problems in the emergency room: A rapid alcohol problems screen. *Drug and Alcohol Dependence, 40,* 133–137.

Cook, R., & Schlenger, W. (2002). Prevention of substance abuse in the workplace: Review of research on the delivery of services. *The Journal of Primary Prevention, 23,* 115–141.

Cook, R. L., Sereika, S. M., Hunt, S. C., Woodward, W. C., Erlen, J. A., & Conigliaro, J. (2001). Problem drinking and medication adherence among persons with HIV infection. *Journal of General Internal Medicine, 16,* 83–88.

D'Amico, E. J., & Fromme, K. (2002). Brief prevention for adolescent risk-taking behavior. *Addiction, 97,* 563–574.

Dawson, D. A. (2003). Methodological issues in measuring alcohol use. *Alcohol Research and Health, 27,* 18–29.

DeJong, W., & Winsten, J. A. (1999). The use of designated drivers by U.S. college students: A national study. *Journal of American College Health, 47,* 147–150.

Dufour, M. C. (1999). What is moderate drinking? Defining "drinks" and drinking levels. *Alcohol Research and Health, 23*, 5–14.

Éduc'alcool. (2009). *Be prepared to talk to your children about drinking.* Montreal: Author.

Elder, R. W., Shults, R. A., Sleet, D. A., Nichols, J. L., Thompson, R. S., Rajab, W., et al. (2004). Effectiveness of mass media campaigns for reducing drinking and driving and alcohol-involved crashes: A systematic review. *American Journal of Preventive Medicine, 27*, 57–65.

European Forum for Responsible Drinking (EFRD). (2008). *Drinks industry initiatives 2008: Voluntary initiatives by the EU spirits industry to reduce alcohol-related harm.* Brussels, Belgium: Author.

Finfgeld-Connett, D. L. (2004). Treatment of substance misuse in older women: Using a brief intervention model. *Journal of Gerontological Nursing, 30*, 30–37.

Foxcroft, D. R., Ireland, D., Lister-Sharp, D. J., Lowe, G., & Breen, R. (2003). Longer-term primary prevention for alcohol misuse in young people: A systematic review. *Addiction, 98*, 397–411.

Foxcroft, D. R., Ireland, D., Lowe, G., & Breen, R. (2002). Primary prevention for alcohol misuse in young people. *Cochrane Database System Review, 3.* Retrieved March 11, 2009, from http://www.cochrane.org/reviews/en/ab003024.html

Giesbrecht, N. (2007). Reducing alcohol-related damage in populations: Rethinking the roles of education and persuasion interventions. *Addiction, 102*, 1345–1349.

Gill, J. S., & Donaghy, M. (2004). Variation in the alcohol content of a "drink" of wine and spirit poured by a sample of the Scottish population. *Health Education Research, 19*, 485–491.

Global Road Traffic Safety Partnership (GRSP). (2007). *Drinking and driving: A road safety manual for decision-makers and practitioners.* Geneva, Switzerland: Author.

Go, V. F., Solomon, S., Srikrishnan, A. K., Sivaram, S., Johnson, S. C., Sripaipan, T., et al. (2007). HIV rates and risk behaviors are low in the general population of men in southern India but high in alcohol venues: Results from two probability surveys. *Journal of Acquired Immune Deficiency Syndromes, 46*, 491–497.

Gorgulho, M., & Tamendarova, D. (2008). Tackling extreme drinking in young people: Feasible interventions. In M. Martinic & F. Measham (Eds.), *Swimming with crocodiles: The culture of extreme drinking* (pp. 219–259). New York: Routledge.

Grant, M., & Litvak, J. (Eds.). (1998). *Drinking patterns and their consequences.* Washington, DC: Taylor & Francis.

Graves, K., & Kaskutas, L. A. (2002). Beverage choice among Native American and African American urban women. *Alcoholism: Clinical and Experimental Research, 26*, 218–222.

Gruenewald, P. J., Millar, A. B., Treno, A. J., Yang, Z., Ponicki, W. R., & Roeper, P. (1996). The geography of availability and driving after drinking. *Addiction, 91*, 967–983.

Heath, D. B. (2000). *Drinking occasions: Comparative perspectives on alcohol and culture.* Philadelphia: Brunner/Mazel.

Homel, R. (1988). *Policing and punishing the drinking driver: A study of general and specific deterrence.* New York: Springer-Verlag.

Homel, R., Carvolth, R., Hauritz, M., McIlwain, G., & Teague, R. (2004). Making licensed venues safer for patrons: What environmental factors should be the focus of interventions? *Drug and Alcohol Review, 23,* 19–29.

International Center for Alcohol Policies (ICAP). (1998). *What is a "standard drink"?* (ICAP Report 5). Washington, DC: Author.

International Center for Alcohol Policies (ICAP). (2003). *International drinking guidelines* (ICAP Report 14). Washington, DC: Author.

International Center for Alcohol Policies (ICAP). (2005a–ongoing). Examples of targeted interventions. In *ICAP Blue Book: Practical guides for alcohol policy and prevention approaches.* Retrieved on March 5, 2009, from http://www.icap.org/Publication/ICAPBlueBook/tabid/148/Default.aspx

International Center for Alcohol Policies (ICAP). (2005b–ongoing). *ICAP Blue Book: Practical guides for alcohol policy and prevention approaches.* Retrieved on March 5, 2009, from http://www.icap.org/Publication/ICAPBlueBook/tabid/148/Default.aspx

International Center for Alcohol Policies (ICAP). (2008). *Informing consumers about beverage alcohol* (ICAP Report 20). Washington, DC: Author.

International Center for Alcohol Policies (ICAP). (2009a). *Industry codes of practice on self-regulation of beverage alcohol advertising.* Washington, DC: Author.

International Center for Alcohol Policies (ICAP). (2009b). *Policy table: International guidelines on drinking during pregnancy.* Retrieved March 8, 2009, from http://www.icap.org/Table/InternationalGuidelinesOn DrinkingandPregnancy

International Center for Alcohol Policies (ICAP). (2009c). *Policy table: Minimum age limits worldwide.* Retrieved March 5, 2009, from http://www.icap.org/Table/MinimumAgeLimitsWorldwide

International Center for Alcohol Policies (ICAP). (2008d). *Policy table: International drinking guidelines.* Retrieved March 5, 2009, from http://www.icap.org/Table/InternationalDrinkingGuidelines

International Center for Alcohol Policies (ICAP) & European Forum for Responsible Drinking (EFRD). (2008a). *Responsible service of alcohol: A server's guide.* Washington, DC: International Center for Alcohol Policies.

International Center for Alcohol Policies (ICAP) & European Forum for Responsible Drinking (EFRD). (2008b). *Responsible service of alcohol: A trainer's guide.* Washington, DC: International Center for Alcohol Policies.

Johnston, L. D., O'Malley, P. M., Bachman, J. G., & Schulenberg, J. E. (2008). *Monitoring the Future national survey results on drug use, 1975–2007. Volume I: Secondary school students.* Bethesda, MD: National Institute on Drug Abuse.

Kalichman, S. C., Simbayi, L. C., Vermaak, R., Jooste, S., & Cain, D. (2008). HIV/AIDS risks among men and women who drink at informal alcohol serving establishments (*shebeens*) in Cape Town, South Africa. *Prevention Science, 9*, 55–62.

Kerr, W. C., Greenfield, T. K., Tujague, J., & Brown, S. E. (2005). A drink is a drink? Variation in the amount of alcohol contained in beer, wine and spirits drinks in a U.S. methodological sample. *Alcoholism: Clinical and Experimental Research, 29*, 2015–2021.

Kerr, W. C., Patterson, D., Koenen, M. A., & Greenfield, T. K. (2008). Alcohol content variation of bar and restaurant drinks in northern California. *Alcoholism: Clinical and Experimental Research, 32*, 1623–1629.

Kumpfer, K. L., Alvarado, R., Tait, C., & Turner, C. (2002). Effectiveness of school-based family and children's skills training for substance abuse prevention among 6–8-year-old rural children. *Psychology of Addictive Behaviors, 16*(Suppl. 4), S65–S71.

Kumpfer, K. L., Alvarado, R., & Whiteside, H. O. (2003). Family-based interventions for substance use and misuse prevention. *Substance Use and Misuse, 38*, 1759–1787.

Kypri, K., Langley, J. D., Saunders, J. B., Cashell-Smith, M. L., & Herbison, P. (2008). Randomized controlled trial of web-based alcohol screening and brief intervention in primary care. *Archives of Internal Medicine, 168*, 530–536.

Kypri, K., McManus, A., Howat, P. M., Maycock, B. R., Hallett, J. D., & Chikritzhs, T. H. (2007). Ingredient and nutrition information labelling of alcoholic beverages: Do consumers want it? *Medical Journal of Australia, 187*, 669.

Kypri, K., Stephenson, S., Langley, J., Cashell-Smith, M., Saunders, J., & Russell, D. (2005). Computerised screening for hazardous drinking in primary care. *New Zealand Medical Journal, 118*, U1703.

Larimer, M. E., Cronce, J. M., Lee, C. M., & Kilmer, J. R. (2004). Brief intervention in college settings. *Alcohol Research and Health, 28*, 94–104.

Lubman, D. I., Hides, L., Yucel, M., & Toumbourou, J. W. (2007). Intervening early to reduce developmentally harmful substance use among youth populations. *Medical Journal of Australia, 187*(Suppl. 7), S22–S25.

Marlatt, G. A. (Ed.). (1998). *Harm reduction: Pragmatic strategies for managing high-risk behaviors*. New York: Guilford Press.

Marshall, M. (Ed.). (1979). *Beliefs, behaviors, and alcoholic beverages: A cross-cultural survey*. Ann Arbor: University of Michigan Press.

Martinic, M., & Measham, F. (Eds.). (2008). *Swimming with crocodiles: The culture of extreme drinking*. New York: Routledge.

Martinic, M., Tamendarova, D., & Houghton, E. (2005). Alcohol education. In M. Grant & J. O'Connor (Eds.), *Corporate social responsibility and alcohol: The need and potential for partnership* (pp. 151–175). New York: Routledge.

Masten, A. S., Faden, V. B., Zucker, R. A., & Spear, L. P. (2008). Underage drinking: A developmental framework. *Pediatrics, 121*(Suppl. 4), S235–S251.

Mattern, J. L., & Neighbors, C. (2004). Social norms campaigns: Examining the relationship between changes in perceived norms and changes in drinking levels. *Journal of Studies on Alcohol, 65*, 489–493.

McCammon, K. (2001). Alcohol-related motor vehicle crashes: Deterrence and intervention. *Annals of Emergency Medicine, 38*, 415–422.

Morojele, N. K., Kachieng'a, M. A., Mokoko, E., Nkoko, M. A., Parry, C. D., Nkowane, A. M., et al. (2006). Alcohol use and sexual behaviour among risky drinkers and bar and *shebeen* patrons in Gauteng province, South Africa. *Social Science and Medicine, 62*, 217–227.

Nayak, M. B., Kerr, W., Greenfield, T. K., & Pillai, A. (2008). Not all drinks are created equal: Implications for alcohol assessment in India. *Alcohol and Alcoholism, 43*, 713–718.

Paine, A., & Davan, A. D. (2001). Defining a tolerable concentration of methanol in alcoholic drinks. *Human and Experimental Toxicology, 20*, 563–668.

Papas, R. K., Sidle, J. E., Wamalwa, E. S., Okumu, T. O., Bryant, K. I., Goulet, J. L., et al. (2008). Estimating alcohol content of traditional brew in western Kenya using culturally relevant methods: The case for cost over volume. *AIDS and Behavior* [OnlineFirst]. Retrieved July 7, 2009, from http://www.springerlink.com/content/m73xuj000nn57x04/

Perkins, H. W. (Ed.). (2003). *Social norms approach to preventing school and college age substance abuse: A handbook for educators, counselors, and clinicians.* San Francisco: Jossey–Bass.

Perkins, H. W., & Craig, D. W. (2002). *A multifaceted social norms approach to high-risk drinking: Lessons from Hobart and William Smith Colleges.* Newton, MA: Higher Education Center for Alcohol and Other Drug Prevention.

Pernod Ricard. (2009). *Raising awareness among pregnant women.* Retrieved March 5, 2009, from http://www.pernod-ricard.com/en/pages/2844/pernod/Corporate-responsibility/Responsible-consumption/Raising-awareness-among-pregnant-women.html

Plant, M., Single, E., & Stockwell, T. (Eds.). (1997). *Alcohol: Minimising the harm.* London: Free Association Press.

Portman Group. (2009). *Proof of age scheme.* Retrieved on 5 March 2009 from http://www.portman-group.org.uk/

Reid, R. J., Hughey, J., & Peterson, N. A. (2003). Generalizing the alcohol outlet-assaultive violence link: Evidence from a U.S. Midwestern city. *Substance Use and Misuse, 38*, 1971–1982.

Roman, P., & Blum, T. (2002). The workplace and alcohol prevention. *Alcohol Research and Health, 26*, 49–57.

Saitz, R., Helmuth, E. D., Aromaa, S. E., Guard, A., Belanger, M., & Rosenbloom, D. L. (2004). Web-based screening and brief intervention for the spectrum of alcohol problems. *Prevention Medicine, 39*, 969–975.

Saitz, R., Sullivan, L. M., & Samet, J. H. (2000). Training community-based clinicians in screening and brief intervention for substance abuse problems: Translating evidence into practice. *Substance Abuse, 21*, 21–31.

Saunders, J. B., Kypri, K., Walters, S. T., Laforge, R. G., & Larimer, M. E. (2004). Approaches to brief intervention for hazardous drinking in young people. *Alcoholism: Clinical Experimental Research, 28*, 322–329.

Semple, S. J., Patterson, T. L., & Grant, I. (2003). HIV-positive gay and bisexual men: predictors of unsafe sex. *AIDS Care, 15*, 3–15.

Sloan, F. A., Stout, E. M., Whetten-Goldstein, K., & Liand, L. (2000). *Drinkers, drivers, and bartenders. Balancing private choices and public accountability.* Chicago: University of Chicago Press.

Sorocco, K. H., & Ferrell, S. W. (2006). Alcohol use among older adults. *Journal of General Psychology, 133*, 453–467.

Spear, L. P. (2002). Alcohol's effects on adolescents. *Alcohol Research and Health, 26*, 287–291.

Spear, L. P., & Varlinskaya, E. I. (2005). Adolescence: Alcohol sensitivity, tolerance, and intake. *Recent Developments in Alcoholism, 17*, 143–159.

Stimson, G., Grant, M., Choquet, M., & Garrison, P. (Eds.). (2007). *Drinking in context: Patterns, interventions, and partnerships.* New York: Routledge.

Stockwell, T. (2001). Responsible alcohol service: Lessons from evaluations of servers training and policing initiatives. *Drug and Alcohol Review, 20*, 257–265.

Stockwell, T., Blaze-Temple, D., & Walker, C. (1991). The effect of "standard drink" labelling on the ability of drinkers to pour a "standard drink." *Australian Journal of Public Health, 15*, 56–63.

Stockwell, T., & Single, E. (1997). Standard unit labelling of alcohol containers. In M. Plant, E. Single, & T. Stockwell (Eds.), *Alcohol: Minimising the harm. What works?* (pp. 85–104). London: Free Association Books.

Thom, B., & Bayley, M. (2007). *Multi-component programmes.* York, U.K.: Joseph Rowntree Foundation.

Treno, A. J., Grube, J. W., & Martin, S. E. (2003). Alcohol availability as a predictor of youth drinking and driving: A hierarchical analysis of survey and archival data. *Alcoholism: Clinical and Experimental Research, 27*, 835–840.

Varlinskaya, E. I., & Spear, L. P. (2004). Changes in sensitivity to ethanol-induced social facilitation and social inhibition from early to late adolescence. *Annals of the New York Academy of Sciences, 1021*, 459–461.

Weir, S. S., Pailman, C., Mahlalela, X., Coetzee, N., Meidany, F., & Boerma, J. T. (2003). From people to places: Focusing AIDS prevention efforts where it matters most. *AIDS, 17*, 895–903.

Weitzman, E. R., Folkman, A., Folkman, M. P., & Wechsler, H. (2003). The relationship of alcohol outlet density to heavy and frequent drinking and drinking-related problems among college students at eight universities. *Health Place, 9*, 1–6.

Windle, M., Spear, L. P., Fuligni, A. J., Angold, A., Brown, J. D., Pine, D., et al. (2008). Transitions into underage and problem drinking: Developmental processes and mechanisms between 10 and 15 years of age. *Pediatrics, 121*(Suppl. 4), S273–S289.

World Health Organization (WHO). (2004). *Global status report on alcohol.* Geneva, Switzerland: Author.

Worldwide Brewing Alliance (WBA). (2007). *Global social responsibility initiatives.* London: British Beer and Pub Association.

Zunino, H., Litvak, J., & Israel, Y. (1998). Public and private partnerships in prevention and research: IV. The case of the College of Pharmacy, University of Chile. In M. Grant & J. Litvak (Eds.), *Drinking patterns and their consequences* (pp. 282–285). Washington, DC: Taylor & Francis.

8
WORKING TOGETHER

BRETT BIVANS AND JOHN ORLEY

Introduction

There is growing international recognition of the importance of building and strengthening relationships among governments, non-governmental organizations (NGOs), the private sector, and others to address complex social issues. Research has demonstrated the effectiveness and efficiency of such interactions at international, national, and local levels (Donahue & Zeckhauser, 2006; Nelson, 2002; Nelson & Zadek, 2000; Reinicke, 1998). They can enhance the provision of goods and services and offer innovative solutions to myriad social, economic, and environmental challenges. This chapter presents a framework for how different sectors, including the industry, can work together in the alcohol field. The case studies, featured throughout the text, highlight the wide range of areas where joint efforts have made a contribution to reducing harmful drinking.

Working Together to Reduce Harmful Drinking

Governments and society have high expectations that the beverage alcohol industry is seriously active in helping combat the misuse of its products. The International Center for Alcohol Policies (ICAP) sponsor companies believe that a systematic integration of corporate social responsibility (CSR) into their business practices makes a positive impact on their economic, social, and environmental performance (Grant & O'Connor, 2005). The CSR framework provides an enabling environment for collaboration among sectors. Successful collaborations involve a range of skills and determination to follow key steps that will enhance the quality of these endeavors (International Center for Alcohol Policies [ICAP], 2002a, 2002b, 2008).

The broad range of possible interventions to target harmful drinking will necessarily involve an equally broad range of stakeholders in their implementation. Historically, beverage alcohol producers have partnered on and funded many such programs. These initiatives are highlighted on a regular basis in annual corporate reports as well as in company reporting on corporate citizenship, CSR, and sustainability. ICAP and many of its sponsor companies are members of the United Nations (UN) Global Compact, a voluntary initiative launched in 2000 by UN Secretary-General Kofi Annan. By reporting their accomplishments on the UN website, Global Compact members seek to advance responsible corporate citizenship and to enhance the role business plays in responding to social, economic, and environmental concerns.

Dimensions of Working Together

There are many shapes and contexts for what we term in this book "working together." Collaborations are influenced by the various roles and responsibilities undertaken by the stakeholders of a joint activity. Despite considerable diversity, a number of prerequisites and values underpin effective and sustainable collaboration, particularly embracing inclusivity and shared values.

Embracing Inclusivity

Development and implementation of alcohol policies, as well as monitoring their outcomes, are enhanced by a broad-based involvement of stakeholders. Inclusion of all relevant sectors is a critical feature of effective engagement in the beverage alcohol field. Sustainable policy approaches rely on consultation and collaboration among the following stakeholders: government at the regional, national, and local levels; intergovernmental organizations; the private sector; NGOs and the civil society; healthcare professionals; researchers; and the media (Orley & Logan, 2005). There are many levels of inclusivity, just as there are many roles for stakeholders. The critical feature of effective engagement is the recognition of the interdependence of many actors with a shared purpose, accountability, and a real stake in the success or failure of addressing the issues. The beverage alcohol industry—not only producers but also retailers and the hospitality sectors—has a legitimate interest and contribution to make in the alcohol policy arena (see Chapter 1).

Shared Values

The goal of working together must rely on basic core values. Is there sufficient understanding, trust, and mutual interest for government and business to combine forces in the delivery of policies and programs to reduce harmful drinking in ways that balance the public and private interests? The guidelines of the World Health Organization (WHO) (2000) for interaction with commercial enterprises characterize the general principles of partnership as mutual respect, trust, transparency, and shared benefits. When all stakeholders apply these four principles to the area of reducing harmful drinking, there exists the greatest potential for impact (Grant, 2005).

Models for Working Together

In this chapter, we highlight the validity of all sectors working together in pursuit of common goals. However, considerable effort is still required from stakeholders to move from an abstract desirability of collaboration to putting it into practice. The following five models present a scale for describing various levels of multi-sector engagement. This section showcases the key areas in which working together has led to the delivery of innovative programs and creative solutions. These initiatives are examples of the types of interventions that beverage alcohol members are already doing and that they are willing to replicate, scale up, and help adapt to different national, religious, and cultural contexts. The topics included are by no means exhaustive of the areas in which industry can be involved. On the contrary, industry invites an innovative approach, much needed to enhance feasible and effective pathways to promoting responsible drinking.

Model 1: Identifying and Sharing Best Practice

The simplest form of working together involves identifying and sharing best practice among stakeholders. In this model, the key feature is the public exchange of knowledge and ideas for strengthening programs that can contribute to promoting responsible drinking and reducing potential harm.

BEST PRACTICE IN SELF-REGULATION

Following a meeting organized in 2003 by WHO with representatives of the alcohol industry, ICAP convened a series of workshops to exchange best practice on self-regulation in advertising and marketing of beverage alcohol (ICAP, 2004, 2006a, 2006b, 2007). As self-regulation takes different forms in different markets—appropriately reflecting the many ways in which alcohol is regulated, sold, and consumed in diverse cultures—in addition to a global workshop in 2004, regional workshops were held in 2006 and 2007 in Africa (Cape Town, South Africa), Asia-Pacific (Tokyo, Japan), and Latin America (Santiago, Chile). The workshops afforded opportunities for industry to interact with a wide range of stakeholders, from self-regulatory bodies and advertisers to governments and public health experts, and included observers from intergovernmental organizations.

COMMON THEMES

The main themes that emerged during the workshops should be considered in light of the varying cultural and regulatory environments in the three regions. Six common issues were identified, however, as central to strengthening self-regulation.

1. **Leadership.** Leadership from the most senior levels of company management was seen as an important success factor in implementing companywide standards on self-regulation and codes of practice.
2. **Comprehensive Coverage.** To be effective, the self-regulatory systems must cover all aspects of alcohol

marketing, including packaging, promotion, and the new media.

3. **Compliance With Regulation.** Given the considerable variation in the scope and complexity of government regulation, codes need to be cognizant of the different legislative contexts. Close communication between government and industry is necessary to establish the place of self-regulation in the regulatory mix.

4. **Training.** A system of training on applying codes of practice and existing regulation is required for company employees responsible for marketing and promotions. Regular refresher courses are essential given the high staff turnover and the frequent changes in the regulatory environment.

5. **Recognition of Cultural Differences.** Sensitivity to the local context is an important factor in the way companies are perceived as good corporate citizens, both in developed and developing markets. While there has been some movement toward consistency at an international level among existing codes, there are important local differences that require specific consideration. Examples of such differences include issues of taste, custom, culture, and religion, which can vary significantly from country to country. Companywide codes set a minimum standard—often quite high—but where stricter provisions are mandated locally, either because of cultural considerations or existing legislation, the more rigorous provisions take precedence.

6. **Copy Advice, Prevetting, and Internal Reviews.** Thorough reviews of proposed marketing initiatives, applied at appropriate stages during the creative and design processes, can aid an effective and efficient implementation of a company's codes of practice, in terms of both the letter and the spirit of the particular code. Existence of a sound system of reviews contributes to the

credibility of self-regulatory systems. In many contexts, such reviews give marketers and advertisers the benefit of advice and input from a wider perspective, both from within and outside the company. Reviews or prevetting can reduce the potential for public concern and lower costs associated with changing or removing promotions deemed to be in breach of self-regulatory codes.

REGIONAL THEMES

While emphasizing the differences among regions, ICAP's regional workshops highlighted the need to improve understanding of self-regulation and to strengthen implementation of self-regulatory systems internationally, regionally, and locally. At the end of each workshop in Africa, Asia-Pacific, and Latin America, participants endorsed joint statements that recognized their collective responsibility to improve the scope and the effectiveness of self-regulation through collaboration with other stakeholders. There was a general consensus that it is important for all sectors of the beverage alcohol industry to participate in effective self-regulatory systems, and that such systems must reflect different market, cultural, and regional circumstances.

FUTURE DIALOGUE

The value of these international and regional workshops lies in the opportunity to share best practice and establish commitments from a range of stakeholders whose involvement is crucial for a well-functioning self-regulatory system. The identification of areas of ongoing concern in relation to alcohol marketing by the healthcare professionals was a significant contribution to the workshops. Industry representatives acknowledged the benefit of getting a clear understanding of the issues that are likely to have most impact on the regulatory environment. The public sector participants noted the high level of industry activity to strengthen existing codes. Monitoring the efficacy of self-regulation is as important to the industry as it is to governments and the public health community. The workshops helped document recent advances in this area. Furthermore, there was an enthusiasm for continued multi-sector engagement on a more frequent and targeted basis.

Model 2: Developing and Implementing Codes of Practice

At the next level of collaboration, stakeholders contribute to developing and implementing codes of practice. This approach can involve any mix of actors from various companies and sectors participating in a joint activity. Here, competitors work together to compose and follow rules that will govern their activities in an arena where they exercise influence.

BEER PROMOTERS IN CAMBODIA

Sale of beverage alcohol by female beer promoters (BPs) is a common and accepted practice in many countries, particularly in Asia (International Labour Organization [ILO], 2006). Women are recruited to promote and sell specific brands of alcohol beverages in bars, nightclubs, and restaurants. In essence, these women are waitresses dressed in the colors and logos of a particular alcohol brand. Surveys indicate that BPs are typically young—starting such work between 18 and 21 years of age—and come from households that rely on agriculture as the main family activity (ILO, 2006). BPs tend to live separately from their families and supplement the families' income; some portion of their salaries is frequently based on commission calculated as a percentage of sales. These young women are often presumed by bar patrons to be indirect sex workers and can thus be exposed to sexual harassment, aggression, and violence, both at the workplace and in the community. BPs may also feel pressured to drink with patrons, particularly in establishments where health and safety provisions are weak.

Following a benchmark study in 2003 (Quinn, 2003), local and international stakeholders began working together to develop standards to protect and improve the status and wellbeing of BPs. The recommendations from the study were incorporated into CARE International's collaboration with Heineken, Asia Pacific Breweries, and Cambodia Breweries. The implementation of the Selling Beer Safely—a Cambodian Women's Health Initiative from 2003 to 2005 explored the key issues that affect the safety and protection of BPs and highlighted the need to develop an industry code of practice.

Selling Beer Safely provided training and support for BPs, with an objective to equip them with the skills necessary to manage difficult customers and remain in control. The program emphasized three areas:

- **Work organization**, addressing such issues as interaction with supervisors, transportation, skill levels, provision of counseling, hygiene, and uniforms
- **Information, instruction, and training** on such topics as selling beer, personal health and safety, alcohol and its effect on the body, and appropriate behavior in dealing with customers
- **Human resources (HR) issues**, including hiring practices, contracts, working conditions, safety, medical care, and privacy

The initiative demonstrated the breweries' commitment to improving health and general wellbeing of BPs.

RULES AND GUIDELINES FOR BEER PROMOTERS IN CAMBODIA

Building on the successful implementation of the Selling Beer Safely program, alcohol companies in Cambodia have advocated for continued industrywide work on BPs. Heineken took the lead in creating Beer Selling Industry Cambodia (BSIC), a membership organization of national and international brewers and beer distributors. BSIC's code of practice emphasizes the occupational health and safety issues of BPs to organization members, outlet owners, and consumers. The code's objectives are to improve the health, safety, and working conditions of BPs by setting industry standards in seven broad areas: employment status, work organization, uniform, transportation, training and information, harassment, and drinking behavior.

1. **Employment Status.** The code stresses that BPs' employment status must comply with the Cambodian Labor Law (National Assembly of the Kingdom of Cambodia, 1997). Regardless of whether they are casual workers, part-time employees, or full-time staff, BPs must have a transparent, written contract and receive a copy of this contract from their employer; they should also receive a fixed monthly base salary and be remunerated in accordance with the Cambodian rules and regulations. Incentive systems can be put in place in addition to the base salary, but this should be done in such a way that it avoids unhealthy or unsafe situations. BSIC rejects commission-only work.

2. **Work Organization.** BPs should have, and be clearly informed about, a supervisor. Procedures must be in place for BPs to express any grievances in relation to their work. This includes the use of a database to register all grievances.

3. **Uniform.** BPs who sell BSIC member products should receive company-branded uniforms or sashes so that they are clearly visible and identifiable as workers selling or promoting beer. BPs who are off duty should not wear the uniform. Uniforms must be decent, taking into account the input from the BPs themselves.

4. **Transportation.** The employer should ensure transportation from the venue to a BP's home, including if she lives in a rural area. This will minimize the risk of

BPs being harassed on their way home. They should be offered and encouraged to use the company transport.

5. **Training and Information.** All BSIC members should offer a standard and comprehensive training package to BPs as part of the orientation training, focusing on the following topics: managing difficult customers; alcohol consumption and drug use; workplace harassment; relationships between men and women and healthy gender roles; healthcare options; and sexual and reproductive health, including information about contraception methods and sexually transmitted infections (e.g., HIV/ AIDS). Refresher training is to be implemented at least once a year.

6. **Harassment.** BSIC declares a zero-tolerance approach with respect to abuse and sexual harassment of BPs. All BSIC members are to develop and implement company policies against sexual harassment for staff as a part of personnel contracts and codes of conduct. Policies should be clearly communicated to employees, and sufficient training is to be provided to emphasize that sexual harassment will not be tolerated. Sanctions must be taken if rules are broken.

7. **Drinking Behavior.** BSIC acknowledges that many BPs may be pressured to drink to support their sales or to please the customer. It is the organization's policy that, during working hours, BPs should not sit or drink with customers. All BSIC members should inform their employees about this rule and train BPs to refuse offers of a drink and take appropriate steps if they are being forced to consume alcohol.

MONITORING, TRAINING TOOLS, AND SUPPORT

Local NGOs monitor and evaluate compliance with the BSIC code on a regular basis. Beverage alcohol producers who are BSIC members are required to inform their distributors about the code, supervise and monitor their compliance, and take action if the distributor does not comply with the code.

Training for BPs has been developed in cooperation with several NGOs, of which CARE International is the prominent partner in Cambodia. These NGOs have experience in working with women on a range of issues, such as reproductive and sexual health, gender, life skills, women's empowerment, labor rights, and alcohol consumption. Collaboration with government agencies (e.g., the ministries of labor, interior, commerce, and women's affairs) contributes to enhancing best practice approaches throughout the country.

Model 3: Providing Resources to Develop and Implement Programs

The beverage alcohol industry can also provide resources that other stakeholders can use to develop and implement independent programs. By supporting independent organizations, the industry helps leverage the knowledge and access these organizations have to groups and individuals at risk for harm.

STRENGTHENING FAMILIES PROGRAM

The Strengthening Families Program: For Parents and Youth 10–14 (SFP 10–14) is designed to reduce substance use and other problematic behaviors in children aged 10 to 14 years. The primary author of SFP 10–14 is Dr. Virginia Molgaard, a research scientist at the Institute for Social and Behavioral Research (ISBR) at Iowa State University (USA). SFP 10–14 resulted from a major revision of the original Strengthening Families Program developed by Dr. Karol Kumpfer and colleagues at the University of Utah, with funding from the U.S. National Institute on Drug Abuse (NIDA), part of the National Institutes of Health (NIH). In the United States (U.S.), a Spanish language version, El Programa Familias Fuertes, has been developed and supported by the Pan American Health Organization (PAHO) and international development agencies.

SFP 10–14 COMPONENTS

SFP 10–14 is delivered through parent, family, and youth sessions using narrated videos that portray typical situations related to alcohol and drugs. Sessions are highly interactive and include role-playing, discussions, learning games, and family projects designed to improve parenting skills, build life skills in children, and strengthen family bonds. Youth sessions help children develop the skills necessary for managing stress and strong emotions, effective communication and goal setting, responsible behavior, and dealing with peer pressure. Youth booster sessions focus on making good friends, handling conflict, and reinforcing skills learned earlier. Parent and family sessions discuss the importance of both nurturing children and setting rules as well as monitoring compliance and applying appropriate discipline. Specific topics include making house rules, following up with consequences, encouraging good behavior, building bridges, and protecting children against alcohol and drug use. Booster sessions focus on handling parents' stress, communicating when partners do not agree, and reinforcing earlier skills training.

SFP 10–14 IN EUROPE

A large program of research is now under way to bring SFP 10–14 to a number of European countries, with support from governments, universities, charities, and industry. For example, the Alcohol Education and Research Council (AERC), the Home Office, and Diageo Great Britain are funding a project to adapt, test, and pilot the program in the United Kingdom (U.K.). Starting in 2007, the Maraton Foundation, supported by Diageo Great Britain, has been working on adapting SFP 10–14 for Poland. In Spain, the program is being developed by the Addictive Behavior Group at the University of Oviedo and was financed initially by the Spanish National Plan on Drugs and, subsequently, by the Spanish Psychological Association, with support from Diageo España. In Greece, SFP 10–14 is being adapted and tested by the National and Kapodistrian University of Athens, with support from Diageo Hellas. In all these countries, the intention is to carry out a rigorous assessment to check whether the European versions of the program have the same effects as the American original. All the academic institutions involved are receiving advice and support from Oxford Brookes University, which led the work to adapt SFP 10–14 for the United Kingdom.

IMPACT OF SFP 10–14

The SFP 10–14 program has been rigorously tested and highlighted in an International Cochrane Collaboration systematic evidence review, funded by WHO and AERC. The Cochrane review pointed to the program's potential for preventing substance use and other problematic behavior in young people (Foxcroft, Ireland, Lowe, & Breen, 2002). Evaluation highlighted the following:

- Children attending SFP 10–14 demonstrated significantly lower rates of alcohol, tobacco, and marijuana use and fewer conduct problems in school compared to their peers who did not attend the program (the control group).
- The differences between program and control young people actually increased over time, indicating that skills learned and strong parent-child relationships continued to have positive influence over the years.
- Adult SFP participants showed gains in specific skills, such as setting appropriate and consistent limits, monitoring children, and building a positive parent-child relationship.

Further information about the program and its application in different countries is available at http://www.mystrongfamily.org/.

Model 4: Developing and Implementing Programs

The next level of working together moves toward a closer collaboration between industry and other stakeholders: The industry is a direct participant in the development and implementation of programs. This model may be particularly suited for areas with close links to the industry's business interests.

RESPONSIBLE HOSPITALITY

Hospitality is the art and science of creating space for people to socialize. Many people enjoy beer, wine, and spirits as part of socializing, while others choose to abstain from alcohol. Responsible hospitality measures have been useful in creating safe and comfortable drinking venues (Homel, Carvolth, Hauritz, McIlwain, & Teague, 2004; Quigley, Leonard, & Collins, 2003). The objective of such measures is to ensure that risk for harm to individuals is minimized while safeguarding the quality of life in the surrounding community. As a policy approach, responsible hospitality hinges on the involvement of those who operate alcohol-serving establishments, those who enforce the existing laws, and the community as a whole (see Chapter 6; see also Saltz & Stanghetta, 1997; Smith, Wiggers, Considine, Daly, & Collins, 2001; Stockwell, 2001; Turrisi, Nicholson, & Jaccard, 1999).

Many alcohol-serving establishments train their staff—servers and security personnel—in handling drunk patrons, liability issues, and using server judgment to prevent such incidents as alcohol-impaired driving (Burns, Nusbaumer, & Reiling, 2003; Johnsson & Berglund, 2003; Single, 1990; Sloan, Stout, Whetten-Goldstein, & Liand, 2000; Stockwell, 2001). Other practices that have complemented server training include the provision of alternate means of transportation for patrons who may no longer be fit to drive or incentives for individuals willing to refrain from drinking alcohol and act as "designated drivers" (Dresser & Gliksman, 1998). Where the minimum drinking age limit is set, servers and other personnel may also be trained to enforce these laws, requesting identification from patrons and refusing service to minors (Freisthler, Gruenewald, Treno, & Lee, 2003; Toomey et al., 1998; Wagenaar et al., 1996).

TRAINING FOR INTERVENTION PROCEDURES (TIPS)

In 1982, Dr. Morris Chafetz, the founding director of the U.S. National Institute on Alcoholism and Alcohol Abuse (NIAAA), developed the first Training for Intervention Procedures (TIPS) program with support from the beverage alcohol industry. TIPS is an interactive, skills-based learning tool designed to prevent intoxication, alcohol-impaired driving, and underage drinking by enhancing the fundamental "people skills" of servers, sellers, and consumers of alcohol. Initially developed for on-premise establishments (e.g., restaurants, bars, cafés, and nightclubs), TIPS was later expanded to include off-premise retail outlets and provide targeted training for special venues (TIPS for Concessions and TIPS for Gaming) and consumer groups (TIPS for the University, TIPS for Seniors, and TIPS for the Workplace). In over 25 years, TIPS has certified over 3 million servers and has been offered across the United States and in more than 30 countries worldwide.

The program includes a robust record-keeping system to verify training and certification. Working with clients, TIPS assists in developing model venue policies and internal procedures for reducing risks. The tangible benefits of such training include insurance discounts for liquor liability premiums, legal recognition as a good practice standard, a professional staff, and more satisfied customers.

TIPS Training

TIPS sessions vary in length from 2 to 5 hours. They can be administered by a certified trainer or through eTIPS, an online training program. The former employs video and printed materials to facilitate discussion of the course content; the material is presented in three sections: information, skills training, and practice/rehearsal.

1. **Information.** The training may begin with a video presentation, followed by a discussion to cover basic information about alcohol, its effects, and effective intervention strategies. Some of the topics include behavioral cues (visible progressive signs of intoxication); blood alcohol concentration (BAC); alcohol metabolism and factors that influence it; effective intervention strategies for servers; checking for age (specifying proper formats of identification and how to check their authenticity); relevant legislation; server liability (instances when servers can be held responsible for alcohol-related problems in patrons); and proper documentation (the importance of keeping an incident log of alcohol-related situations).

2. **Skills Training.** Once the information is provided, the program participants try to put it to use. Through role-playing exercises, they demonstrate their ability to intervene effectively in difficult alcohol-related situations using the guidelines and strategies they have learned. The participants are encouraged to use past experiences for the exercise or choose a sample situation from the manual. This section is presented in two parts: evaluating cues (learning to determine intoxication levels for customers and guests) and evaluating responses (determining the effectiveness of server response as portrayed in the course video).

3. **Practice/Rehearsal.** After the skills training segment, the participants receive feedback from both the certified trainer and their classmates on the intervention techniques they used; this is to help them discover and develop their own skills and confidence to intervene with customers. The participants thus demonstrate their ability to use the information and skills learned in the program and receive immediate feedback on their effectiveness.

Impact of TIPS

TIPS has been reviewed, particularly in the university setting, with the following results:

- The Center for Studies on Alcohol, an independent research organization working with NIAAA, has reported a 20% reduction in risky drinking behavior within the first year of implementing TIPS among students at fraternities, male student organizations in the United States and Canada that traditionally report high levels of heavy drinking (Caudill et al., 2007).
- A private U.S. university in Decatur, Illinois, credited TIPS training for a 55% reduction in alcohol violations from 2000 to 2003. As a result, the school now mandates that all first-year students go through TIPS training as part of their orientation.
- Beginning in the fall semester of 2001, Millikin University committed to training all of its incoming freshmen with TIPS. The university received donations from local alcohol-selling establishments, student housing centers, and an Anheuser-Busch wholesaler. Benefits, as measured by the university, included a reduction in disciplinary referrals related to harmful drinking by students. Ninety-three percent of students said that, after receiving TIPS training, they felt comfortable intervening with a peer who was intoxicated.

Model 5: Partnership

The highest level of working together describes what is appropriately termed "partnership." Real partnership can be transformational. It embraces new mindsets, overcomes polarization, and delivers mutually beneficial impact and relationships. Thus, partnership can result in service that otherwise would not be provided, reach populations otherwise not served, help generate new knowledge and innovation, empower individuals and organizations, and reinforce the wellbeing of society. While polarizing points of view create more fragmentation, partnership can help bridge those gaps and provide tools to better meet community needs.

ROAD TRAFFIC SAFETY

The *World Report on Road Traffic Injury Prevention* (Peden et al., 2004) indicates that the number of people killed in road crashes worldwide amounts to more than 1 million each year; as many as 50 million people are injured. Low- and middle-income countries account for about 85% of all road traffic deaths. Road crashes have a disproportionate impact on the poor, who have limited access to emergency care and often face long-term medical costs and loss of income that can push families into poverty. While it is anticipated that road traffic deaths will decline in high-income countries between 2000 and 2020, they are projected to rise significantly in low- and middle-income countries over the same period. Road crashes therefore are not only a problem for the transport sector but also a global public health, development, and equity issue.

The *World Report* (Peden et al., 2004) identified six recommendations that should guide national road safety programs: (1) identify a lead agency in government to guide the national road safety effort; (2) assess policies and institutional settings related to road traffic injury and the capacity for road traffic injury prevention in each country; (3) prepare a national road safety strategy and plan of action; (4) allocate financial and human resources to address the problem; (5) implement specific actions to prevent road traffic crashes, minimize injuries and their consequences, and evaluate the impact of these actions; and (6) support the development of national capacity and international cooperation. Low- and middle-income countries that lack sufficient resources to implement the recommendations are encouraged to seek partnerships with international organizations and other relevant entities, including the private sector.

GLOBAL ROAD SAFETY PARTNERSHIP

The Global Road Safety Partnership (GRSP), initiated by the World Bank in 1999, brings together business, civil society, and governmental organizations to improve road safety conditions around the world. The International Federation of Red Cross and Red Crescent Societies hosts the GRSP Secretariat at its headquarters in Geneva, Switzerland; over 200 organizations have participated in GRSP and contributed to its activities.

Today, it is widely acknowledged that many sectors have a role to play in the prevention of crashes, deaths, and injuries. GRSP facilitates collaboration among these sectors globally, nationally, and locally to help create sustainable partnerships and implement effective road safety programs. It shares knowledge, provides advice on good practice, and implements projects in a growing number of countries.

ALCOHOL-IMPAIRED DRIVING

Alcohol impairment, both by drivers and pedestrians, is acknowledged as an important contributing cause of road traffic injuries, identified as one of the "critical risk factors" in the *World Report* (Peden et al., 2004). The alcohol industry's involvement in road safety generally, and combating impaired driving in particular, has been extensive, global, and long running (European Forum for Responsible Drinking [EFRD], 2008; Worldwide Brewing Alliance [WBA], 2007).

ICAP is a founding member of GRSP, and ICAP staff contributed to the development of *Drinking and Driving: A Road Safety Manual for Decision-makers and Practitioners*, produced by GRSP (2007) under the UN Road Safety Collaboration. With its sponsors, ICAP supports the recommendations of the *World Report* (Peden et al., 2004) and the *Drinking and Driving* manual. Industry members are already making positive contributions that build on the recommendations (EFRD, 2008; WBA, 2007), including the following:

- public awareness campaigns—advertisements and messages by government, public health, and private sector organizations about the effects of alcohol on driving
- designated driver campaigns and programs
- ride-share/free-taxi or taxi-call programs—schemes organized in collaborations with local government to provide alternative transportation for those who have been drinking
- server training and responsible hospitality programs
- support for setting maximum BAC limits for driving, public awareness campaigns about these limits, and collaboration with local authorities to improve enforcement
- development of national alcohol policies and plans of action

There is considerable scope for these programs to be improved. Industry members are keen to develop their actions further and to explore increasing collaboration with governments, the public health community, and others involved in road safety.

RESULTS OF THE PARTNERSHIP

In 2002, PricewaterhouseCoopers conducted an evaluation of GRSP and other partnership programs initiated by the World Bank and highlighted the process of engagement with the private sector in social development issues. In 2004, the Norwegian Institute of Transport Economics (Transportøkonomisk institutt, TØI) evaluated GRSP on behalf of the Swedish International Development Cooperation Agency (SIDA). The TØI evaluation concluded that GRSP had largely met its partnership objectives with regard to relevance of activities, effectiveness, efficiency, impact, and sustainability.

1. **Relevance.** In the 10 years since its inception, GRSP has become a global leader in road safety and is delivering innovation and new resources to address a significant

health and development issue through partnership with a wide range of stakeholders, including the private sector.

2. **Effectiveness.** Through targeted work in focus countries and implementation of good practice, GSRP contributes to the reduction of road traffic casualties in both developing and transition countries.

3. **Efficiency.** The efficiency of the GRSP approach can be measured by the leverage of additional resources committed to road safety in low- and middle-income countries during the years of GRSP's existence. Current direct funding of GRSP is on the order of USD 6 million per year, and leveraged funding (funds raised by others but used by GRSP programs) is approximately three-fold.

4. **Impact.** In the face of rapid growth in motorization in low- and middle-income countries, GRSP is facing a mounting tide. Yet, GRSP and its partners can point proudly not only to raising awareness about the crisis but also to new programs, standards, and, in some areas, improved safety. Going forward, growing reliance on evaluation of projects and assistance to governments and other partners in this respect will improve GRSP's ability to target those at risk.

5. **Sustainability.** At the global level, GRSP has a professional secretariat and sound relations with contributing partners. Few international initiatives, particularly in relatively new areas such as road traffic safety, can match the scope and strength of country-level activities that GRSP has achieved over its 10-year history.

As a further indication of GRSP's unparalleled track record of facilitating road safety partnerships, a 5-year (2005–2009), USD 10 million program—the Global Road Safety Initiative (GRSI)—was established by seven large automotive and oil companies (Ford, General Motors, Honda, Michelin, Renault, Shell, and Toyota). GRSI chose GRSP to implement a program of work to promote good practice guides on key risk factors for road safety—helmet wearing, seat belts, speed management, and alcohol-impaired driving. The purpose of this initiative is to establish regional "centers of excellence" to deliver training in the application of good practice and implementation of road safety projects in collaboration with governments, donor agencies, the private sector, and the civil society. The success of GRSP initiatives emphasizes again the multidimensional nature of the road safety challenge. It also highlights the significant advantages of developing partnerships to tackle road safety problems.

Conclusion

Actions aimed at reducing harmful drinking are being supported by the beverage alcohol industry at local, national, and international levels and in collaboration with a wide variety of stakeholders from the public and private sectors. No single prescription or approach can be offered to society as the ultimate solution to alcohol-related problems. But, by investing in joint actions, stakeholders are investing in the promise of greater sustainability.

Meeting complex social challenges cries out for more varied collaborations, including public-private partnerships, multiagency coalitions, and harm reduction responses. Such actions look beyond immediate opportunities (and beyond the status quo) by seeking potential linkages that create new solutions or strengthen existing structures and programs.

The WHO global strategy on reducing harmful drinking ought to be a clarion call to recognize and address issues facing all stakeholders—including government, public health, and the industry. ICAP and the industry leaders that support it believe that there are many ways and models for stakeholders to work together in the implementation of a sound, balanced strategy. As the WHO global strategy moves into its implementation phase, there will be many opportunities for different stakeholders to work together effectively.

References

Burns, E. D., Nusbaumer, M. R., & Reiling, D. M. (2003). Think they're drunk? Alcohol servers and the identification of intoxication. *Journal of Drug Education, 33*, 177–186.

Caudill, B. D., Luckey, W., Crosse, S. B., Blane, H. T., Ginexi, E. M., & Campbell, B. (2007). Alcohol risk-reduction skills training in a national fraternity: A randomized intervention trial with longitudinal intent-to-treat analysis. *Journal of Studies on Alcohol and Drugs, 68*, 399–409.

Donahue, J. D., & Zeckhauser, R. (2006). Public-private collaboration. In M. Moran, M. Rein, & R. F. Goodin (Eds.), *Oxford handbook of public policy* (pp. 496–527). Oxford, U.K.: Oxford University Press.

Dresser, J., & Gliksman, L. (1998). Comparing statewide alcohol server training systems. *Pharmacology, Biochemistry and Behavior, 61*, 150.

European Forum for Responsible Drinking (EFRD). (2008). *Drinks industry initiatives 2008: Voluntary initiatives by the EU spirits industry to reduce alcohol-related harm.* Brussels, Belgium: Author.

Foxcroft, D. R., Ireland, D., Lowe, G., & Breen, R. (2002). Primary prevention for alcohol misuse in young people. *Cochrane Database System Review, 3.* Retrieved March 5, 2009, from http://www.cochrane.org/reviews/en/ab003024.html

Freisthler, B., Gruenewald, P. J., Treno, A. J., & Lee, J. (2003). Evaluating alcohol access and the alcohol environment in neighborhood areas. *Alcoholism: Clinical and Experimental Research, 27*, 477–484.

Global Road Safety Partnership (GRSP). (2007). *Drinking and driving: A road safety manual for decision-makers and practitioners.* Geneva, Switzerland: Author.

Grant, M. (2005). Alcohol policy through partnership: Is the glass half empty or half full? In M. Grant & J. O'Connor (Eds.), *Corporate social responsibility and alcohol: The need and potential for partnership* (pp. 57–62). New York: Routledge.

Grant, M., & O'Connor, J. (Eds.). (2005). *Corporate social responsibility and alcohol: The need and potential for partnership.* New York: Routledge.

Homel, R., Carvolth, R., Hauritz, M., McIlwain, G., & Teague, R. (2004). Making licensed venues safer for patrons: What environmental factors should be the focus of interventions? *Drug and Alcohol Review, 23*, 19–29.

International Center for Alcohol Policies (ICAP). (2002a). *Alcohol policy development: Partnership in practice.* Washington, DC: Author.

International Center for Alcohol Policies (ICAP). (2002b). *Creating alcohol policies in the 21st century: A best practice approach.* Washington, DC: Author.

International Center for Alcohol Policies (ICAP). (2004). *Sharing best practice in self-regulation: An international workshop.* London, United Kingdom. Washington, DC: Author.

International Center for Alcohol Policies (ICAP). (2006a). *A workshop on self-regulation: Asia-Pacific Region. Meeting report.* Washington, DC: Author.

International Center for Alcohol Policies (ICAP). (2006b). *A workshop on self-regulation: Africa Region. Meeting report.* Washington, DC: Author.

International Center for Alcohol Policies (ICAP). (2007). *A workshop on self-regulation: Latin America Region. Meeting report.* Washington, DC: Author.

International Center for Alcohol Policies (ICAP). (2008). *A guide to building partnerships.* ICAP Policy Guides. Washington, DC: Author.

International Labour Organization (ILO). (2006). *The Mekong challenge. Cambodia's "beer promotion girls": Their recruitment, working conditions and vulnerabilities.* Bangkok, Thailand: ILO Mekong Sub-regional Project to Combat Trafficking in Children and Women.

Johnsson, K. O., & Berglund, M. (2003). Education of key personnel in student pubs leads to a decrease in alcohol consumption among the patrons: A randomized controlled trial. *Addiction, 98,* 627–633.

National Assembly of the Kingdom of Cambodia. (1997). *Labour law.* Retrieved March 5, 2009, from http://www.scribd.com/doc/7997364/Cambodian-Labour-Law

Nelson, J. (2002). *Building partnership cooperation between the United Nations system and the private sector.* New York: United Nations Global Compact Office.

Nelson, J., & Zadek, S. (2000). *Partnership alchemy: New social partnerships in Europe.* Copenhagen, Denmark: Copenhagen Centre.

Orley, J., & Logan, D. (2005). Perspectives on partnership for corporate social responsibility in the beverage alcohol industry. In M. Grant & J. O'Connor (Eds.), *Corporate social responsibility and alcohol: The need and potential for partnership* (pp. 43–55). New York: Routledge.

Peden, M., Scurfield, R., Sleet, D., Mohan, D., Hyder, A. A., Jarawan, E., et al. (Eds.). (2004). *World report on road traffic injury prevention.* Geneva, Switzerland: World Health Organization.

Quigley, B. M., Leonard, K. E., & Collins, R. L. (2003). Characteristics of violent bars and bar patrons. *Journal of Studies on Alcohol, 64,* 765–772.

Quinn, I. (2003, September). *Selling beer safely: A baseline survey and needs assessment of beer promoters in Phnom Penh.* London: CARE International.

Reinicke, W. (1998). *Global public policy.* Washington, DC: Brookings Institute.

Saltz, R. F., & Stanghetta, P. (1997). A community-wide responsible beverage service program in three communities: Early findings. *Addiction, 92*(Suppl. 2), S237–S249.

Single, E. (1990). *Paths ahead for server interventions in Canada.* Rockville, MD: Office for Substance Abuse Prevention, U.S. Department of Health and Human Services.

Sloan, F. A., Stout, E. M., Whetten-Goldstein, K., & Liand, L. (2000). *Drinkers, drivers, and bartenders: Balancing private choices and public accountability.* Chicago: University of Chicago Press.

Smith, K. L., Wiggers, J. H., Considine, R. J., Daly, J. B., & Collins, T. (2001). Police knowledge and attitudes regarding crime, the responsible service of alcohol and a proactive alcohol policing strategy. *Drug and Alcohol Review, 20,* 181–191.

Stockwell, T. (2001). Responsible alcohol service: Lessons from evaluations of servers training and policing initiatives. *Drug and Alcohol Review, 20,* 257–265.

Toomey, T. L., Kilian, G. R., Gehan, J. P., Perry, C. L., Jones-Webb, R., & Wagenaar, A. C. (1998). Qualitative assessment of training programs for alcohol servers and establishment managers. *Public Health Reports, 113,* 162–169.

Turrisi, R., Nicholson, B., & Jaccard, J. (1999). A cognitive analysis of server intervention policies: Perceptions of bar owners and servers. *Journal of Studies on Alcohol, 60,* 37–46.

Wagenaar, A. C., Toomey, T. L., Murray, D. M., Short, B. J., Wolfson, M., & Jones-Webb, R. (1996). Sources of alcohol for underage drinkers. *Journal of Studies on Alcohol, 57,* 325–333.

World Health Organization (WHO). (2000). *Guidelines on working with the private sector to achieve health outcomes: Report by the Secretariat.* Geneva, Switzerland: Author.

Worldwide Brewing Alliance (WBA). (2007). *Global social responsibility initiatives.* London: British Beer and Pub Association.

9

IMPLEMENTING THE WHO GLOBAL STRATEGY TO REDUCE HARMFUL USE OF ALCOHOL

The Producers' Contributions

MARK LEVERTON AND MARCUS GRANT

Introduction

This book is intended to provide input into the World Health Organization's (WHO) global strategy to reduce harmful use of alcohol (WHO, 2008). The purpose of this chapter is to set out how alcohol producers can contribute to reducing harmful drinking in countries where they are present. The specific areas are a menu of options rather than a proscriptive plan for all producers to implement in all countries. It has been compiled by drawing on existing efforts by producers and the views expressed by those in the public health community—for example, concerns about young people's drinking—as well as on the various recommendations made by authors in preceding chapters of this book. Producers currently undertake a number of the actions listed in a range of developed and developing countries; however, plenty of scope remains for building and expanding these existing contributions. It is important to emphasize that the focus of this chapter is on producers; the roles of other economic operators—in particular retailers (both on- and off-premise)—are not included here, although, of course, they are relevant to reducing alcohol-related harm and to implementing the WHO global strategy.

We believe that producers are legitimate stakeholders in government and public health initiatives to reduce harmful drinking; that it is essential to engage and integrate them continuously in the process of strategy development and its implementation; and that, with producers' support and involvement, efforts to reduce alcohol-related harm will have a much higher chance of success. This chapter is therefore in that spirit—that is, a constructive and sincere contribution to reduce alcohol-related harm.

Either alone or in partnerships, in both the developing and developed world, producers have for many years been involved in promoting consumer awareness of the risks of harmful drinking. These efforts include, for example, programs to build parents' skills to discuss alcohol with children and initiatives to prevent alcohol-impaired driving, underage drinking, "binge" drinking, and drinking during pregnancy. In addition, producers make continuous efforts to ensure that their core business activities, from production to the "end consumer," do not have a negative impact and, as far as possible, have a positive impact on public health, such as by working in the retail environment to prevent underage access (e.g., with help of proof-of-age schemes), stop alcohol-impaired driving, and encourage and support server training. We recognize that the contribution these efforts make to reducing problematic drinking would be better appreciated if more of them were independently evaluated. In practice, high-quality rigorous evaluation of programs is complex and challenging and would benefit from greater dialogue between industry and the public health community. While producers will continue with and expand their efforts to promote responsible drinking and address harmful drinking, the focus of this chapter is primarily on how producers can help reduce harmful drinking through their core business activities. This chapter therefore approaches this subject somewhat differently than in the past, concentrating more on what producers can do practically in their day-to-day business and using industry strengths.

Producers also recognize that harsh social and economic living conditions contribute to alcohol abuse as well as to a range of other problems, as described by WHO and others (Commission on Social

Determinants of Health, 2008), and that it is crucial to address social deprivation in which alcohol problems are rooted. Alcohol producers make an important contribution to social and economic wellbeing by bringing significant benefits to the countries in which they do business (see Chapter 2). Producers help improve economic welfare through tax revenues, employment, and development, as well as by implementing a broad range of social responsibility programs—for instance, providing fresh water to communities and healthcare access to employees and their families, including access to antiretroviral treatment, in a number of developing countries. These contributions to sustainable development help alleviate poverty and reduce the socioeconomic drivers of harmful drinking.

The following are areas for producers' continuing contributions: high-quality and alternative-strength products, data sharing, responsible innovation and packaging, counterfeiting, illicit noncommercial alcohol, responsible marketing and self-regulation, responsible retailing, responsible drinking initiatives, community partnerships, and taxation and regulation.

High-quality and Alternative-strength Products

Producing high-quality products by striving to have production processes, product standards, and quality controls in place to make high-quality products (Chapter 2, pp. 26–28).

Providing alternative-strength products by monitoring consumer trends to identify market-driven opportunities to produce lower-strength alcohol beverages to offer wide consumer choice (Chapter 2, pp. 32–35).

Data Sharing

Providing production/consumption data by sharing noncommercially confidential data with WHO, national governments, and the public health community to help contribute to a better understanding of drinking patterns (Chapter 2, p. 21).

Responsible Innovation and Packaging

Taking public health perspectives into account when developing new products by considering public health issues, such as avoiding products that might primarily appeal to those underage or that might encourage excessive consumption, in producers' internal processes to develop new products (Chapter 2, pp. 28–32).

Using only responsible packaging by not using containers for alcohol drinks that, for example, may primarily appeal to those underage or that might encourage excessive consumption (Chapter 2, pp. 28–32).

Counterfeiting

Stepping up efforts to combat counterfeiting of legitimate products by enhancing collaboration with governments and other relevant authorities, providing training to customs and enforcement officers, and investing in and deploying relevant technologies (Chapter 3, p. 56).

Illicit Noncommercial Alcohol

Improving understanding of the illicit noncommercial sector by collaborating with governments and others in public health, for example, to provide certain noncommercially confidential production and consumption data and by supporting independent research into the health, economic, and social impacts of noncommercial alcohol (Chapter 3, pp. 57–58).

Discouraging consumption of illicit and harmful noncommercial products by seeking opportunities to reduce the harm from noncommercial alcohol through, for example, supporting efforts to educate consumers about potential risks and producing high-quality affordable alternatives (Chapter 3, pp. 52–58).

Responsible Marketing and Self-regulation

Strengthening self-regulatory codes and systems by seeking continual improvement of established self-regulatory and co-regulatory systems based on best practice by promoting systems that comprehensively cover the entire range of marketing communications, including, for example, new/electronic and digital media and sponsorship (Chapter 4, p. 84).

Expanding self-regulation systems across the world by working with governments and other stakeholders to set up robust and enforceable self-regulation or co-regulation systems in countries where they are lacking; these should be inclusive of all industry players, cover all media, address marketing content and placement, and have provisions for independent resolution of complaints and consequences for noncompliance (Chapter 4, pp. 83–84).

Evaluating the effectiveness of self-regulatory systems by undertaking regular independent audits of compliance and publishing the results (Chapter 4, p. 83).

Promoting best practice of self-regulation and responsible marketing practices by organizing workshops and other educational platforms, working in partnership with self-regulatory organizations, the media and advertising industries, and public health stakeholders (Chapter 4, pp. 83–85).

Encouraging Responsible Retailing

Encouraging responsible retail practices by working with retailers and other stakeholders to encourage responsible retailing practices and discourage irresponsible price promotions such as "all-you-can-drink" specials (Chapter 5, pp. 109–110).

Encouraging responsible marketing in retail establishments by working with retailers to provide point-of-sale marketing and promotion materials in retail outlets that comply with best practice codes of responsible conduct (Chapter 6, pp. 123–125).

Encouraging responsible drinking in retail establishments by working with retailers to reduce alcohol-related harm in the retail environment; this includes, for example, preventing underage drinking through proof-of-age schemes, preventing sale to intoxicated persons, providing designated driver schemes, and supporting training of staff in retail establishments on measures to reduce alcohol-related harm (Chapter 6, pp. 126–135).

Responsible Drinking Initiatives

Promoting responsible drinking through social marketing campaigns by using producers' marketing expertise, skills, creativity, and knowledge to run social marketing campaigns to promote responsible drinking (e.g., discouraging drinking and driving and young adult "binge" drinking) based on research of what consumers find persuasive (Chapter 4, pp. 72, 83–84).

Providing consumer information by using various channels, such as packaging, websites, customer care lines, point-of-sale material, and advertisements to provide useful information (i.e., on alcohol content, nutrition, ingredients, and allergens) to help consumers make informed choices (Chapter 7, pp. 144–151).

Collaborating with the scientific and public health community to identify rigorous and effective methods of evaluation of responsible drinking initiatives and programs (Chapter 7, pp. 162–163).

Preventing alcohol-related harm in the workplace by putting in place policies and programs to address workplace drinking issues for employees and by sharing best practice with others in the private sector (Chapter 7, p. 158).

Community Partnerships

Supporting communities to address local alcohol-related harm by working at local level in multi-stakeholder partnerships to mobilize communities to address, for example, underage access to alcohol (Chapter 6, pp. 126–135).

Taxation and Regulation

Collaborating to identify effective taxation policies by working with governments to identify policies and other measures that

avoid fostering unrecorded cross-border trade, illicit production, and smuggling; provide a fair and sustainable source
of public revenue; and take into account public health issues
(Chapter 5, pp. 103–106).

Supporting appropriate regulation by encouraging governments to
enforce existing laws and regulations, backed by appropriate
penalties, and by supporting the introduction of effective regulations where they do not already exist, for example, licensing of retail outlets, purchase age restrictions, and drink-drive
laws (Chapter 1, pp. 13–14).

Conclusion

To inform stakeholders and in the interest of transparency, producers
intend to report regularly on progress in the implementation of these
areas, for example, via the International Center for Alcohol Policies
(ICAP) website (www.icap.org) and through other means, including
the possibility of convening a multi-stakeholder conference by 2014.

Producers recognize and wish to emphasize that, although their
contribution to reducing harmful use of alcohol is significant and
important, it alone cannot solve these complex problems. This requires
an integrated strategy of targeted interventions in which multiple
stakeholders work in partnership, both within the drinks industry—
producers, retailers, and the hospitality sector—and involving governments, public health, and nongovernmental organizations (NGOs),
all of whom have a role to play (Chapters 7 and 8). Producers are
willing to play their part, preferably working with others who share
their goal to reduce harmful drinking.

References

Commission on Social Determinants of Health (CSDH). (2008). *Closing the
gap in a generation: Health equity through action on the social determinants
of health. Final Report of the Commission on Social Determinants of Health.*
Geneva, Switzerland: World Health Organization.

World Health Organization (WHO). (2008). WHA 61.4. Strategies to reduce the harmful use of alcohol. In *Sixty-first World Health Assembly: Geneva, 19–24 May 2008. Resolutions and decisions* (pp. 7–8). Retrieved February 9, 2009, from   http://www.who.int/gb/ebwha/pdf_files/WHA61-REC1/A61_REC1-en.pdf

Index

Drunk driving
    enforcement, 151–153
    Global Road Safety Partnership,
        189, 190–192
    national road safety/traffic safety
        programs, 188
    prevention, alcohol industry's role
        in, 189–190
    server training to reduce,
        184–185

E

El Programa Familias Fuertes, 181

F

Fetal alcohol syndrome, 153–154

G

Gender and alcohol consumption
    guidelines, drinking, 147
    increase in female consumption,
        117
    metabolic differences, 117
    pregnancy awareness, 153–154
Global Alcohol Producers Group, 75
    best-practices for self-regulation,
        77–78
Global Road Safety Partnership,
    189, 190–192. *See also*
    drunk driving

H

Hospitality industry, 160–162,
    184–186

I

Industry Association for Responsible
    Alcohol Use (ARA)
    code of conduct, 55, 109–110
    corporate social responsibility,
        role of, 171–172
International Center for Alcohol
    Policies, 51–52

K

Kumpfer, Karol, 181

L

Leverhulme, Lord, 64–65
Licensing restrictions, alcohol sales,
    121–123
Lower alcohol products
    acceptance of, 33
    demand for, 32, 34–35
    ready-to-drink beverages, 33–34
    technological advances in
        producing, 33

M

Marketing, alcohol, 10
    adolescents/youth (*see* youth and
        alcohol industry)
    advertising bans, 79, 80–81
    beverage marketing, 66–67
    co-regulation, industry, 78
    codes of conduct, 75, 76–77
    demand saturation, 65
    education, role of, 85
    governmental regulations, 67–68,
        78
    history of, 64–65, 66–67
    media role, 71, 84
    overview, 63–64

youth drinking, as factor in (see youth and alcohol industry)
Production of alcohol. See alcohol production
Project-10, 72

R

Ready-to-drink beverages, 33–34
Respect 21 retailing program, 129–130
Responsible drinking. See also cultural factors in alcohol consumption
alcohol education (see alcohol education)
at-risk individuals, 153
definition of, 4
drinking guidelines, 147–150
harmful drinking, versus, 5
hospitality industry, 160–162
labels, 145–147
overview, 143–144
partnerships to encourage, 187–188
risky behaviors, preventing, 150–151
screening, 157
Retail alcohol sales. See alcohol sales, retail

S

Self-regulation of alcohol marketing by industry, 74–76
areas of importance, 174–176
Servers
beer promoters, 177–178, 179–180
judgment of, developing, 184
TIPS training, 185–186, 187

training, retail establishments, 134–135
SFP 10-14, 182–183
Shebeens, African, 39–40
Social influences on drinking, 116–117
age, 118
aggregate consumption, 116–117
behaviors, 119–120
context, 115–116, 118–119
cultural factors (see cultural factors in alcohol consumption)
gender (see gender and alcohol consumption)
traditions, 119–120
Socioeconomic factors in alcohol use, 5–6
Spirits, history of, 18–19
STOP! Underage Drinking (Japan), 131–132
Strengthening Families Program, 181–183
Surrogate alcohol, 42
Sustainability in alcohol industry
Asahi Breweries Group initiatives, 24–25
defining, 24
inclusivity, role of, 172–173
initiatives, 24–25
overview, 24
Water Mandate, United Nations CEO, 24

T

Test marketing, alcohol beverages, 28–30
Tourism, role in alcohol consumption, 8
Training Intervention Procedures, 185–186, 187